ARKANA
THE LONG TRIP

For the past twenty-five years Paul Devereux has pursued his twin passions: the study of ancient sites and the study of consciousness. He has written numerous books in these fields and has been made a Fellow of the Royal Society of the Arts. He has edited the journal *The Ley Hunter* since 1976 and is the Director of the Dragon Project Trust, a research effort that studies claims of unusual energies at prehistoric sites. He is also Director of the Environic Foundation International, an organization that applies geomantic research in architecture and town planning, and was recently appointed one of ten members of an interdisciplinary think-tank at Princeton University designed to probe the interaction of consciousness and the physical world. He is a frequent lecturer and workshop leader and has broadcast widely on British radio. His most recent book is entitled *Re-visioning the Earth: Guide to Opening the Healing Channels Mind & Body*.

PENGUIN
ARKANA

In the Aztec language, the hallucinogenic experience was called *temixoch*, the "flowery dream." This is an early sixteenth-century Aztec statue of Xochipilli, the Prince (or God) of Flowers, in the Museo Nacional de Antropología in Mexico City. With his face wearing an awe-filled expression, he seems frozen in rapture. His body and the plinth on which he sits are covered in depictions of intoxicating plants, including the flower of the morning glory, the flower of tobacco, the sacred auditory hallucinogen *sinicuichi*, and stylized hallucinogenic mushrooms. This graven image gazes at us across the centuries to remind us of knowledge that has been lost. *(Peter T. Furst)*

the
Long Trip

A PREHISTORY
OF PSYCHEDELIA

PAUL DEVEREUX

PENGUIN/ARKANA

ARKANA
Published by the Penguin Group
Penguin Putnam Inc., 375 Hudson Street,
New York, New York 10014, U.S.A.
Penguin Books Ltd, 27 Wrights Lane,
London W8 5TZ, England
Penguin Books Australia Ltd, Ringwood,
Victoria, Australia
Penguin Books Canada Ltd, 10 Alcorn Avenue,
Toronto, Ontario, Canada M4V 3B2
Penguin Books (N.Z.) Ltd, 182–190 Wairau Road,
Auckland 10, New Zealand

Penguin Books Ltd, Registered Offices:
Harmondsworth, Middlesex, England

First published in Arkana 1997

10 9 8 7 6 5 4 3 2 1

LIBRARY OF CONGRESS CATALOGING IN PUBLICATION DATA
Devereux, Paul.
The long trip : a prehistory of psychedelia / Paul Devereux.
p.   cm.
Includes bibliographical references and index.
ISBN 0 14 01.9540 8 (pbk.)
1. Hallucinogenic drugs and religious experience. 2. Hallucinogenic drugs and re-
ligious experience—History. 3. Hallucinogenic drugs and religious experience—
Cross-cultural studies. I. Title.
BL65.D7D45   1997
394.1´4´0901—dc21   96–53444

Printed in the United States of America
Set in Weiss
Designed by Claudyne Bedell

FOR CHRISTOPHER CASTLE,
*visonary artist and old
comrade-in-arms of the sixties*

"Among the Jívaro, it is felt that part of the soul may leave the body, with the subject having the sensation of flying, returning when the effects of the drug wear off. This is actually referred to as a 'trip' by the Jívaro. . . ."

Michael J. Harner
"Hallucinogens and Shamanism:
The Question of a Trans-Cultural Experience"
Hallucinogens and Shamanism

"The role of hallucinogens in societies other than ours has considerable relevance to our own time and place. . . . The fact is that we still know far too little of this important area of the study of man."

Peter T. Furst
Introduction,
Flesh of the Gods

Preface

One aim of this book is to demonstrate (rather than to merely state) that our modern culture stands out in the long record of human history because of its difficulty in accepting in an orderly and integrated way the role natural substances, primarily from the plant kingdom, have played in aiding mind expansion. This book provides a thorough overview of what is currently known about the ancient use of psychedelic drugs for ritual and spiritual purposes. It offers the interested general reader a useful single source of information on the whole subject area. As part of this inquiry, it is important to evoke some understanding of actual experiences with psychedelic substances. A failure to register the experiential qualities of hallucinogens would make it more difficult for us to understand the fascination they have held for human beings throughout all known time. So although the main focus here is on the long human usage of hallucinogenic substances—the "Long Trip"—we will also hear first-person accounts of those pioneers who have studied the substances in recent and modern times.

This book is not a specialized work of ethnobotany, archaeology, anthropology, plant chemistry, or the modern social history of psychedelia. It is nevertheless uniquely updated and comprehensive, and provides far more than a superficial study of the overall subject area. I trust that it will provide a worthwhile general reference for a variety of readers. The later sections of the book examine generally overlooked evidence showing that a record of archaic ecstatic experience was "written" on the landscape in various parts of the world. I suspect this material is unfamiliar to most readers.

The fact that we have, indeed, been on a Long Trip raises deep questions that humanity needs to address. So profound are these questions that it will take a tremendous effort on the part of the scientific community to explore them adequately.

PAUL DEVEREUX,
Cotswolds, United Kingdom, and New York, 1996

Acknowledgments

I have been blessed in the writing of this book with exceptional help and goodwill from numerous people—it really has made the task a pleasure. I am grateful to numerous people who over the years helped me develop the background knowledge and perspective that proved useful in this work. But I want to specifically thank those who have been of major help to me on this project.

I recall a most enjoyable afternoon spent in Oxford in the lively company of Andrew Sherratt, whose important work on the use of psychoactive substances in the Neolithic period and the Bronze Age has been a guiding beacon, and Richard Rudgley, the author of *Essential Substances*. I thank them both for the time they took out of their busy schedules and for their generous provision of information. I also greatly enjoyed meeting with Mark Patton at Carmarthen, and appreciated his frank, open comments and his pointing me toward additional sources regarding the archaeological evidence of drug usage in the prehistory of the British Isles and Brittany.

Thanks and appreciation are due to Rick Strassman for his willingness to answer questions on his key research into DMT and to offer some of his own views for publication in these pages.

David Lewis-Williams and Thomas Dowson were their usual cordial and helpful selves, and I am grateful to them not only for permissions regarding a large number of illustrations of southern African rock art, but also for their formidable and ongoing trailblazing research into the trance aspects of prehistoric rock art in general. Likewise, David S. Whitley has been exceptionally helpful in providing information about his valuable work on visionary Native American rock art in the Great Basin. I thank Shirley-Ann Pager for allowing use of the rock art tracings by her late husband, Harald Pager. I must also express my thanks to Jeremy Dronfield for so promptly answering my urgent plea for his papers on his fascinating new analyses of Neolithic rock art, which reached me just in time to be included in this work.

Special mention must be made of Peter T. Furst for so effectively answering my SOS for certain illustrative material, and for his decades of work in chronicling many aspects of the Long Trip.

For various items of information or insight given or sent to me personally at various times on matters associated in one way or another (not always obvious at the time) with ancient psychedelia, I wish to acknowledge Chris Ashton, David Browne, Isabelle Druc, Albert Hofmann, Mike Ibison, Julian Jaynes, Bob Jones of Coventry University, Charles Laughlin, Christian Rätsch, and Thomas Sever, among others. Of course, I also am indebted to the many pioneers in ethnobotany and psychedelic research who are widely cited throughout this book—all of them are an inspiration, and in a real way this book is a testament to their work.

I appreciated the effectiveness of the Blodgett Memorial Library in Fishkill, New York, the friendly, efficient service of the FS Book Company in Sacramento, and that likewise of David Goldstein of the PHD in New York City.

For formal permissions I thank John Wiley and Sons and Harvard University Press. I also thank the efforts of Nicky Badman at Duckworth, and McGraw-Hill and the University of California Press for attempting to track down elusive copyright sources.

Finally, I want to thank my agent on this particular book, Stephany Evans of Imprint Agency, for her enthusiasm; my son, Solomon, for reliably ensuring that essential information was communicated to me transatlantically; and my wife, Charla, for her ongoing support, suggestions, and discussions.

Contents

Coming to Terms

There are a few specific terms that are so fundamental to the subject matter we will be exploring that we need to be clear about their definitions at the outset.

ARCHAEOLOGY

This is the scientific study of the material remains of past peoples, cultures, or societies. Such remains can include monuments, inscriptions, pottery, tools and other small artifacts, burial sites—even ancient refuse heaps (middens). When dealing with prehistoric remains (see Prehistory, page xvii) there are no written records to guide the archaeologist, so interpretation of the remains becomes an essential skill. Such interpretive work is usually aided by cross-reference with similar finds, computer modeling, a growing battery of scientific dating methods, and the archaeological equivalent of forensic chemical analysis. In recent years, some archaeologists have extended the interpretive process to create models of the ancient mind—thus bringing nonmaterial remains such as ancient religious beliefs and ritual activity into the realm of archaeology. This approach can be loosely termed "cognitive archaeology." We will see examples of this still-developing approach in this book.

ECSTASY

Today we tend to use this word loosely, to mean "very happy," "extreme pleasure," and so on. However, "ecstasy" has a more profound definition. It really means visionary rapture, mental transport, altered state of consciousness. The term derives from the Greek *ekstasis*, meaning displacement, trance, out of the senses—the flight of the soul from the body. While such altered states can involve ineffable pleasure, they can also cause terror, deep fear, and ontological shock.

ETHNOLOGY

This branch of anthropology is concerned with how various cultures develop and change, the patterns of thought and behavior of people belonging to them, and how and why peoples today and in the past differ in their ways of thinking and acting. Ethnologists tend to collect data by observing and interviewing living people. An ethnologist who spends time actually living with other cultures is called an *ethnographer*, and an *ethnography* is a detailed study of a society resulting from such fieldwork. *Ethnobotany* is the study of plant knowledge, lore, and usage in traditional societies and the further botanical investigations that are derived from this study.

HALLUCINOGEN

This is but one of many words that have been used to describe substances that produce mind-altering effects. These effects include visionary elements, but also other hallucinatory experiences that can be auditory, tactile, olfactory, and gustatory in nature. Furthermore, hallucination may be just one part of the overall experience triggered by a hallucinogen. Another term that was proposed early on was *psychotomimetic*, meaning "psychosis-mimicking," but since the hallucinogenic experience can produce beatific, meaningful, nonpathological states, *psychotomimetic* seemed inadequate. Indeed, it is a biased and misleading term that betrays our culture's assumption that any state of consciousness that is not centered in what we consider "normal reality" is pathological. *Psychotropic* and *psychoactive* are more useful, neutral terms, but most researchers agree that there is, in fact, no single word that adequately describes the vast range of mental experience that these various remarkable substances can provoke. The most workable broad definition is probably that provided by Abram Hoffer and Humphry Osmond. Hallucinogens, they say, are chemicals that, when used in nontoxic doses, produce alterations in perception, thought, and mood, but that rarely produce mental confusion, loss of memory, or disorientation.

PREHISTORY

This term does not describe a specific period on a single time line. Rather, it describes a state in which written and other forms of documentation were not yet available. Historical time began when events were continuously and systematically recorded. Prehistory came to an end and historical time began at different moments in different parts of the world.

PSYCHEDELIC

This term developed out of correspondence between Aldous Huxley and Humphry Osmond, both of whom were pursuing the subject. Both wanted a term that described the visionary, arguably mystical, and possibly healing nature of hallucinogens, but that did not have a pathological inference. In 1956, Osmond proposed *psychedelic*, deriving from the Greek *psyche*, soul, and *delos*, visible or manifest, hence meaning soul- or mind-manifesting. Huxley proposed *phanerothyme*, and the men exchanged ditties. Huxley wrote:

> To make this trivial world sublime,
> Take half a gram of phanerothyme.

But Osmond won out with:

To fathom Hell or soar angelic,
Just take a pinch of psychedelic.

The term came into common usage in the 1960s, and was applied not only to the psychoactive substances themselves, but to everything that seemed to either inspire or be inspired by their use—in music, art, or fashion. Because of this generalized usage, and because of its inadequacy as a precise descriptor of the otherworldly effects associated with psychoactive substances, some people dislike the term. Some researchers have proposed—rather forcefully—that *psychedelic* should be replaced with *entheogenic*, which has Greek origins meaning "realizing the divine within." They would also replace *hallucinogens* with *entheogens*. As laudable as this attempt may be, it is unlikely that the unwieldy "entheogenic" will ever replace "psychedelic" in common parlance.

SHAMANISM/SHAMAN

The religious historian Mircea Eliade defined shamanism as the technique of ecstasy. The scholar I. M. Lewis defined a shaman as being an inspired prophet and healer, a charismatic religious figure who had the power to control spirits, often by incarnating them, and had the capacity to engage in mystical soul flight and other out-of-body experiences. Jerome Rothenberg described shamans as "technicians of the sacred." Shamanism was and is a phenomenon of tribal societies, and the shaman is the person who acts as an intermediary between the tribe and the otherworld. A shaman may heal sick tribal members by locating their lost souls, perhaps entering the otherworld to reclaim them, or by deflecting bad spirits and invisible influences. There can be a variety of other reasons for entering the spirit realms: for example, the shaman might act as a *psychopomp*, accompanying the souls of dying people into the spirit world, or he or she may travel there to seek information or gain prophetic insight. When in the otherworld, the shaman is considered to have temporarily died. Another role is as the protector of the tribe, combating the malevolent actions of rival shamans in other tribes. The shaman must be proficient in using sorcery as both a defensive and offensive tool: shamanic "wars" are, in some cultures, a fact of life. Contrary to the common "New Age" assumption, the world of traditional shamanism was and is not necessarily one of sweetness and light.

The shaman employs a wide range of techniques to produce the trance states necessary for the ecstatic experience, and these can include drumming, dancing, chanting, fasting, sensory deprivation, hyperventilation, and the ingestion of hallucinogenic substances. Often, there is a combination of such methods.

Although the role of the shaman is common to many cultures, the word itself was originally used among Siberian and central Asian tribes. It derives from the Tungus word *saman* (though actually there is argument that the word may be foreign to even that language). Today the word is used—even by anthropologists—to describe healers and practitioners anywhere in the world who employ ecstatic soul-flight in trance. So not all witch doctors, medicine men, or sorcerers are necessarily shamans. Shamanism, which evolved out of animism, is one of the oldest and most universal expressions of human spiritual sensibility. Although it was incorporated into larger and more organized religions in many parts of the world, it still survives today in some tribal societies. From those societies we have increasingly come to understand that shamanism plays a central role in the story of humanity's Long Trip.

the Long Trip

A Head of
the Times

Sugar had never seemed so sweet. I walked with quickening step, barely able to curb my anticipation as I hurried from the college building to the nearby house I had rented as lodgings with a few fellow students. As I lovingly cradled the small bag containing the two sugar cubes, I realized that Aldous Huxley's prophecy for me was coming true. Here it was, March 1966, a few days before my twenty-first birthday, and I at last possessed the passport to instant "is-ness," a ticket to the Magic Theater, a front row seat at the cinema of cellular memory. What a perfect way to celebrate my "coming-of-age"!

Only a few years earlier, in my last school year before college, I had written to Huxley. Like many of my generation I had been fascinated by his essays "The Doors of Perception" and "Heaven and Hell," in which he described his experiments with the hallucinogenic drug mescaline. Huxley was no drug fiend, but a famous literary figure of exceptional erudition and spiritual insight. He wrote vividly and inspiringly of seeing the mundane world transformed into paradisal vistas drenched with intense colors that shone with visionary light. "Brick chimneys and green composition roofs glowed in the sunshine, like fragments of the New Jerusalem," Huxley said of his mescaline revelation. "Flowers in the gardens still trembled on the brink of being supernatural, the pepper trees and carobs along the side streets still manifestly belonged to some sacred grove. Eden alternated with Dodona, Yggdrasil with the mystic rose." The "ludicrous" gleaming cars of Sunset Boulevard convulsed him with laughter. "Azure furnace-doors separated by gulfs of unfathomable gentian" became for him "a Last Judgement which, after a long time and with considerable difficulty, I recognized as a chair." Indoors, the bookshelves appeared to contain glowing jewels rather than the colored covers of books, and the folds in his trousers became as intricate and meaningful as a great work of art. Huxley's mescaline-enriched perception was based entirely in the outer world, but, citing the experiences of other experimenters, he described entrancing visions from the "mind's antipodes, in which seemingly autonomous bejewelled landscapes inhabited by heroic beings unrolled before the inner eye." Despite Huxley's warning that under some circumstances the visionary gleam can be replaced by a hellish glare, causing angelic revelations to become demonic, I felt I had to have the mescaline experience. I was an aspiring artist, and I figured that my doors of perception could surely do with a little cleansing. But how, trapped in my provincial English school, could I get mescaline? With the breathtaking naïveté of a schoolboy, I decided to write to the great man himself, and ask him where I could buy some. I knew he lived in California, but I didn't know his address, so I sent him a letter via Penguin, the publishers of my well-thumbed edition of his essays.[1]

Some weeks later, a reply from Huxley arrived. In retrospect, I am positively staggered that he bothered to respond, knowing as I do now that he was then in the last year of his life, suffering from cancer. But he did, and wrote that he had obtained his mescaline from research groups and did not know where it could be obtained outside of such sources. But he added that I wasn't to be downhearted: I could be sure that when the time was right, the opportunity to experience the wonders of altered consciousness provided by such sacramental substances would doubtless come my way. He was right, for the following years led me to an art college on the fringes of London, which enabled me to move in circles where I could obtain LSD. It wasn't mescaline, but as far as I was concerned in those days it was a very similar substance. If anything, it seemed likely to be an even more powerful visionary tool.

And here I was.

As soon as I got home, I poured a tall glass of water in which I dissolved both sugar cubes. I waited impatiently for friends who were to accompany me on my "trip"—I knew enough not to take such a substance alone. When the first couple of people showed up, one of them sipped a teaspoonful of the solution, and I downed the rest. A few other student friends arrived as I settled down and waited for the psychedelic movies to begin.

OUT ON THE ETERNAL HIGH WIRE

Nothing unusual happened for what seemed an interminable period—in actuality, about half an hour. Then I became increasingly aware of the ceiling light shining above the lone daffodil in its slim, elegant vase on the table. I realized with some surprise that I could actually feel the heat from the bulb. I had the palpable impression of being in a bright sandy desert beneath a raging sun in a deep blue sky, but this was not what I was looking for—I wanted visions, not impressions. But almost imperceptibly, I began to realize that I could hear a pure, ringing tone. What was it? The blood pumping through my body? No. I moved around the room, cocking my head to one side, then another. I knew my behavior looked odd to my companions, but I couldn't locate the source of the sound. Then a tsunami of understanding flooded over me: I was listening to silence. More precisely, I was tuned into The Silence. All sounds were like bees in amber; they were sealed within this all-pervading no-sound. No amount of noise could shatter this awesome, deep, rich silence. Louder than any sound, it was the matrix that contained all acoustical vibration. It was The Silence that gave sound the space to be. In a flash I understood the biblical phrase "The peace which passeth understanding." At the same time, I noticed that I had arrived at a state of bliss. In fact, it was a holier feeling than that, more a state of grace. In a serene way I reasoned that this was because I was simply here: the trains of thought that normally chained me mentally and emotionally to yesterday and tomorrow had dissolved. I was experiencing the truth of the matter—this is always all that I ever am, just here and now. Everything else is an illusion. What passes for normal ra-tional mentality is in fact the grossest of illusions. I had read these kind of ideas in literature dealing with various forms of mysticism, but I wasn't intellectualizing now. This was simply the direct experience of a fact. "Now" was clearly and obviously a movable feast that persisted forever. Linear, sequential time and the cargo of memories, regrets, concerns, images, and emotions that time brings with it, had been removed. When the grime of time was washed away, I saw with astounding clarity that the pristine undersurface of eternity was always there. Yet things still happened around me. Time took its course, but, just as sound was encased in silence, time was suspended within the greater medium of eternity. Eternity was not endless time or some future state, eternity was here and now, that was its very nature. Eternity was always present; time was merely a glinting reflection off its surface, like the sparkle of sunlight in the waters of a stream. Truly, as Blake wrote, "If the doors of perception were cleansed, everything would appear to man as it is: infinite." His phrase about holding "Eternity in an hour" was simply stating the obvious. The idea that this was "poetry" fell away. I had much the same feeling when someone put Bob Dylan's "Tambourine Man" on the record player. What had previously seemed to me a string of marvelously poetic images now turned out to be clear descriptions of the states I was experiencing. The Silence was simply an aspect of the eternity that I felt all around me and all through me, and both were, in turn, just other facets of this bliss. Yet why couldn't I always think, move, and have my being like this? What had changed? Nothing had seemingly happened, yet everything was different! Zen writings that had seemed entertainingly half-baked to me suddenly took on deep meaning. "A split hair's difference and heaven and earth are set apart." (How very true.) "What is gained is no gain, yet there is something truly gained in this." (Absolutely. I couldn't have put it better myself.) Far from appearing paradoxical, such sparse, well-honed statements were now seen as the equivalent of engineering specifications describing the structure of reality. I began to appreciate with some amusement that this profound state of mind I was experiencing did not come with mental fireworks, cosmic visions, clouds of angels, or hordes of hobgoblins. It was not the result of hallucinatory additions; quite the contrary, the process was one of *paring away*. The culture I normally inhabited was the hallucination. This was unadulterated, primal consciousness, and here there was only here. And now. Here was infinity; now was eternity. This most simple yet vastly complex truth was the joyous, glorious news of liberation. I thrilled with the exultation of salvation.

I was no mystic or sage, however, and my untrained, ungainly mind could not balance on the high wire for long. I lost my footing, and all hell broke loose as the LSD experience took its course. I spent several hours falling back to Earth.

I started to disappear down brilliant, swirling tunnels formed from kaleidoscopic colors hurtling along at light speed. I'd stop back at the room, wondering where I had been. Then the hurricane of consciousness would blast through me again. I felt myself going away without myself, as if my mind were draining away. Except that wasn't possible, because I didn't have a separate mind anymore. There were no boundaries: the whole cosmos was passing through me and the edges that formed my personality became invisible, because what was inside me also surrounded me. And it was moving fast. I tried to hold on, coming to the verge of screaming panic on several occasions. "This must be what it's like to go mad," I whimpered. "Oh God . . . oh God . . ." I wanted to be able to go to sleep to get my consciousness out of this situation, to block off this ontological hurricane, but at this level of awareness there was no waking and no sleeping; there was only an endless, impersonal cosmic flux within and without, with no distinction.

As I calmed down a little, I flopped onto a bed. The colors were gone now, but I was still experiencing powerful surges washing me toward invisibility, as if I were afloat on a huge, deep swell flowing in from a dark, shoreless ocean that filled the whole universe. I felt that if I washed away, I would dissolve into such an infinity that I could never return. Why was I disappearing? I realized (actually, in some completely indescribable way, I saw) that both time and space were dissolving. I was entering eternity through some other door this time. It became transparently obvious to me that if time and space unraveled, then the coordinates that defined my existence as a person would also disappear. With an inexpressible flood of fear, I realized that I would, in effect, die. My ego-self was bouncing in and out of existence as time and space waxed and waned around me, in me, through me, but when I finally went "out" something that was still me, though beyond the confines of the personality that I identified with, still existed. I can't reconstitute a memory of where I went; it is beyond even imagery, let alone description. I just remember trembling with raw awe as I passed into the beyond, and feeling that I was unworthy—too dense, too unclean—to be entering this exquisitely rarefied and awe-full place of sanctity, this ultimate holy of holies. I was a trespasser. To enter I must die.

So I died.

Several eternities later, I found myself staring at the corner of the ceiling. Space had returned. Then time, slightly out of sync, seemed to somehow somersault into the scene over the top of my head. I was back in the room, and I began to sink slowly down levels of consciousness that were lower, though still elevated compared with my normal, daily waking state.

I had only a few visions—a short version of the kind of "movie show" I'd been expecting. Some were odd, and had an almost cartoon-like corniness about them, such as the robed angelic arms appearing out of a cloud offering me a quill pen and an open, blank book. It seemed to be an invitation, but at that time my intentions were set on painting, not writing. Other visions had more gravity to them, such as when I was floating through interstellar space and coming upon what looked at a distance like a flaming star. As I drifted closer to it, I saw it was a great, spoked wheel, carved with all manner of arabesques and filigree, silhouetted against a vivid glow of multicolored, fiery light. This majestically rolling wheel was thousands of miles across, and what I thought at first was an intricate pattern around the rim turned out to be the flickering silhouettes of countless human beings, engaged in myriad activities. From across the universe a pure, godlike voice rang out: *"This* is the human race."

Things were equally weird when I opened my eyes and looked

around the room. The fellow who had sipped a teaspoonful of the LSD solution had himself gone on quite a trip, so I didn't wonder that I was being hung out to dry in the cosmic gales. He was engrossed in the folds of the (undrawn) window drapes. He stirred himself and pulled out his crumpled cotton handkerchief, which I saw as a dove that my friend was holding by the beak. It was a dead dove, but exact in its lineaments and totally convincing. I marveled at the way consciousness could mold realities. At that moment I realized that our normal perceptions are simply the possibilities that get "frozen" within the consensual cultural frame. There simply isn't one set reality "out there" in the environment. The fabulous processing capabilities of the brain-mind can conjur any appearance out of the matrix of energies that bombard our sensory receptors from the environmental world. I understood what Blake had been talking about with his "double the vision my eyes do see, and double the vision is always with me." He could see a thistle across his way as an old man gray, and so could I. Or a handkerchief as a dove.

I moved around the room, stretching my legs. A dull glow of color around someone's shoulder caught my eye. I looked closer and focused on the effect. I saw bands of very soft, almost ethereal color surrounding the person's head and shoulders. I could easily see the wallpaper pattern through this delicate, slowly shifting rainbow atmosphere. It suddenly dawned on me that I was looking at the human aura, the stock-in-trade of clairvoyants and other occult practitioners. "Jesus! The aura is a real thing!" I thought in amazement. I knew then, as I remain convinced, that this was a true observation. It was no hallucination, but a phenomenon that I was able to closely and repeatedly observe. In later years I managed to clearly observe it on one or two occasions without the use of drugs. Somehow this observation worried me. It was one thing having high experiences that partook of the mystical and the visionary, but this was *occult*. Prejudices I had inherited surfaced in me. And it worried me in another way: if the aura really was a feature of the human being (it clearly was), and if that feature was denied and even derided by our mainstream society, it meant that our society had a significantly incomplete model of reality. What else had it got wrong? What else was missing from its world picture? Shouldn't we be equipping our doctors with the technical skills to explore this phenomenon and conduct rigorous clinical experiments looking into the correlation between aura and medical conditions?

I sat down at the table, smiling at my companions, who had shown enormous patience and were quietly keeping an eye on me and my unplanned-for fellow traveler. I looked at the lone but elegant daffodil. As I gazed at its yellow petals, I saw that they were moving in a subtle way. I looked closer: yes, the petals really were making minute waving motions. It was like a modest version of one of those time-lapse films that massively speed up the opening and closing of a flower. For me, time was not yet settled into place, I recognized, and I was watching the flower in a speeded-up time frame. I wanted to ensure that this was no hallucination. I changed my position and was able to plot the movement of the petals' peripheries against the "grid" formed by the windowpanes beyond the table. As with the aura, I was convinced (and remain convinced) that I was making an accurate observation. I sat back in my chair and various events diverted my attention for a while. When my gaze reverted to the vase and daffodil, I was horrified to see tiny bugs crawling up the flower's stem. I looked more closely. They were not bugs, but very small droplets of moisture moving by capillary action up the inside of the stem. I realized with shock that I could only be seeing this because I had X-ray vision. Is it possible for the visual cortex to process energy outside the visible spectrum? While I struggled to understand how this could happen, I lost the novel visual ability and the daffodil became just a daffodil once more.

But interaction between myself and the flower wasn't yet over. Some time later, I entered into a most curious empathic relationship with it. There was no visual component, it was strictly an emotional link. Without losing my own (admittedly by now somewhat bruised and fragile) sense of identity, I found my awareness slipping inside that of the daffodil. While still being conscious of sitting in a chair, I could also sense my petals! Then an exquisite sensation cascaded through me, and I knew I was experiencing light falling on those petals. It was virtually orgasmic, the haptic equivalent of an angelic choir. At every moment I felt, repeatedly, as if I were receiving the first ray of sunshine on the first morning in Eden. The world was unutterably new and innocent. I knew why one got such a refreshing, uplifting feeling being in a garden. I understood the lyrics of "All Things Bright and Beautiful"! This was myth brought to life. This was Eden. This was the dawn of the first day. A mythic atmosphere hung like the most delicate gossamer in the air. Then the student who had taken his psychedelic spoonful leaned forward, grasped an apple from the fruit bowl, and unceremoniously crunched his teeth into it. This broke the Eden-like spell. I was wrenched out of the daffodil, and fell back into my chair, horrified at the spectacle of the apple being devoured. "That's how it happened," a girl sitting nearby muttered. She had a tear in her eye, it seemed, and was inside the same sad myth. I smiled at her, though rather weakly—I had, after all, just been cast out of Eden.

For the first time in the session, I focused my attention outside the room and looked out of the window. It was nighttime and overcast, yet I could see very dim streaks of light flashing through the clouds, their subtle trails crisscrossing. I was sure yet again I was making an actual observation, though one related to physics this time. Perhaps secondary particles triggered by cosmic ray activity? Again I wondered about the potential for using substances like LSD as research tools in various scientific disciplines.

I wanted to go outside, so my companions put me in a car, and we drove around for half an hour. I shall never forget that view of my society. We passed a house where a young couple were saying good-bye to an older woman. The gray-haired lady stood in her doorway waving to the youngsters. I could see laughter and tears simultaneously on her face. I knew that without my enhanced perception I would only have seen her smiling.

It felt as if I was seeing beyond the surface of the social and physical environment in subtle ways. Driving down the main street, we passed two girls walking home from a club or party. I thought they were animated manikins out of a store window, and it took me some moments to appreciate that they were living beings. I pointed out to a companion that a multistory building had an additional set of stories beyond the "real" number. When I mentioned this, he suggested that I might be picking up on the original ambitions of the building's architect, or perhaps its sponsor within the town council. Perhaps those stories existed in someone's mind and I'd somehow "seen" them.

The next day I felt fragile. My sense of identity had reassembled itself, but I felt that I was on the verge of a steep precipice. I could not understand how one could come back from such mental vastness and drop into one's identity again. It seemed to me like the equivalent of flying across intergalactic space to find one strand of hair on a person's head. I couldn't get back to painting. I gazed out of the window: a beam of pale golden sunlight was shining through a gap in the clouds. The sight generated in me an awareness of the vulnerable yet paradoxically indestructible gentleness at the innermost heart of existence. It overwhelmed me, and I cried. I took a lone walk in a nearby wood. I almost expected to encounter Buddha among the trees. A startled bird flew rapidly across my field of vision, and I simultaneously felt it fly through my cranium; inner and outer interacted in a symbiosis I had never experienced prior to my LSD session. Over the following days, however, my ego boundaries hardened again, and my exposed psyche grew protective layers to insulate it from the world. But these layers were to be forever thinner than before.

TUNING IN

This account of one psychedelic session shows just how complex and far-reaching such an experience can be. The workings of the mind are revealed, aspects of the environment can be observed in ways impossible in ordinary consciousness, and profoundly deep (and, yes, sometimes painful) spiritual and philosophical insights are gained by direct experience. The experience is far too important and complex to be dismissed as "bad." Today it is the fashion to talk of "drugs" in a monolithic sense, as if they were all the same, all harmful. Because Western society in general, and American society in particular, is failing in various ways, the use of some drugs, including alcohol but also other more dangerous substances such as crack cocaine, amphetamines, and heroin, further alienates and fragments individuals within that failing society, causing physical harm, illness, crime, and despair. This of course has to be addressed. But in societies where hallucinogenic substances were, and in some cases still are, regarded in a sacramental way, they actually help bind and order society. With suitable safeguards, organization, and planned application, some of those substances could have a similarly important function within our society. From one perspective, our failure to incorporate hallucinogenic experience into our culture puts us out of step with the entire record of human experience. It is our culture that is eccentric. Unfortunately, the ignorance about and indiscriminate prejudice against "drugs" have made it difficult to conduct scientific research on hallucinogens or even talk clearly and openly about them.

At the same time it also has to be said that the situation has not been helped by the attitudes toward hallucinogens by some of their users. Hallucinogens tend to be abused in today's society and not properly valued as serious, powerful tools for extending our understanding of consciousness, which is what, with careful and considered use, they can be. It is difficult now to remember the fact that in the 1960s substances like LSD, mescaline, and even marijuana tended at first to be used in a genuinely exploratory way, by a relatively small number of people.

No one was more serious about and ultimately responsible for the notoriety of LSD and other hallucinogens during the 1960s and 1970s than Timothy Leary. For a period of time after my initiatory LSD session, students, friends, and acquaintances would come to our house— sometimes from considerable distances—to spend a weekend having a psychedelic session. Rooms were carefully prepared, guides were on hand, and nothing ever went wrong on those sessions. One of our bibles was *The Psychedelic Experience: A Manual Based on the Tibetan Book of the Dead* by Leary, Ralph Metzner, and Richard Alpert (later to be known as Ram Dass). Although Leary came to be seen as a modern Pied Piper leading the youth of the Western world astray, he started out as a respected professor of psychology at Harvard University. While on holiday in Mexico in 1960, he took some hallucinogenic mushrooms, which gave him the deepest religious experience of his life up to that point. Back at Harvard, Leary and associates, including Alpert and Metzner, conducted group experiments using psilocybin tablets obtained for research from the pharmaceutical firm of Sandoz, where Albert Hofmann had synthesized the active components of the sacred mushrooms of Mexico. On having his first LSD experience in 1961, Leary went on to publicly extol its virtues. He conducted experiments that made Harvard authorities wary and question the "scientific" methods practiced. Leary went on and politicized LSD more and more, however, and he and Alpert were dismissed from Harvard in 1963. By then they had already established an off-campus organization called the International Federation for Internal Freedom (IFIF) to train people in conducting hallucinogen sessions that would be spiritually enhancing, and they planned a psychedelic center in Mexico. Leary vainly attempted to order large quantities of LSD and psilocybin from Sandoz, but by then a black market in such substances was already beginning to emerge. The Mexican center didn't last long, and Leary and his colleagues eventually moved to a country house in the town of Millbrook, north of New York City. Here the Castalia Foundation was established, the *Psychedelic Review* was published, and a community devoted to the study and development of psychedelic mysticism was formed. Representatives of a wide range of American society were influenced by the experientially based work of the Millbrook group, which seems to have alternated dynamic insight with way-out psychedelic buffoonery and recklessness. Leary was arrested in 1965 for transporting a small amount of marijuana across the Mexican border, and eventually Millbrook was raided, under the direction of the Dutchess County prosecutor, G. Gordon Liddy, who would later be a central figure in the Watergate scandal. The raid failed in court, but the Millbrook commune disbanded in 1967. In 1970, Leary was sentenced to twenty years in jail for possession of a small amount of pot, a ridiculous term that was clearly meant to make an example of him. Leary escaped from jail with the help of the Weathermen, an underground revolutionary group, and made his way to Algeria, where he lived for a time in exile with the Black Panthers, including Eldridge Cleaver. After various escapades he was arrested and extradited to the United States, and in 1973, Leary was sentenced to twenty-five years in jail. In 1976 he was released on parole.

Despite his notoriety, Leary's writings *on the subject* of running psychedelic sessions are full of sound, sensible, and informed advice. He emphasized that set and setting were crucial if a session was to go well; he urged that no one take a substance like LSD on his or her own, so that other people would be there to diffuse panic reactions should they arise. The presence of an experienced guide during a psychedelic session was central to Leary's research approach. He always stressed the seriousness of the experience itself. In an interview Paul Krassner once said to Leary: "A lot of people smoke pot for what they consider pleasure, simply to get high. Are you copping out on them by fighting your marijuana case on the grounds of religious freedom?"

"They have a perfect right to defend their use of marijuana or LSD as an instrument for getting high," Leary smoothly replied. "The pursuit of happiness is the first sentence in the Declaration of Independence, which founded this republic. But most people who use LSD and marijuana to get high don't really know how to *do* it, because the science and discipline of ecstasy is probably *the* most demanding yoga that I can think of."[2] In his long and well-known interview in the September 1966 issue of *Playboy*, he skillfully parried leading questions, titillating with his answers yet always ramming home points: that it was important to have a guide during an LSD trip; that LSD was a powerful releaser of energy not yet fully understood; that the experience of sex under LSD (about which *Playboy* pressed him repeatedly) could involve making love with candlelight or a bowl of fruit and wasn't simply centered on genital energy; and that one could be frightened and confused by the LSD experience as well as overwhelmed and delighted by it.

Nevertheless, some scientific researchers who worked on hallucinogens (and those that would want to if they could obtain government permission) complain bitterly that it was largely Leary's public antics and promotion of LSD that brought on the backlash that made it impossible to continue unfettered scientific research into the substance. There is little doubt that Leary was much less cautious with his public pronouncements on the social aspects of LSD taking than he was in his writings on its actual use, and he appeared to revel in being provocative about the use of the substance, and in entreating youth to "Turn On, Tune In, Drop Out." "When I first learned about psychedelic drugs I tried to apply them in a humanist context, not in a medical context or a psychiatric context or a CIA brainwashing context, but as a tool for the individual to activate and operate his or her own brain," he was to write much later. "I was never advocating LSD. I was advocating something much more subversive: Think for yourself."[3]

In his "Politics of Ecstasy," Leary reported on his tackling a member of "one of America's top acid-rock bands" who was complaining that "Hey, man, the English run a tight scene. Too literary . . . Always analysing and rapping about books . . . The head trip." "I think that's great of Britain," Leary retorted. "The trouble with our hippies is, they aren't connected. Rootless. Turned on but not tuned in." (Leary confessed to preferring a "high church" approach to psychedelia.) In actual fact, few in my generation in Britain knew enough to put LSD or the psychedelic experience in either its contemporary or historical context—a common condition, I suppose, when one is in the midst of events. It was simply a terrific scene to be part of. For me as a young student, it was enough that London was swinging, and it was great to hang out in Portobello Road mixing with like minds or catching sight of famous figures in Finches Pub, to browse through the esoteric literature in Watkins Bookshop off Charing Cross Road and casually note a white-suited Mick Jagger breeze in to get a stack of occult books, to take part in late-night sessions with hip psychiatrist R. D. Laing or Beat poet Allen Ginsberg at the Dialectics of Liberation symposium at the Round House, or to visit the pad of Beat writer Alexander Trocchi.

It was at this gathering that Trocchi motioned me toward Michael Hollingshead. I wasn't interested. He seemed to me to be just a quiet Englishman sitting in an upright chair, his back to the wall. Little did I know that this was the man who, it was generally revealed the following decade when he wrote *The Man Who Turned On the World*, had been keeper of a legendary and influential mayonnaise jar. At the beginning of the 1960s he had been associating with Leary and his Harvard colleagues during their psilocybin days, and had received part of a gram of pure LSD ordered by pediatrician John Beresford from the Sandoz laboratories in Switzerland, where LSD-25 had been synthesized. Only when he had to handle it did Hollingshead realize that it was so incredibly potent that he didn't have the means to measure out doses accurately (LSD can be active in doses as small as ten to twenty millionths of a gram). So he randomized it by mixing it thoroughly with powdered sugar and distilled water into a mayonnaise jar. Hollingshead claimed that his share of the Sandoz gram was given to a galaxy of musicians, including Paul McCartney, as well as to writers, anthropologists, and philosophers in the United Kingdom and the United States, and that it was how Leary received his first dose of LSD. It is said that Leary took one and a half tablespoonfuls out of the magical mayonnaise jar and didn't talk for five days afterward.[4] "There is some possibility that my friends and I have illuminated more people than anyone else in history," Hollingshead wrote.

In 1962, Beresford (also originally from England) formed the Agora Scientific Trust, an LSD research organization in Manhattan, with Jean Houston and Michael Corner, and useful psychedelic research was conducted. He maintained that the term "psychedelic" does little to describe altered states of consciousness, and defines nothing. "Calling something 'psychedelic' merely suggests a similarity perceived by people who experience the effect of first one psychedelic drug and then another. That is a rather loose unifying principle."[5] Beresford is credited with inventing the sugar cube method of dispensing LSD, but I didn't know that when I had my first sugar cube. I *did* know that the man who had synthesized LSD was the Swiss chemist Albert Hofmann, who specialized in the chemistry of medicinal plants.

THE KINDLING OF THE FIRE

At Sandoz, Hofmann researched the alkaloids of ergot (*Claviceps purpurae*), a lower fungus parasite that grows on rye, and to a lesser extent on other species of grain and on wild grasses. Ergot was potently psychoactive. In the Middle Ages and since, there have been mass poisonings of whole communities caused by bread baked with ergotized flour. The convulsions, gangrene, and hallucinations triggered by this fungus were referred to as "Saint Anthony's fire" (among other names). In the early 1930s researchers at the Rockefeller Institute had studied ergot alkaloids and discovered that they shared a common nucleus. They named that common nucleus lysergic acid. Lysergic acid is one of the components of the alkaloid ergobasine, and Hofmann successfully prepared this alkaloid synthetically. In the course of this work, he also synthesized new lysergic acid compounds. In 1938 he produced the twenty-fifth in this series—LSD-25 (lysergic acid diethylamide)—for laboratory use. Animal tests of LSD-25 showed a strong effect on the uterus, and a restlessness during the narcosis, but nothing especially interesting over and above what had already been observed in other ergot alkaloids was noted. Testing was discontinued. Hofmann continued his investigations, which produced substances of medical value. Nevertheless, he had a "peculiar presentiment" that LSD-25 had properties that had yet to be discovered. In April 1943 he produced some more for further tests. During the final phase of this work he was "interrupted . . . by unusual sensations." He was forced to go home, being affected by "a remarkable restlessness" and dizziness. There he lay down "and sank into a not unpleasant intoxicated-like condition, characterized by an extremely stimulated imagination. In a dreamlike state, with eyes closed . . . I perceived an uninterrupted stream of fantastic pictures, extraordinary shapes with intense, kaleidoscopic play of colours."[6] He was so affected for two hours. He surmised that the lysergic acid material he had been handling had been the cause of this experience, yet he had employed meticulous work habits. If he had picked any of it up on his fingertips it could only have been a minute amount, suggesting the drug had "extraordinary potency."

A few days later he deliberately ingested a quarter of a milligram of lysergic acid diethylamide tartrate (one milligram equals one thousandth of a gram). Within forty minutes he was experiencing "dizziness, feeling of anxiety, visual distortions, symptoms of paralysis, desire to laugh," and could not continue with his notes. He started to undergo what he called a "most severe crisis," and asked his laboratory assistant to accompany him home. Due to wartime restrictions they rode bicycles. Hofmann had the sensation that he was pedaling but getting nowhere, but his assistant later assured him that he had travelled "very rapidly." At home, he instructed his assistant to call the doctor and ask the neighbor for some milk as "a nonspecific antidote for poisoning," then collapsed onto a sofa. The room seemed to spin round, and objects took on grotesque and threatening forms. They were in continuous animated activity. When the lady from next door brought his milk he could hardly recognize her: she appeared as "a malevolent, insidious witch with a coloured mask." No effort of will could "put an end to the disintegration of the outer world and the dissolution of my ego." The LSD-25 had become a demon that had vanquished him. "I was taken to another world, another place, another time," Hofmann recalled.[7] He feared that he was dying, and that these were the sensations of transition, for at times he felt himself to be outside his body. He could see his physical body on the sofa while his disembodied self moved around the room in a distressed state. What would his wife and children think when they returned? And the irony of the situation was not lost on him: if he was now to die, it was because of a substance that he himself had created. And if not death, then madness, perhaps?

By the time the doctor arrived, the peak—or depth—of the experience had passed. Since he could find nothing wrong with Hofmann, the doctor put him to bed and kept him under observation. With fears of death and insanity rapidly receding, Hofmann was gradually able to enjoy the experience. He was fascinated by the remarkably colored, glowing geometric patterns and fantastic images that surged in on him. In particular, he noticed how every sound he heard, even noises as inconsequential as the turning of a door handle or of a passing car, would generate "a vividly changing image, with its own consistent form and colour." He later described parts of his experience as "deeply religious."

The next day Hofmann awoke with a sensation of well-being to a world that seemed fresh and new. Food was experienced as being extraordinarily delicious, and foliage in the garden, glistening after a spring shower, sparkled in the sunshine with a fresh light. "All my senses vibrated in a condition of highest sensitivity, which persisted for the entire day," he wrote.[8] He was able to remember the entire experience, and realized that he had been fully conscious of what had gone on during the course of the experience. The LSD-25 had caused no impairment of mental faculties. His superiors at Sandoz could hardly believe that such a minute dose of any substance could have such powerful psychoactive effects, but further self-tests among Sandoz personnel showed that even lesser dosages gave impressive results. Up to three hundred thousand substantial doses could be obtained from one ounce: they had discovered the most powerful psychoactive substance known.

Sandoz felt sure that they had a drug that would be of great use to psychiatry and psychology. Experimental sessions were undertaken at the University of Zurich and the first paper on LSD's mental effects was published in 1947. LSD was handed informally to American psychiatrist Nicholas Bercel in 1949 by Werner Stoll of Sandoz and he took it to Los Angeles to test. Some was requested by and mailed to Boston's Psychopathic Hospital. A 1950 paper by psychiatrists A. K. Busch and W. C. Johnson appeared in an American academic journal recommending that LSD-25 be investigated for psychotherapy potential. Sandoz saw the drug as being a "psychotomimetic" able to produce "model psychosis," and although it was eventually realized that the effects of LSD had characteristics distinguishable from those of schizophrenia, numerous psychiatrists and psychologists at the time were keen to test it. More papers on the medical effects of the substance appeared in the early 1950s, and by 1953 Dr. Ronald Sandison opened the world's first public LSD clinic, in England. Similar centers sprouted up throughout Europe. One of these was the Psychiatric Research Institute in Prague, where a young medical researcher, Stanislav Grof, worked. Grof took his first LSD trip in 1956, and, according to psychedelic chronicler Peter Stafford, tried the substance in conjunction with a strong flashing light, designed to "drive his brainwaves."[9] (Stroboscopic lighting at certain frequencies can entrain brain rhythms at those frequencies.) "And this incredible blast of white light came," Grof wrote of this experiment. "And the next thing I knew was that my consciousness was leaving my body. Then I lost the clinic. Then I lost Prague. Then I lost the planet. Then I had the feeling of existing in a totally disembodied state and literally becoming the universe—experiencing it."[10] Grof went on to conduct and observe thousands of LSD sessions with patients, initially in Czechoslovakia, and subsequently in the United States, where he currently practices. He is one of the most experienced LSD therapists alive, and has been instrumental in developing nondrug methods of achieving psychedelic states. Grof insists that the doses used for LSD and other psychedelics are too low for there to be a specific pharmacological effect. The fact that people experience different sensations—and that even the same subject will have distinct experiences—argues against a simplistic toxic effect. "The content and nature of the experiences that these substances induce are thus not artificial products of their pharmacological interaction with the brain ('toxic psychoses'), but authentic expressions of the psyche revealing its functioning on levels ordinarily not available for observation and study."[11]

Another LSD pioneer was Humphry Osmond, a British psychiatrist based in Canada. He successfully treated alcoholics using LSD and mescaline. It was Osmond who gave Huxley his first mescaline session in 1953. Osmond was also befriended by perhaps the most bizarre figure in the LSD story, Captain Alfred M. Hubbard, a clandestine U.S. intelligence operative in World War II who was responsible for ensuring that Britain received its "unofficial" supply of American ships and war materials at a time when it stood alone against Nazi Germany.

Hubbard received a dose of Sandoz LSD from Sandison in England in 1951. He underwent a profound experience in which he witnessed his own conception, and subsequently became an energetic LSD evangelist, disseminating the drug widely throughout North America. Hubbard understood perhaps earlier than anyone the mystical and therapeutic potential of LSD. Despite his ruggedness, Hubbard got on well with Huxley, the refined intellectual, and gave the writer his first dose of acid in 1955. Huxley also moved in the same circles as Dr. Oscar Janiger, who had an ample supply of LSD from Sandoz, allowing him to make thousands of administrations of the substance to over eight hundred people. These were people from all walks of life—including film stars Cary Grant and Jack Nicholson. In 1959, Beat poet Allen Ginsberg first took LSD as a guinea pig at the Mental Research Institute in Palo Alto, California. Already familiar with some hallucinogens, Ginsberg was anxious to experience LSD, and it was the brilliant intellectual Gregory Bateson who arranged for him to be included in a research program at the institute. Ginsberg had a sober session there, and felt at one time that his soul was being sucked into the monitoring instruments he was hooked up to. But he went on to make contact with Leary, who gave him psilocybin pills—containing the active compounds of hallucinogenic "magic" mushrooms. These had also been synthesized by Hofmann. Ginsberg himself shared and partly encouraged Leary's own psychedelic enthusiasm, so LSD and psilocybin came to be added to the range of psychedelic substances already circulating within the Beat scene. The interest was longstanding. William Burroughs, for instance, had gone to the Amazon in search of hallucinogenic *yagé*. Now it seemed that LSD with the Sandoz label was "leaking" from the Sandoz New Jersey plant into the Beat scene in Greenwich Village.[12] The Beat culture of the late fifties and early sixties became very much a proving ground for the coming psychedelic revolution. Ginsberg felt that the Beats were "part of a cosmic conspiracy . . . to resurrect a lost art or a lost knowledge or a lost consciousness."

Thus the magical power of LSD escaped into popular culture, which was not the intent of some of those who were its strongest advocates initially. Throughout this period, the CIA and military intelligence agencies had been keeping their eyes on who was experimenting with and handling LSD. The sheer power of the drug had raised their interest, for they saw it as a potential weapon capable of altering behavior, and of brainwashing. In addition to encouraging and trying to control research in the United States, they were also concerned that the Russians not obtain supplies from Sandoz. The firm did not release supplies to the U.S. military, but the army approached Hofmann (in vain) every two years or so—until they finally secured a U.S.-based supply of the substance. "I had perfected LSD for medical use, not as a weapon," Hofmann would later remark. But Sandoz did apparently agree to let the CIA purchase supplies and to inform them who was ordering the drug. In most cases, LSD researchers were rubbing shoulders with CIA operatives without knowing it. The likes of Osmond and Huxley didn't appreciate how closely they were monitored, and even Gregory Bateson had been introduced to LSD by Dr. Harold Abramson, one of the CIA's top LSD experts. That was why Bateson suggested to Ginsberg that he should visit the Palo Alto program. This was a covert military operation,[13] and Ginsberg wasn't aware that Dr. Charles Savage, one of the researchers associated with the program, had conducted hallucinogenic drug experiments for the U.S. Navy.[14] Funding for LSD research was plentiful, while the CIA spied on those conducting it. It is an appalling episode in U.S. intelligence operations, consisting of schemes that ranged from the ridiculous to the sinister, involving outrageous experiments on many hundreds of soldiers and civilians, including the use of a brothel to observe unwitting subjects, and a proposal for testing hallucinogenic gases on subways. At least one suicide resulted from earlier experimentation.[15]

The CIA's disturbing involvement with LSD renders the legal crackdown on LSD use by the U.S. establishment all the more hypocritical. In 1962, authorized distribution of LSD became tightly controlled; it was classified as an "experimental drug." This meant it could only be used for research purposes, which in effect excluded therapeutic studies conducted by psychiatrists within their general practice. Many groundbreaking researchers were not able to continue their work. Certain researchers—such as the CIA—could be exempted, however, and covert experimentation was clearly not hampered. Even tighter restrictions were applied in 1965 in the United States, preventing work with LSD by anyone who did not have the FDA-approved exemption. Illicit manufacture and sale of LSD became a misdemeanor. Despite concern voiced by Senator Robert Kennedy about such a heavy-handed approach, most normal scientific research was curtailed. In 1967 it worsened: a committee was established to closely vet all research applications. In 1968 sale of LSD was upgraded to a felony, and possession now became a misdemeanor. By 1970 psychedelic drugs were assigned to Schedule I status, which meant that they were officially considered drugs of abuse with no medical value.

But by then interest in LSD was public and widespread, and it was inevitable that as a result of the government's actions an even larger black market in LSD flourished. When Stanislav Grof arrived in the United States from Czechoslovakia in 1967, he was surprised and perplexed at the legal situation he found with regard to LSD. When he left his home country, LSD was being manufactured there legally. It was in the official medical pharmacopoeia as a therapeutic agent with specific indications and contraindications listed. Those administering LSD sessions had to be properly qualified, but it was freely available to trained professionals as both a therapeutic and an experimental substance. Research reports circulated among academics and scientists, so there was no strong public knowledge about or interest in the drug (and consequently no black market in it). In any case, anyone interested in self-experimentation could have an LSD session, provided it was conducted in approved circumstances. By contrast, hundreds of thousands of Americans were experimenting willy-nilly with acid. Black-market LSD was readily available, and psychedelic subcultures were developing within the main body of society. Public knowledge about the substance was confined to sensationalist reports in the media, but the impact of psychedelics on the culture was evident in the arts, in popular music, in fashion, in the movies, and on TV. "The legislative measures undertaken with the intention of suppressing dangerous self-experimentation proved rather ineffective in curbing nonmedical use of LSD," Grof observed, "but had adverse direct and indirect consequences for scientific research."[16] Peter T. Furst, a distinguished professor of anthropology with a research interest in ethnobotany, has also commented: "It must seem to many the height of irony and of official cynicism that even as civilian medical research with LSD was being severely hampered by legal restrictions, and thousands of Americans, mostly young people, were being jailed and marked for life with felony records on LSD-related charges, the drug was being covertly administered to other thousands to see if it might prove useful for chemical warfare, while the Army was seeking ways to have it manufactured in quantities equivalent to literally tens of millions of individual experimental doses!"[17]

ANCIENT FLOWER POWER

LSD-25 is the product of the laboratory. In the sixties, it was considered somewhat ironic that a modern chemical took a person into realms that seemed to manifest the antithesis of the secular, technoscientific culture of which we were heirs, and in many cases provided a link back to nature. It was as if at the eleventh hour, perhaps to balance out the advent of the nuclear age, some higher power had created a way for modern society to innoculate itself against its own narrow vision and claustrophobic, single-phase brand of consciousness. Yes, the substance had been derived from something in the natural world, the lowly ergot parasitic fungus, but that seemed inconsequential. Nature didn't figure much in the image of LSD, which seemed to have more to do with white-coated laboratory workers. It seemed obvious that the psychedelic revolution was unique in the history of the world. Yet at this very time, Hofmann himself had been ushering into his laboratory substances that had been used centuries ago by great, lost civilizations from the Americas—psychoactive mushrooms and morning glory seeds. The story of the morning glory seeds relates to the LSD story, and leads us on to the main subject of this book.

A year after Hofmann had synthesized LSD-25, some time before his involuntary first trip, another brilliant, dedicated researcher was combing the remote wilds of Mexico, seeking, among other things, a legendary psychoactive plant. The researcher was the great Harvard ethnobotanist Richard Evans Schultes, and the plant was the mysterious *ololiuhqui* ("round things," "pellets") of the Aztecs. In 1629, Spanish chronicler Ruiz de Alarcón wrote in his *Tratado* on "the superstition of the *ololiuhqui*." He noted that the Indians attributed divinity to an unspecified plant, which was pictured in the 1651 chronicle of Francisco Hernández. The Indians addressed the plant with special incantations, and even swept the ground around the bushes that provided the seeds.

The seeds were venerated on altars, and made into drinks to be used for both divinatory and healing purposes. Hernández wrote: "When drunk, it acts as an aphrodisiac. It has a sharp taste and is very hot. Formerly, when the priests wanted to commune with their gods and to receive a message from them, they ate this plant to induce a delirium. A thousand visions and satanic hallucinations appeared to them." The Spaniards attempted to curtail use of the plant, burning the seeds they found and uprooting the bushes. But the practice survived by acquiring a Christian veneer, and disappeared from European view. Botanists started looking for it in the twentieth century.

In 1919, Mexican scholar Dr. Blas Pablo Reko had collected *ololuc* seeds and identified them as a species of morning glory, *Rivea corymbosa*. Because no intoxication resulted from ingestion of the seeds, and because no psychoactive alkaloids had been found in any of the Convolvulaceae, the noted American botanist William Safford felt that *ololiuhqui* had to be the seeds of *Datura inoxia*, which were known to be intoxicating. (Safford also dismissed the idea that psychoactive mushrooms were used by the Aztecs.) In 1937, C. G. Santesson confirmed that the morning glory family of plants, including *R. corymbosa*, could have hallucinogenic properties, but the active components were not identified. On a field trip with Reko in 1939, Schultes encountered a cultivated species of *R. corymbosa* in the garden of a Zapotec Indian healer, the first recorded sighting by a scientist. He uncovered the continuing use of the brown, oval seeds of this plant amongst the Zapotec and other Indian groups, and published a paper on the subject in 1941. Later, Gordon Wasson was to discover that the seeds of another major hallucinogenic morning glory, *Ipomea violacea* (often going by the name Heavenly Blue in gardening circles), were also used, and were called *Tlitliltzen* by the Indians in ancient times.[18] Its black seeds are known as *badoh negro* or *badungás* in Oaxaca today. Learning of Santesson's claims that as yet unidentified psychoactive alkaloids were likely present in morning glory seeds, Humphry Osmond ate approximately a hundred seeds, but his symptoms—listlessness, visual sharpness, and finally a sense of well-being—did not match the effects as reported in Aztec times. Later tests by other researchers failed to show any inebriating effects, and the rumor began to circulate that the ancient Indians must have been susceptible to autosuggestion. But Wasson, primarily engaged in a study of the traditional use of hallucinogenic mushrooms in Mexico, pointed out that the researchers were not preparing the seeds in the same way the Indians did, grinding the seeds on a stone (metate) and reducing them to flour. This flour was soaked in cold water, then strained and drunk. Wasson had used the seeds in this way himself, and had found their potency to be "undeniable." Taking the seeds whole simply meant that they passed through the digestive system with little or no effect.

In 1959, Wasson, knowing of Hofmann's work on LSD, sent him samples of *R. corymbosa* and *I. violacea* he had collected in Mazatec and Zapotec Indian areas of Mexico. Initial analysis by Hofmann showed that indole compounds related to LSD and the ergot alkaloids were present in the seeds. Analysis of further samples sent by Wasson in 1960 revealed that their main active constituents were ergot alkaloids *d*-lysergic amine and *d*-isolysergic acid amide, closely related to *d*-lysergic acid diethylamide. Hofmann self-tested lysergic acid amide and "established that it likewise evoked a dreamlike condition, but only with about a tenfold to twentyfold greater dose than LSD."[19]

The finding of LSD in such a species as morning glory was startling, for these plants were very much different from lower fungi such as ergot, and had a different evolutionary history. In fact, when Hofmann announced his findings at a conference in Australia in 1960, delegates had difficulty accepting them.[20] Some claimed that Hofmann's samples must have been contaminated by traces of LSD derivatives in the laboratory, or that they had been infected with alkaloid-producing fungi. But there had been no such circumstances, and Hofmann's discovery was confirmed by other researchers.

THE CIRCLE IS UNBROKEN

The finding of LSD in morning glory seeds on the one hand provoked Hofmann into studying and confirming that other botanical sources also contained psychoactive alkaloids, and on the other made him feel that a "magic circle," beginning and ending with LSD, had closed for him. He had discovered for modern society the profound mind-changing properties of LSD, while his work with the seeds had revealed that it occurred naturally in the higher plants and that it had been used in cultures before our own—indeed, long before our own. The Aztecs, whose culture was at its peak in the sixteenth century when the Spanish arrived, were continuing a tradition that went back at least to Teotihuacán, a remarkable Native American city in the Valley of Mexico that was active A.D. 100 to 650.[21] It was possibly the largest city of its age in the Western Hemisphere, and no one knows who built and inhabited it. When the Aztecs encountered its awesome ruins they considered it the birthplace of the gods, and consequently named it Teotihuacán, which means "birthplace of the gods." A mural in a sacred building there shows a great Earth Mother Goddess with a stylized depiction of *R. corymbosa*.

These interactions between researchers in Mexico and Switzerland marked developments that led to the closing of a "magical ring" of my own. All the complex history of LSD and the emerging ethnobotanical dimensions were largely unknown to most of my contemporaries and me in 1966; I knew something about Leary's troubles, knew that Hofmann had synthesized LSD-25 and that he worked at Sandoz in Switzerland. I was locally famous for having received a letter from Aldous Huxley, and I decided to take up my pen again. This time, I wrote to Hofmann, and asked how to secure supplies of LSD. This time, no reply came back. As the years passed, we attempted to alter our consciousness in new ways. We heard about morning glory seeds—and other psychedelic exotica—and tried them. But either because I did not know how to properly prepare them, or because the seeds had been sprayed,* the only effect I experienced was exceptional gas for about a week afterward.

---

*The consumption of morning glory seeds soared to such an extent that they were chemically treated by seed distributors and suppliers to render them useless for hallucinogenic purposes.

Eventually, the great wave of psychedelia spent itself, and I and many of my contemporaries became more or less respectable members of society, our mystical zeal tempered by reality. But I guess many of us never became "normal" in the full sense: those gleams of the other-world that we had glimpsed, though dimming in our memories, were never quite extinguished. I turned to an interest in ancient societies, sites, and lifeways, especially those areas considered heretical by mainstream scholarship and those specifically to do with the history of human consciousness, such as shamanism. After my experiences during the psychedelic sixties, the next couple of decades seemed dreadfully gray, and dismissal by the mainstream cultures of—and even antagonism toward—the idea of exploring altered states was almost discouraging.

So I set out to find if ancient worldviews contained elements that were missing from our own, and if so, to see if their principles could be reintegrated into our ways of thinking today. This inevitably made me aware of the discoveries within ethnobotany, eventually leading me to become particularly involved with uncovering evidence of "shamanic landscapes," which have considerable relevance to the use of hallucinogens in ancient cultures. Through my work in this area I participated in numerous conferences worldwide. At a symposium in Munich in 1992, I was delighted to meet Albert Hofmann. By now, of course, I knew of his important contribution to the study of hallucinogens in ancient societies, but I had heard little about him in the years just prior to the symposium. I found Hofmann to be a sprightly man now in his eighties, bright and charming. In one of our conversations I couldn't resist telling him of the letter I had sent him as a callow youth so many years earlier. "I did not reply?" he asked, clearly quite shocked, for he prided himself on being very orderly with his correspondence. "I must go back over my files!" We both chuckled, and I assured him that would not be necessary, that the letter had most probably not even reached him. More to the point was to thank him for his remarkable contribution to the field: he had been a catalyst for research developments and social events that he could never have foreseen when he took his cosmic bike ride in 1943.

As that callow youth, I had not been equipped to put the whole psychedelic issue into its proper context, which was so much greater than merely the social upheavals of the 1960s. I had thought then that I was part of a revolutionary movement the likes of which the world had never seen before; I smugly thought I was one of those way ahead of the times, but in truth I was just another "head" of my times. I couldn't then have guessed that, in fact, humanity has been on a long, long trip—it has been tripping out through all recorded history, and long before, perhaps from the dawn of humanity. It is even possible that the use of hallucinogens encouraged the evolution of higher forms of mentation in early humans, elaborating language, memory, and other skills.

This book offers some snapshots of that long, strange trip, which will help us gain a perspective and provide a larger context in which to evaluate the views our mainstream culture has developed toward hallucinogens and altering states of consciousness. It will also remind us that peoples long gone, or now on the brink of extinction, may have had a richer, subtler knowledge of consciousness than we modern, Western-style societies possess today. We may have a rapidly growing understanding of the brain, but the ancients had the technology of the mind. In terms of understanding consciousness, we are as yet primitives. "I think in antiquity," Albert Hofmann has said, "they had institutions where people who wanted to be initiated could, under well-elaborated conditions, derive a beneficial effect from it. That is a problem which our society has not yet solved."[22]

one
Stoned at
the Bones

Archaeologists Go to Pot: Opium
and Cannabis in Stone Age Europe?

Legend has it that long ago a land sank beneath the sea that now washes the shores of Cornwall, the most southwesterly peninsula of England, and "Armorica," the ancient name for that portion of northwestern France that now includes Brittany, part of Normandy, and the Channel Islands. Both Cornwall and Brittany have strikingly similar landscapes—rocky coasts punctuated by sandy coves, and a rather bare, undulating interior—and there is indeed evidence in both lands that parts of their coastal areas were subject to inundation, probably a few thousand years ago. In Cornwall the legendary lost land is referred to as Lyonesse; in Armorica, it is called Ynys ("island"). This legend keeps alive the idea, or memory, of a mysterious land to the west, in the waters beyond the edge of the world.

The eerie power of this myth-memory was brought home to me one gray March day when a few companions and I arrived at the quayside at Locmariaquer, a small community on the shores of Quiberon Bay, not far from Carnac. Armorica, and this region particularly, has arguably the greatest concentration of prehistoric standing stones and megalithic ("big stone") monuments in the world. There are several thousand standing stones—some isolated menhirs, some in stone circles or enclosures, some lined up in rows that extend for miles. There are also chambered mounds from various periods of prehistory, including "passage graves" and "gallery graves." The Breton passage graves may be as much as six thousand years old. We had arrived at Locmariaquer on this particular day to visit Gavrinis, one of the largest and most famous examples, situated on a tiny island a short distance off the mainland in Quiberon Bay. It was not the tourist season, so there were no boats available, but we were in luck, for Charles-Tanguy Le Roux, a leading French prehistorian and specialist on Gavrinis, was taking a party of local dignitaries out to see the monument. So we hitched a ride.

Our boat took a wide, curving course, and passed close to an islet on which stand the remains of two stone circles that almost interlink. This is the site known as Er Lannic. It presented a dramatic scene as we passed by: the dark waters of the wintry sea were rolling right up to the circles and sluicing between the gray, gaunt stones. The greater part of the circles disappeared beneath the waves. I had never seen a stone circle flooded by the tide before, and it brought to life the legends of lost Ynys. A small valley and a river had separated the hilltops holding Er Lannic and Gavrinis some thousands of years ago, where now they were divided by the swirling waters leading out into Quiberon Bay.

Er Lannic has other significance than just dramatizing the inundation of the coastline. It was an important ceremonial center in Neolithic times, when it could be approached on foot. This is indicated not only by the presence of the large stone circles themselves, but also by the fact that intriguing finds were unearthed among the stones by archaeologists. One discovery was a hoard of stone axes. These were ceremonial objects for ritual use, not for chopping firewood. Some were polished, and are remarkably fine, sophisticated artifacts, while others were unfinished, "suggesting that the site was involved in the production of stone axes," archaeologist Mark Patton observes.[1] The source for the stones was nearby, and it seems the roughs were brought to Er Lannic for finishing. Carved representations of axes are found on two of the stones of the circles. "This suggests an important link between axe production and megalithic ritual," Patton deduces. Archaeologists at Er Lannic also found evidence of a series of hearths, which they likewise interpreted as being associated with ritual activity. In addition, they found the fragments of at least 162 ceramic objects known as "vase supports." It is with these objects that our journey into Stone Age psychedelia begins.

POPPY FIELDS OF DREAMS

These so-called vase supports are shallow bowls set within cylindrical or cubic stands. They are usually richly decorated. Archaeologists had previously interpreted them as being stands for round-bottomed vessels, but some of the shallow bowls show traces of burning, prompting archaeologist Andrew Sherratt to suggest that they are, in fact, braziers.[2] He has further argued that they were designed to burn substances such as opium or cannabis (both of which can produce hallucinogenic effects)—and he feels it most likely that opium was the substance used at the Er Lannic finds.

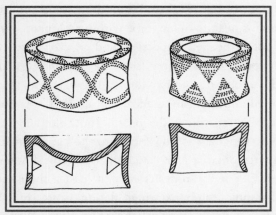

Pottery vase supports (probably braziers) from the ceremonial site of Er Lannic, Brittany. *(Andrew Sherratt, 1991)*

Opium derives its name from the Greek *opos*, "juice," and comprises a complex of nearly forty alkaloids such as morphine (named after Morpheus, the god of dreams), codeine, papaverine, thebaine, neopine, laudanidine, and so on. The effects of this complex are closely related to brain chemicals known as endorphins: our cerebrospinal fluid naturally contains these opiumlike chemicals. (So, deep inside, we are all illegal!) "Juice" is a reference to how opium is collected: a milky sap exudes from slits cut in the partly ripened seed capsule of the opium poppy (*Papaver somniferum*) and this is allowed to congeal to a rubbery substance before collection. The opium poppy is a flowering annual not known in the wild state, so it must have been cultivated in ancient times—it may be a cultigen of *Papaver setigerum*, which is indigenous to the Mediterranean region, which would mean that the opium poppy was domesticated in this area, its use for nutrition, medicine, and religious purposes diffusing out from there in all directions.

We see ample testimony to the importance of opium in Mycenaean and Minoan societies in relics from Bronze Age Greece and Crete: terra-cotta figurines from Knossos with incised capsules as coronas;[3] the three-foot-tall Cretan "Poppy Goddess" effigy with poppy pods sticking out of her headband, found buried by volcanic ash and earthquake debris near an opium pipe within an "opium den";[4] the curiously long poppy-headed needles found at Mycenae, which were eventually recognized as being tools for handling small pieces of opium;[5] and various decorative depictions of poppies. The opium poppy remained important in Greece, as indicated by a 600 B.C. statue of Aesculapius, which shows the healing god clutching a handful of poppy capsules. Opium was also known to the Egyptians. For example, the Ebers Papyrus of circa 1500 B.C. contains medical notes containing opium references copied from a source at least a thousand years earlier,[6] and pharaonic tomb paintings dating from 1600 to 600 B.C. show opium poppies and other psychoactive plants. And we can track the use of opium even further through cuneiform tablets that are the world's oldest surviving written documents. These tablets from Sumer, a region between the Euphrates and Tigris Rivers, now in southern Iraq, date from the third millennium B.C. and earlier, and mention the use of opium.

Much of this has long been known, but it now seems that opium also has a presence in northern and western Europe at least as old as that recorded in Sumer. Hard archaeological evidence for the religious

Upper part of "Poppy Goddess" figure from Bronze Age Crete. *(Author's drawing)*

use of the opium poppy in the early Neolithic period in Europe is provided by a site called the Cueva de los Murciélagos ("Bat Cave") located about 150 feet up the side of a ravine at Albuñol near the coast of Granada in southern Spain. When Spanish archaeological researchers investigated it in 1868, this prehistoric burial cave had been largely destroyed by people seeking bat guano and minerals. Nevertheless, some intriguing finds were made. A number of burials within the cave were found to be accompanied by bags made from esparto grass. These globular bags contained, among other items, large numbers of opium-poppy capsules. "This find suggests that poppy-heads had a symbolic significance beyond the simple use of their seeds as a source of food, and that this symbolism was particularly appropriate as an accompaniment for the dead," Sherratt remarks.[7] These items were reexamined in 1980, and yielded a radiocarbon date of around 4200 B.C.—the early Neolithic period contemporary with the onset of the era of passage graves in Brittany.

Poppy seeds have been uncovered at Neolithic lake villages, and at some seventeen other Neolithic sites in Switzerland. Seed heads found in Neolithic contexts in Switzerland and Spain are from domesticated poppies. Seeds have also been found at ten sites of the later Bronze Age in Switzerland, and similar finds have been made in Italy and Germany, where complete seed heads have been recovered from lakeside sites and arid caves.

Sherratt sees a slow shift from a "smoking complex" to a "drinking complex" in prehistoric Europe. It seems that the introduction of alcohol occurred in Mesopotamia and the eastern Mediterranean region in the fourth millennium B.C. It slowly spread westward, reaching the Atlantic coast of Europe by about 2500 B.C. Sherratt suspects that a mysterious type of British Neolithic pottery called "Grooved Ware" (on account of its characteristic incised markings) may have been used for a ritual drink. Grooved Ware has unknown origins,[8] and is frequently found in ceremonial sites such as stone circles and henge monuments. This kind of pottery "seems to have had a special quality which set it aside from everyday containers," Sherratt notes. (We shall come to further revelations about Grooved Ware later.) The "smoking complex" and the "drinking complex" coexisted for some time, and the hallucinogens that had previously been smoked—opium and cannabis particularly—were prepared as liquid concoctions. Ultimately alcohol assumed dominance in Europe.[9–12]

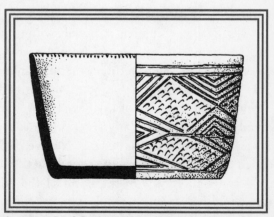

An example of Grooved Ware. Neolithic. *(After Stuart Piggott)*

This emerging preference for liquid intoxicants can be seen in the form of Bronze Age pots—jugs, bottles, and flasks—from Cyprus. These have been found in Egypt dating from the Eighteenth Dynasty of the New Kingdom in Egypt (1550–1307 B.C.), and later sets have been recovered from the remains of Tell el-Amarna (Akhetaten), the short-lived capital city of Egypt built by the deformed heretic king Akhenaten, who reigned from 1353 to 1335 B.C. The jug was the most common of these Cypriot pots. In commenting that the apparent importance of these jugs must reflect the importance of their content, Richard Rudgley goes on to note:

> We know that the narrow necks of the juglets point to liquid contents, as solid substances could not have been emptied through such small apertures. Working along a line of highly innovative thinking, Robert Merrillees has argued that the Cypriote export merchants of the Bronze Age could have best announced the nature of their product by designing a vessel whose shape would easily communicate the nature of its contents. That many of their foreign customers would not have understood any written language except

A schematic comparison of the shapes of an imported Cypriot jug from Egypt and an inverted poppy capsule.

their own, while others would have been altogether illiterate, makes this the most viable method of advertising their wares.[13]

Today, as Merrillees pointed out, plastic vessels in the shape of, say, a tomato, for tomato ketchup, or a squeezable, yellow plastic lemon for lemon juice, serve the same purpose. The alarmingly obvious fact is that the standard shape of these Bronze Age jugs strongly suggests an opium poppy capsule held upside down: the long thin neck of the jug is like the stalk of the poppy, the rounded body of the vessel takes almost precisely the form of the poppy capsule itself, and the base ring of the jug spreads out in a manner strongly imitative of the stigma on top of the poppy capsule. This clearly suggests that the contents of such vessels were probably an infusion of opium (the Cypriots are known to have produced a liquid opium preparation in an olive oil base). In fact, the suspicion originally raised by Merrillees has now been confirmed by British biochemist John Evans using chromatographic and spectroscopic techniques on the Bronze Age Cypriot pottery. His analysis of organic residues found there shows that opium was indeed present in at least some of the jugs.[14]

CULTURE SHOCK

But let us return to the much older Breton vase support/braziers. These objects are decorated with distinctive "sunburst" motifs that Sherratt tells us are "associated with a particular style of pottery decoration, which seems to have spread from south to north." This is the same presumed direction as the diffusion of opium usage from its home base in the eastern Mediterranean region. "These objects occur in caves in the south, and in ditched enclosures in the Paris Basin, and they occur not infrequently in megaliths in the west," Sherratt continues. "Their use in group ritual . . . seems rather clear; and their inter-regional distribution suggests that they were associated with a cult which spread from south to north over a large area of western Europe, uniting groups of different origins."[15] We must also remember that at the ceremonial site of Er Lannic, these objects were found in association with "ritual hearths"—

some of the stones even showed evidence of fire damage.

The timing of the appearance of the vase support/braziers in Armorica is intriguing. Those found at Er Lannic have been dated to between 4250 and 3750 B.C.[16] This seems to coincide with a period of considerable change in the area, when, most notably, the passage graves first started to appear. Patton explains the significance:

> The appearance of passage graves apparently represents an independent development within the Armorican region, and must relate *to fundamental cultural and religious change* [italics mine]: in Northwestern Brittany, large passage graves appeared in areas where monumental ritual was previously unknown, whilst in southern Brittany and the Channel Islands, they supplanted an earlier megalithic tradition, the monuments of which were, in some cases, deliberately destroyed.[17]

This evidence of a change from some earlier tradition is particularly strongly marked at Gavrinis, Er Lannic's neighboring monument. Excavation there has revealed that the massive capstone forming the ceiling of the chamber is a broken segment of a reused standing stone. On its upper side, therefore hidden from view within the chamber, are large carvings of horned animals and other objects. By matching the fragments of the representational carvings, it was confirmed that two other passage graves (La Table des Marchand and Er-Vingle) had segments of this same huge former standing stone built into their fabric too. (The original stone from which these segments originated must have stood around forty feet tall.) Reused fragments of earlier megaliths have been found as part of the fabric of other passage graves too. It is of further significance that the style of the carvings on this reused monolith is completely different from the abstract patterns carved into the walls within the passage and chamber of Gavrinis. The nature of this later art style is, as we shall see, evidence of the use of altered states of consciousness at the site.

It clearly seems that something rocked the cultural boat in Armorica around the time those braziers arrived. Could it have been the mysterious, waking dreamworld of the opium poppy? Although the use of the vase support/braziers for the inhalation of opium fumes is as yet just unconfirmed interpretation, it is an extremely likely scenario. Although scientific analysis has not yet confirmed opium residues on any of the ceramic objects, Sherratt feels it is really just a matter of time. He is certain the technical evidence will be found to confirm the obvious nature of the artifacts. Similarly, Patton says he is just waiting for the uncontaminated remnants of one of these ceremonial vessels to be excavated at a ceremonial site—perhaps in Brittany or the Channel Islands. The next time one is uncovered he will have the residue analysis done immediately. It seems that many of the objects already recovered were excavated at a time when the modern, high-tech methods of analysis were not developed or known about. Shards were routinely washed or otherwise altered, making it impossible for technical analysis to be meaningfully carried out on them. In Patton's own excavations at La Hougue Bie, an important passage-grave monument on the Channel Island of Jersey, where numerous vase support/braziers were found, it was bad luck that none of the samples proved suitable for testing. Even today pottery items with the potential for trace analysis sometimes get washed by the excavator before they can be looked at. It may seem odd that such a thing could happen, but it is important to note that there are two general approaches in present-day archaeology. One, mainly displayed by archaeologists in France, Germany, and southern Europe, is to stick pretty rigidly with the hard, empirical evidence of archaeological excavation, limiting theory to only what can be actually observed. The other, found primarily among archaeologists in Britain, the United States, and Scandinavia, considers it possible to extrapolate information which can't be directly observed, such as social structure, religious beliefs, and ideology, from the physical evidence. Adherents of this approach point out that even interpreting empirical data draws on inherent assumptions.

I suspect that until the psychedelic sixties the possibility that hallucinogens were not only being used in prehistoric cultures, but might even be responsible for the appearance of certain types of pottery, not to mention economic and social aspects of prehistoric society, was al-

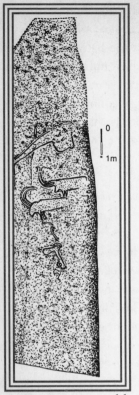

The huge capstone from Gavrinis, a segment of an even larger monolith, showing the representational imagery engraved on it. *(After C-T Le Roux)*

most certainly inconceivable to most archaeological investigators. It simply did not occur to researchers to look for this evidence. Over the last forty years, general familiarity with the idea of psychedelic experience has become widespread throughout Western culture. Virtually all of the archaeologists, anthropologists, and ethnobotanists who are now looking at the nature of hallucinogens and their effects on ancient societies were attending universities during the sixties or in the decades afterward. (The few older ethnobotanists and anthropologists had in many cases experienced for themselves the effects of psychoactive plants earlier, in the course of their fieldwork.) With either personal experience with hallucinogens or awareness that such experiences are possible, it is perhaps not surprising that researchers are now finding evidence previously overlooked in the archaeological record.

HOLY SMOKE

According to Sherratt's model, then, the inhalation of fumes preceded the "drinking complex" and was the most ancient method of taking in aromatic and psychoactive substances (if these two categories are actually distinct). The practice is remembered in the word *perfume* (*par fume*, "by smoke"), and derived from or was closely related to the nearly universal archaic tradition of using incense in rituals and ceremonies. The Greek term *cannabeizein*, for instance, refers to a method of inhaling vapors from an incense burner containing hemp (cannabis) mixed with a variety of resins such as frankincense, balsam, and myrrh. The Ashera priestesses in ancient Jerusalem were one of the groups who employed this method in their temples.[18] It is claimed that the Babylonians used cannabis as an incense in their temples in the third millenium B.C., as did the Assyrians in the seventh and eighth centuries B.C., because its aroma was pleasing to the gods. The classic account of the use of the inhalation of mind-altering fumes in antiquity is that given by the "first historian," the Greek writer Herodotus (born c. 485 B.C.), in his *Histories*:

> I must mention that hemp grows in Scythia, a plant resembling flax, but much coarser and taller. It grows wild as well as under cultivation, and the Thracians make clothes from it very like linen ones. . . . And now for the vapour-bath: on a framework of three sticks, meeting at the top they stretch pieces of woollen cloth, taking care to get the joins as perfect as they can, and inside this little tent they put a dish with red-hot stones in it. Then they take some hemp seed, creep into the tent, and throw the seeds on to the hot stones. At once it begins to smoke, giving off a vapour unsurpassed by any vapour-bath one could find in Greece. The Scythians enjoy it so much that they howl with pleasure (IV:73).

The name "Scythians" was given by the Greeks to nomadic tribes originating in central Asia who inhabited the steppes to the north and east of the Black and Caspian Seas from around the eighth century B.C. Herodotus's description refers to activities associated with their standard funerary observances, and followed an account of their method of burying a king, which involved, among other things, the interment of horses with him. The Swiss scholar K. Meuli felt that Herodotus had mistaken the "howls of pleasure" for the characteristic shouting of the Scythian *Kapnobatai* or shamans during their trances as part of the funerary rites.

Little of all this was understood by most scholars, and many frankly doubted the veracity of Herodotus's account, until archaeological findings confirmed it. This verification resulted from the work of

Russian archaeologist S. I. Rudenko, who in 1924 discovered a set of five burial mounds or barrows in the valley of Pazyryk near the Altai Mountains on the border between Siberia and Outer Mongolia. In a series of excavations spanning the years 1929–48, Rudenko examined all five barrows, which were pit graves or *kurgans*. These tombs had been constructed between 500 and 300 B.C. and were exceptionally well preserved because they had been flooded by water that became frozen. The earth and stone covering the burial chambers prevented this from thawing, so the contents, including normally perishable items, were preserved as in a deep freeze. It was all there, literally frozen in time: textiles, leather, and the bodies of men and horses. In one of the mounds—barrow 2—two copper vessels were found, one contained the charred remains of hemp seeds, the other the stones used to heat them to produce the intoxicating fumes. (The seeds of cannabis are not themselves psychoactive, but the intoxicating flowers and leaves would have been burned away.) Furthermore, a tent frame consisting of six metal rods was also found.[19] Herodotus's account was shown to have been extraordinarily accurate. Rudgley has commented

Copper censors for burning hemp, from barrow 2 at Pazyryk. (*Author's drawing after a photograph by S. I. Rudenko*)

that this shows the remarkable continuity of Scythian practices, because Pazyryk is thousands of miles to the east of the Black Sea, the area where Herodotus had seen the same equipment in use.[20]

In all, there is no doubt that the ritual use of braziers for inhaling intoxicating vapors was well established in antiquity. The question arises, could the Breton braziers have been for cannabis rather than for opium? Mark Patton has remarked that while he personally has no doubt that some form of psychoactive substance was used, exactly what it was is an issue.[21] There are a number of psychoactive herbs that could have been used. Hemp is commonly assumed by scholars to have been introduced into the western fringes of Europe, including the British Isles, in Romano-British or Anglo-Saxon times.[22] But there is some tentative evidence that cannabis may indeed have been present there thousands of years earlier, in the Neolithic period, the time of the great megalithic monuments. Recent archaeological investigation beneath the floor of the passage grave of La Hougue Géonnais, on the Channel Island of Jersey, has revealed traces of ancient pollen that is either cannabis or its close cousin, *Humulus* (genus of hop)[23]—it is notoriously difficult to distinguish the pollen of these two. Robert Jones of Coventry University also has evidence of pollen grains of what may have been hemp found in coastal peat in Jersey, close to archaeological sites. His student, Jim Campbell, has similarly found hemp/hop pollen in later prehistoric contexts on Alderney, the most northerly of the larger Channel Islands, again with nearby archaeological sites. Of course, even if securely identified as cannabis pollen, such evidence does not necessarily mean that the hemp was used for religious intoxication—it could have been used just for making ropes or clothing. But knowing the propensity of human beings in all times and places to seek ways of altering their consciousness, it is unlikely that the psychoactive properties of cannabis would have gone unnoticed. Peter Furst has gone so far as to suggest that the psychedelic effects of cannabis were used "probably long before hemp fiber began to assume economic importance."[24]

The sort of circumstantial evidence Sherratt has assembled still suggests opium as being the most likely substance to have been used in

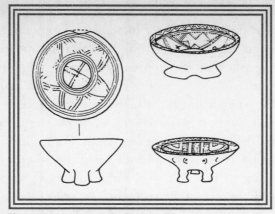

Pottery polypod bowls from eastern and central Europe, possibly braziers for burning cannabis. *(Andrew Sherratt, 1991)*

the vase support/braziers, however. He sees other ceramic artifacts as the most probable candidates for hemp usage. Among these are what are called in Russian *kurilnitsy*—"pipe bowls" or small-footed "polypod" bowls, which have been interpreted as small braziers. The earliest of this type of pottery artifact was found in the steppes, and finds dated to the third millenium B.C. in eastern Europe associate it with cannabis: a pit grave or kurgan at Gurbanestic near Bucharest in Romania contained charred hemp seeds, as did a similar find in the north Caucasus region. Later small-footed bowls have been unearthed in Czechoslovakia and southern Germany, suggesting that this type of pottery spread from east to west. This matches botanical data which indicate that cultivated cannabis originated in central Asia and spread in all directions from there.

The footed or polypod bowl was distinguished by a sunburst decorative motif. The design itself could have been intended to symbolize the psychedelic experience. Its means of execution might also have been symbolically significant: the patterns were made on the surface of the clay with either a cutting tool or by means of *impressed cords*. The cord pattern could—like the poppy-shaped jug—be a reference to the source plant. Hemp was, of course, used for its fiber, especially for making cord and ropes, in addition to its mind-altering properties. We can assume that the cord used for impressing these designs was made of hemp. Sherratt notes that recent study of this cord-impressed design shows that it spread from the steppes westward in the third millenium B.C., contemporaneous with the rise and spread of the polypod bowls themselves. He points out that the highly specific elements of form and decoration retained their characteristics while passing through a thousand miles and half a dozen cultures, spreading from the steppes to temperate Europe. He sees this as evidence of the progression of a cult, and sees the polypod bowls as ritual hemp burners associated with it.

Sherratt also notes other intriguing ceramic items appearing in various parts of Neolithic Europe. In the Balkans, for example, fifth-millenium B.C. dishes standing on three or four legs have been found in both domestic and other contexts (such as in copper mines, which could indicate propitiatory rituals connected with the extraction of ores from the body of the Earth Mother). They are generally interpreted as being small, portable altars or lamps. Sherratt suggests that they may have served this purpose as well as having been burners for aromatic substances, and points out that this domestic and workplace ritual usage underlines the long-established practice of inhaling sacramental fumes. These objects often have animal heads fashioned into their overall design, and are usually richly decorated. The "fret" type of motif often involved would suggest that whatever was burned in the dishes had psychoactive properties, because such designs are indicative of "trance patterns" that are universally used in reference to altered states of consciousness.

Richard Rudgley has succinctly summarized what is known about the prehistoric usage of opium and cannabis in Eurasia:

> There are clear parallels in the use of opium and hemp in prehistoric times. Both grew as weeds near human habitations and are known to have been domesticated in the Neolithic as multipurpose plants. In both cases distinctive ceramic braziers were probably used for the inhalation of the smoke of the respective substances. Although it is only after the Neolithic period (when the ar-

chaeological record becomes sufficiently detailed) that we have direct and irrefutable proof that these plants were used as intoxicants, the circumstantial evidence for their use as such in the Neolithic is highly persuasive.[25]

INSIDE THE OPIUM AND CANNABIS EXPERIENCES

The general impact of the ingestion of opium is to produce waking dreamlike states, relaxation and (usually) a sense of calm, unemotional well-being (a sort of bliss) and, eventually, sleep. Intensive, excessive consumption can cause nightmarish visions, psychological dependency, and, over a period of several months, physical addiction. In other words, it can be used or abused. But opium is less addictive than nicotine,[26] and it has no serious effects on health, other circumstances being equal. It is difficult to categorize most psychoactive substances as being wholly narcotic (that is, having a depressive action on the central nervous system), wholly stimulating, or wholly hallucinogenic, as they can combine differing characteristics at various stages of their psychoactivity. So opium is a narcotic, but it can have hallucinogenic phases of activity. Its hallucinogenic effects, as with all hallucinogens, depend upon *set and setting*. This means that the physical circumstances of a hallucinogenic session and the mental state of the subject can profoundly color the ensuing experience. Set and setting would include the nature of the surroundings (whether sunny, light, and supportive or dark, dismal, and threatening, for example), the expectations and attitude of the hallucinogen taker, the experiencer's physical and psychological state, the belief structure in which the experience takes place, and so on. These and other factors (some researchers consider that even the time of day the opium is administered can be significant) can profoundly affect *and shape* the nature and content of the overall experience. A substance taken with the expectation of having a religious experience would likely result in deeper, or at least more noticeably pronounced, experiences than, say, if it was taken in a casual, secular setting "for kicks." And there are many shades between those extremes of the spectrum. So if we look at a range of firsthand accounts of the hallucinogenic component of opium experience, we can expect to see differences as well as essential similarities, depending on who took what, where, when, and how.

Perhaps the best-known account comes to us from that most artic-ulate of opium addicts, Thomas De Quincey, whose *Confessions of an English Opium-Eater* was a success in his own time and has remained a celebrated account of the trials, agonies, and joys of opium addiction in nineteenth-century England. And addict he was, like many literary figures of his time who had become accustomed to taking the legal and often prescribed laudanum (tincture of opium) for medical reasons. Opium is truly a medicine, with strong painkilling properties, and at the time it was a godsend to medical practice. De Quincey began tak-ing laudanum at the age of twenty-eight to help deal with a gastric ul-cer, which did indeed disappear. But he went on taking laudanum until his habit reached a peak of 8,000 drops a day, against a normal medical dose of 80 to 120 drops daily. Yet he lived on in good fettle as a more moderate addict until his death from natural causes at seventy-four. Al-though he voiced complaint against his addiction, this had something of a theatrical ring to it, and he was actually pretty robust, even boast-ful, about it.

It certainly proved to be the vehicle that boosted his literary ca-reer. He closely observed and studied the nature of the "noon-day vi-sions" his "phantom-haunted brain" produced under the spell of opium. As he put it, he experienced "the re-awakening of a state of eye often-times incident to childhood . . . a power of painting, as it were, upon the darkness all sorts of phantoms . . . at night, when I lay awake in bed, vast processions moved along . . . a theatre seemed suddenly opened and lighted up within my brain, which presented nightly spec-tacles of more than earthly splendour." De Quincey felt that "as the creative state of the eye increased, a sympathy seemed to arise be-tween the waking and the dreaming states of the brain," by which he meant that whatever he voluntarily called up in his visions was liable to become transferred to his actual dreams. "The sense of space, and in the end the sense of time, were both powerfully affected," he further noted about the qualities of his visions. "Buildings, landscapes, etc., were exhibited in proportions so vast as the bodily eye is not fitted to receive. Space swelled, and was amplified to an extent of unutterable and self-repeating infinity. This disturbed me very much less than the vast expansion of time," he confessed. "Sometimes I seemed to have lived for seventy or a hundred years in one night." He also found that he would be precipitated into the "minutest incidents of childhood, or forgotten scenes of later years" with a lucidity that was akin to reliving those moments. In his inner pageants of the night a voice might add commentary to scenes of fine ladies dancing at a royal court, only for the vision to "suddenly dissolve" and "at the clapping of hands" to have a company of Roman centurions sweep by. He was often "transported into Asiatic scenery," which he deeply disliked, as indicated in this splendid outburst in his *Confessions*:

> I was stared at, hooted at, grinned at, chattered at, by monkeys, by paroquets, by cocatoos. I ran into pagodas, and was fixed for centuries at the summit, or in secret rooms; I was the idol; I was the priest; I was worshipped; I was sacrificed. I fled from the wrath of Brama through all the forests of Asia; Vishnu hated me; Seeva lay in wait for me. I came suddenly upon Isis and Osiris: I had done a deed, they said, which the ibis and the crocodile trembled at. Thousands of years I lived and was buried in stone coffins, with mummies and sphinxes, in narrow chambers at the heart of eternal pyramids.[27]

The "swelling space" of De Quincey's visions is echoed in Coleridge's "caverns measureless to man" line from "Kubla Khan," composed in an opium dream, and in the 1842 experience of one William Blair, who attended a theater in New York under the influence of opium: "After I had been seated a few minutes, the nature of the excitement changed, and a 'waking sleep' succeeded," Blair recollected for a New York magazine. "The actors on the stage vanished; the stage itself lost its reality; and before my entranced sight magnificent halls stretched out in endless succession with gallery above gallery, while the roof was blazing with gems, like stars whose rays alone illumined the whole building, which was thronged with strange, gigantic figures. . . ."[28]

In his 1960 autobiography, *My Wicked, Wicked Ways*, roguish film actor Errol Flynn recorded his experiences in an opium den that he attended accompanied by a beautiful Chinese woman, Ting Ling. After a few lungfuls of opium smoked through a pipe, the ceiling took on "a new dimension" and objects seemed larger in size. But then his mind became "as clear as crystal" and he saw his life in sober perspective. An out-of-body experience followed, and Flynn found himself muttering to his companion "Me, up there": the disembodied Errol Flynn watched his reclining physical self for an unknown period of time from a vantage point about four feet above the ground. But he obviously became reattached to his body because he was later able to take Ting Ling to a back room and make love to her "in ways and manners that I would never believe myself capable of."

The English novelist Graham Greene had an altogether more genteel experience of "the white night of opium." For him the opium state was one of supreme calmness that even happiness would have disturbed. He slept more deeply than he ever had for what seemed a whole night but which turned out to be just twenty minutes "of so-called real time." On the other hand, a young doctor in a research laboratory in the late 1960s merely suffered "an hour of sudden shafts of panic and itching".[29] Another doctor, Richard Robert Madden, a century or so earlier, had yet another perspective. He experienced "a universal expansion of mind and matter." For him, the initial hallucinogenic effects of opium acted only on what he saw in the world around him with his eyes open—"in short, it was 'the faint exquisite music of a dream' in a waking moment." Nevertheless, when he finally went to bed the "most extraordinary visions of delight" filled his brain all night long.[30] Around the same period of time as Madden's experimentation, opium bequeathed to the Reverend Walter Colton a range of imagery highly appropriate to a clergyman. He soared "on the pinions of an angel among splendors of the highest heavens" where he heard harps and choral symphonies, and then was hurled down into a "howling gulf" while attached to a thunderbolt. Heaven and hell indeed.

And what of cannabis? Again, it is a substance capable of yielding multiple effects. It may variously act as both depressant and stimulant, and it has hallucinogenic phases of activity in appropriate dosages and conditions. Its effects in general terms involve changes in the perception of time and space—the walls of a room can seem unusually tall, and attention slips in and out of different modes of consciousness so the passage of time appears disjointed. Thought may be strongly associative, skittering off in various directions in response to one stimulus, then another. If the experiencer speaks, the sound of the voice can reverberate within the head in curious ways. Under heavy doses, an ambient sound can become augmented, forming the basis for complex auditory hallucinations—so blood rushing in the ears or wind roaring through the leaves of a forest can transform into angelic choirs. (Other sensory stimuli can also trigger hallucinatory augmentation.) At other times, perception of the outer world can become sharper, more vivid, more "real" in all sense modalities: colors seem brighter, sounds have higher fidelity, touch become highly sensitized, smell and taste enhanced. Occasionally synesthesia can occur, so colors can be heard, sounds seen, and so forth. Normally unconscious bodily processes and states can become more noticeable—muscle tensions, warmth or coldness, posture, and so on. Interestingly, dissociation, the feeling of being outside of or otherwise distant from one's body, is also a surprisingly common experience under cannabis. (A Victorian army manual describing the effects of cannabis for officers serving in India included a drawing of a man lying down on his bed with a superimposed dotted outline of the same fellow sitting up!) Provided dosage is sufficient and attention is being properly directed (especially when the substance is being used in an experimental rather than a social setting), colorful geometric patterns can fill the visual field when the eyes are closed. Sometimes these develop into representational scenes.

In social situations, cannabis can bring on inordinate spasms of laughter. "Great thoughts" can appear and then evaporate like woolly clouds on a summer's day. Sense of meaning can undergo shifts. While a euphoric mood is common, there can be shivering and anxiety attacks too, and dark mood passages. As with all other such substances, set and setting are vital components in determining the overall nature of the experience. Cannabis is nonaddictive, but some people can become psychologically dependent on it so that taking it becomes habitual behavior.

Cannabis emerged into modern European awareness in the nineteenth century. Napoleon's army returned to France from the Egyptian campaign bringing the substance back with it, and the British encountered it in India. Like opium, it became used as a medicine, usually in tincture form, in both Europe and the United States. Some doctors, literary figures, and other intellectuals experimented with its mental effects, individually and in groups. A classic example of group experimentation was Le Club des Haschischins (The Hashish Eaters Club), formed in 1844, composed mainly of artists and writers, including the poets and writers Charles Baudelaire and Le Club's founder, Théophile Gautier. The latter wrote about his first cannabis experience in the following stunning fashion, describing many characteristics of cannabis's hallucinogenic effects:

At the end of several minutes, a general numbness spread through me! It seemed to me that my body dissolved and became transparent. In my chest I saw very clearly the hashish that I had eaten, in the form of an emerald that gave off millions of tiny sparkles. . . . Around me streamed and rolled precious stones of all colors. In space, flower patterns branched off ceaselessly in such a way that I know of nothing better with which to compare them than the play of a kaleidoscope. At certain moments, I saw my comrades again, but they were distorted; they appeared half men, half plants. . . . One of these gentlemen began to converse with me in Italian, but which the hashish by its omnipotence translated into Spanish for me. . . .

Hardly had half an hour passed when I again fell under the sway of hashish. This time the vision was more complicated and extraordinary. In an atmosphere of confusingly flitting lights, there were thousands of swarming butterflies whose wings rustled like fans. Gigantic flowers with crystal calices, enormous hollyhocks, gold and silver lilies rose and opened around me with a crackling like a bouquet of fireworks. My hearing was prodigiously developed: I heard the sound of colors. Green, red, blue, and yellow sounds came to me in perfectly distinct waves. A glass that was upset, a creaking armchair, a softly spoken word vibrated and re-echoed in me like the rumbling of thunder. My own voice seemed to me so powerful and loud that I dare not speak for fear of causing the walls to collapse. . . . Each flowered object emitted a sound of a harmonica or of an aeolian harp. I swam or rather floated in an ocean of sound. . . . Never had such waves of bliss filled my being. I was so much a part of the wave, so far from myself and so devoid of my own being . . . that I understood for the first time what the existence of elementary spirits, of angels and souls separated from the body may be like. . . . Sounds, perfumes, light came to me through multitudes of tubes as thin as hairs, in which I heard the whistle of magnetic currents—According to my calculation, this state lasted about 300 years, for the sensations were so numerous and followed each other so closely that any real appreciation of time became impossible—The attack passed, and I saw that it had lasted a quarter of an hour.

What is distinctive of hashish intoxication is that it is not continuous. It seizes one and leaves one; you rise to the sky and come back to earth without transition. . . . The visions became so queer and whimsical that I was seized by a desire to draw them. . . . Thanks to the hashish I was able to make a portrait of an elf from nature.[31]

Ronald Siegel has pointed out that at the time of Le Club des Haschischins another French group, under the leadership of psychopharmacologist Louis-Alphone Cahagnet, was taking doses of cannabis up to ten times greater than even the generous amounts being consumed by Gautier and his friends. This group was specifically exploring the ability of cannabis to promote the out-of-body sensation and was attempting to trace the soul's journey into the Beyond.[32]

Another version of the cannabis-induced out-of-body experience is well described in the nineteenth-century account of Lord Dunsany:

It [cannabis] takes one literally out of oneself. It is like wings. You swoop over distant countries and into other worlds. Once I found out the secret of the universe. I have forgotten what it was. . . . I have seen incredible things in fearful worlds. . . . Once out in the aether I met a battered, prowling spirit, that had belonged to a man whom drugs had killed a hundred years ago; and he led me into a region that I had never imagined; and we parted in anger beyond the Pleiades. . . . And somehow I imagined my way back, and only just in time, for my body was already stiffening in a chair in my room . . . and I had to move each finger one by one, and there were pins and needles in them, and dreadful pains in the nails, which began to thaw; and at last I could move one arm. . . .[33]

Baron Ernst von Bibra, a traveler, independent scholar, and chemist, took cannabis because of back pains (that was his story, at least) and described its effects on him in his 1855 study of "pleasure drugs," *Die narkotischen Genussmittel und der Mensch*. After a period of restlessness, he found his "plastic sense . . . became activated." He fixed his eyes on a white cloth and "I saw the most magnificent figures modeled from its folds, and a slight alteration sufficed to produce other phenomena. Soon I noticed that I could see whatever I wished at will: heads of bearded men, faces of women, animals of all kinds, for it was sufficient to alter a fold to see the desired pictures. For some time I thus easily modeled the most wonderful busts."[34] By half closing his eyes, he felt he could see windows on a paneled wall, and he could play with the space in his study, making it appear "infinitely large." Closing his eyes while listening to music, he saw a succession of hypnagogic-like images (vivid pictures seen when falling asleep). As the effects wore off he found he had an enormous appetite (a common effect of cannabis intoxication) and ate heartily, finding his back pain was gone and that he could stand upright. He particularly noted that throughout his session, although strange things were happening to his perceptions, he felt calm, neutral, and observing, capable of reverting to his normal state of consciousness at any time. (This is another frequently noted quality of the cannabis experience, and is perhaps a weak form of the sensation of "out-of-body" dual consciousness.)

He persuaded a friend, Dr. Eduard Baierlacher, to try a similar dosage of cannabis and to write up the results for him. Baierlacher did not have a very happy time for much of his session, and overall the sensation he experienced, he said, "could best be compared to falling asleep but at the same time remaining fully conscious." Sounds seemed farther away than they should, he had an urge at times to break out laughing, and he had a ringing sound in his ears. He lost track of whether he had been walking or sitting a minute earlier. "It was a continuous change from consciousness to semi-consciousness," he recalled. "I seemed to be swimming in the sea, a toy in the waves. . . . With my eyelids open, I then saw persons surrounding me whose faces were distorted into horrible grimaces, changing continuously in form; I continued to see these pictures even as I closed my eyes and again fell into a state of almost total unconsciousness."[35]

"Of all the narcotics hashish is most closely related to opium, although it differs from opium in many ways," von Bibra declared. He surveyed its positive effects in a number of medical conditions, and observed that it was included in several German pharmacopoeias—as, indeed, it was in those of other countries.

In America, the youthful Fitz Hugh Ludlow produced the first American writings on self-experimentation with cannabis (a magazine article in 1856 and *The Hasheesh Eater*, 1857). Although tinctures of cannabis were readily available over drugstore counters, few people seemed interested in exploring its mental effects. While living in Poughkeepsie in New York, he obtained a vial of Tilden's Extract of Cannabis Indica from a friend's pharmacy and began his explorations. He saw cannabis as the ideal way to travel to far-off lands without physically having to go there:

> He oscillated between deep beatitude and uncontrollable terror—he was transported to Venice, the Alps, the Nile Valley amid Ethiopians, and even once ended up in Paradise . . . he had numerous hallucinations, both pleasant and frightful. He experienced the sensation of double consciousness . . . he repeated the hashish experience many times, always using Tilden's Extract.[36]

A hashish smoker enjoying his visions. *(M. von Schwind, 1843)*

In one particularly bizarre vision he had an almost opiumlike experience: he saw an old crone who was faultlessly knit in purple yarn, her face formed from stitches. She and other witches were all "knitting, knitting, knitting as if their lives depended on it" while swaying from side to side to music that seemed Ethiopian in tone and style. Each hag was knitting another old woman like herself. When complete, each of the newly knitted crones sprang to work knitting another duplicate. "Here . . . at last, do I realize the meaning of endless progression!" Ludlow cried.

Writer and psychedelic pioneer William Burroughs has described his first cannabis experience, at the age of fourteen. While visiting his father in Tangiers, he scarfed some hashish candies. It combined to a good dose:

> I was so far gone that I couldn't even remember the onset. Only visions of the entire course of human history, from the apeman all

asteam on the hostile plains on through the blessed virgin and plunging into the abyss of technology. After two million years, Ian nudged me gently and said that he'd like to go to sleep.[37]

We can hardly finish our survey of cannabis experiences without noting that that rascally movie actor Errol Flynn tried his hand at the ancient weed as well as opium. He described meeting a Mexican artist who gave him a marijuana cigarette, after which Flynn was able to both see *and hear* the man's paintings. Their colors sounded in symphonies he could see, hear, and even feel.

RITUALS IN THE DARK

Current interpretation of the pottery found at the drowning stone circles around which our boat bobbed and weaved on its way to Gavrinis allows us to conjure up a picture of Neolithic ritualists in Brittany getting stoned at the stones. Perhaps they also got stoned at the bones, for there seem to be a number of associations between the braziers and the mysterious passage graves. Er Lannic and Gavrinis are close to one another, suggesting some association, but these ceramic objects have been found inside six of the Breton passage graves.[38] This suggests that their placement was highly selective, as there are 265 of these ceremonial sites overall in Brittany. Interestingly, five of the passage graves on the Channel Island of Jersey also had these brazierlike objects within them, and La Hougue Bie contained no less than twenty-one of them. Remarkably, no such objects have been found at all on the neighboring island of Guernsey.

If opium or cannabis were used in the braziers, that would add another link to the passage graves, as we have noted that these substances were often used in funerary contexts.

We came ashore at the small island on which Gavrinis stands. From the outside, the passage grave is a massive, tiered cairn (mound of stones) over twenty-five feet high, with an entrance framed by megalithic jambs and a lintel. Inside, a long, stone-faced passage leads into a rectangular chamber constructed from large slabs of stone, now dimly lit by electric lighting. Could this chamber have been intended for getting high—a kind of Neolithic dope den? What was the structure for? What happened here? The rituals that were conducted within Gavrinis took place in the dark, inside this chambered cairn, and remain there, as we can at this point only speculate about their nature.

Archaeologists think the monument was ceremonially sealed sometime between 3340 and 2910 B.C., which means hundreds or even a thousand years after the site had been constructed and the braziers had made their appearance at Er Lannic. Evidence suggests that the closure was preceded by a series of rituals;[39] excavations of the ground beneath a pile of rubble closing off the front of the cairn revealed an extensive area of burning, evidence of postholes and concentrations of flint, three polished ceremonial axes and other stone tools, pottery, and

Exterior of Gavrinis, showing entrance. *(Paul Devereux)*

an animal bone. It was clear to the excavating archaeologists that the pile of rubble had been placed almost immediately after the timber structure indicated by the postholes had been burned. But what had gone on within the chambered cairn during the centuries of its use?

Gavrinis, like other passage "graves," was not, in fact, simply a tomb. The living mixed at times with the bones of the ancestors there. As there appears to be a chronological overlap between the passage graves, the stone circles, and the great stone rows of the region, it may be that these were all part of a single religious system.[40] So the use of braziers at Er Lannic, for example, may have preceded ceremonies within Gavrinis. Furthermore, it is likely that the stone circles and rows were for large-scale public gatherings and ceremonies, while the passage graves by design offer restricted access and so could only have been for the use of a limited group of people—perhaps priests, priestesses, shamans, or religious functionaries. After rituals at the entrance to the passage grave, no one else would be able to see what went on after the elite group had entered the passage and disappeared within. At best outsiders could only hear chanting or other sounds emanating from the activities taking place in the chamber. In short, the passage graves provided the "inner sanctum" function within the system of religious monuments of the time. Sherratt has suggested that the inhalation of opium (or cannabis, or whatever it was) in the braziers took place "perhaps in the context of mortuary rituals and communication with the ancestors."[41]

With some degree of likelihood, we can picture an elite group of Neolithic religious functionaries, perhaps shamans accompanied by a chieftain or tribal elders, sitting with the ancestral bones within the passage grave, experiencing altered states of consciousness in a highly specific setting and with a strongly defined psychological set. Perhaps their aim would have been communing with the spirits of the dead through the medium of visual, aural, and other sensory hallucinations. Or, with their supernatural abilities activated in trance they could listen to the spirits and join with the ancestors in the otherworld by temporarily leaving their physical bodies. What we know of opium, cannabis, and other hallucinogenic experiences tells us that this would be possible with overpowering realism. The bones, especially the skulls, might have provided the frameworks for the appearance of animated spectral forms; the walls of the chamber might have extended to mighty proportions while flickering with kaleidoscopic energy patterns before opening up as portals into the fearsome underworld of the dead, or glorious heavenworlds. These may have been glimpsed first in the form of vistas; then the spirits of the ritual participants would have journeyed into those realms, perhaps guided by the ancestral spirits associated with the bones preserved in the chamber. When archaeologists excavate these sites now, or when we visit them, it is difficult to see them as other than confined, dark, somewhat grim places of the dead, but we must bear in mind that if they were used in trance states of consciousness, in highly focused belief frameworks, they may have been environments bathed in supernatural light, their perimeters extending to infinity, and filled with colorful processions of spirits, exotic perfumes, and the sounds of other worlds.

However, if we are to accept some of the ideas of Princeton psychologist Julian Jaynes, perhaps the critical modality was that of hallucinatory hearing. He has proposed a hypothesis (which many of his colleagues consider debatable) that until a few thousand years ago, human beings had the "software" of their brain configured differently than modern people. He provides a rich and persuasive argument that can only be briefly outlined here.[42] In essence, he maintains that in prehistory the brain functioned as two halves rather than one unified whole. The human brain is divided into two hemispheres, separated by a band of over two million fibers called the corpus callosum. In each hemisphere is an area known as the temporal lobe, which seems to be related to dreaming, hallucinations or visions, language, and other functions. These two are connected across the corpus callosum by a thin bundle of nerve fibers called the anterior commissure. The left brain or hemisphere (to oversimplify a bit) handles speech, logic, analytical thought, stage-by-stage cognition, while the right hemisphere deals with patterns, connections, intuition, *gestalt*. Most of our sensory functions "cross over," so that the left eye, for example, sends its signals to the right hemisphere of the brain. When someone has a problem with his or her anterior commissure, defects are found in perception, although the person usually does not feel that anything is wrong. For instance, such a person could not describe the contents of a slide shown only to the left eye because the right brain does not have speech—but the left hand could point to a matching picture. Since only the left brain has articulate speech (though both hemispheres understand language), it tends to be the hemisphere that dominates in a culture like our own. Jaynes argues that prehistoric people had each hemisphere of their brains operating on separate tracks, as it were, and right-brain thinking was "heard" as voices. Like the voices heard by unmedicated schizophrenics today, these auditory hallucinations, which were taken to be the voices of the ancestors or, later, the gods, had an aura of enormous authority. They gave instructions to the left hemisphere—waking, daily consciousness. Jaynes calls this condition "the bicameral mind." As with schizophrenics today, these voices could seem to emanate from a point in the environment, and were not necessarily heard as if "in the head."

If Jaynes is correct, in the ancient, bicameral world auditory hallucination was highly organized, and in later prehistory it was guided through the use of idols and statues. (It is the case that there were ancient ceremonies involving the mouth washing of idols to keep their speech clear, and the Indians of Mexico told their Spanish conquerors that their statues spoke to them.) Eventually, according to Jaynes, the bicameral condition began to break down, initially in the eastern Mediterranean region, it seems, due to both social and natural changes, and there was a twilight phase between it and the modern mind that was coped with by the use of oracles. Oracular functionaries were usually women (women are more "lateralized" in brain function than men, their psychological functions being less tied to one hemisphere or the other). The locations of oracles were often "hallucinogenic" inasmuch as they were located at sites which had roaring water or wind, or dramatic, elemental settings where the presence of wild nature overpowered human sensibilities. Delphi, in Greece, is a classic example.

Jaynes suggests that the use of idols as conduits for the hallucinated utterances of gods and goddesses may have derived from much older traditions of ancestor worship. He notes that the entire organization of some early communities was designed to place the tomb of a dead chieftain or tribal elder in a position at the center of living activity.[43] He maintains that the "voice" of the dead chief or elder would still have been "heard," if not by the community in general, then by the chief's successor. Jaynes points out that in many Mesolithic and Neolithic burials the arrangement of the ancestral bones, particularly the skulls, and the type of grave goods, along with veneration of the places where the bones were laid, suggest that the ancestors were thought of as if in some way still alive, or at least still present.

There is no doubt that bones were arranged within early Neolithic chambered mounds. The bones of males and females are often separated, and sometimes chambers or "stalls" within megalithic mounds contain no skulls (and certain other bones) whereas other chambers or stalls can contain many skulls or even be filled only with skulls. In the case of the Armorican passage graves, the situation is unclear because the acidic soils of the region destroy bone. Some examples survive, but they are too few to determine a clear pattern of layout within the monuments. Inadequate methodology in early excavations also did not help. It does appear, however, that there tended to be only a small number of individuals laid to rest within the passage graves at any particular time. Sometimes skeletons were kept more or less in one piece. In one instance, a single skeleton was found in what would have been a sitting position in the main chamber.[44] This would certainly favor Jaynes's ideas. But more often the bones were disarticulated, perhaps because the body had been left exposed to be defleshed naturally, or because it had been previously buried. In some cases, the separated bones were found scattered in both the passage and the chamber, while in others the deposition of the bones was more organized, with the skulls carefully placed together in specific locations within the passage grave. Again, this would support the Jaynes hypothesis. In some chambers, pottery was found with the bones, and other items such as polished ceremonial axes and beads were also uncovered. A platform or altar was found within La Hougue Bie, in association with vase support/braziers.

The picture isn't entirely clear, but there is enough to support the idea of the ritualists communing with the skeletal remains of the ancestors. Jaynes has stated that he feels the use of hallucinogens may have emerged as the bicameral mind began to break down. This may be true. Perhaps the change of monumental structures in Armorica coinciding with the arrival of the braziers indicates that through the use of hallucinogens prehistoric people could maintain contact with their ancestors just as they were beginning to fall silent. We have seen that both opium and cannabis sometimes cause auditory phenomena, but it is also true that Jaynes developed his ideas when less was known about the use of hallucinogens in ancient times.[45] It could also be that the extensive use of psychoactive substances in prehistory was itself an element in the creation of a hallucinatory world of spirits and ancestors or, depending on one's cognitive map, in the creation of a way of accessing a spirit world that was beyond the powers of the nonbicameral, nonpsychoactivated mind.

We will probably never know for certain what went on in the Neolithic chambers, but we do know that there is evidence for the wide use of trance states elsewhere in the ancient world, as the reader will discover time and again in the following chapters. At Gavrinis, the evidence is literally in the form of the "writing" on the wall, as we shall see.

two
The Foggy Ruins of Time

Other Aspects of Old World Psychedelia

It was announced in 1975 that one of the oldest stashes in history had been found in a cave in northern Iraq, along with the skeleton of a Neanderthal man. Among the sixty-thousand-year-old burial remains were clusters of pollen from eight kinds of flowering plants. Originally the clusters were thought to be merely the remains of a floral funerary offering, but experts came to realize that the types of plants involved (which included horsetail or ephedra, source of the nerve stimulant ephedrine) had been prominent in herbal curing in the same area and elsewhere in the Old World. The Neanderthal man had likely been a healer of some kind, possibly even a shaman, the flowers perhaps a part of his medicine kit. If herbalism was practiced, then the knowledge of psychoactivity in the plant world was also almost certainly known.

This suggests that the use of hallucinogens in the Old World (which we shall define as everywhere other than the Americas) extends back to the remotest times. Nevertheless, as we shall note in the next chapter, there were far fewer hallucinogens known to have been used in the Old World than in the Americas. But in the Old World, as Schultes and Hofmann have commented, "their use has been widespread and extremely significant from a cultural point of view; furthermore, the use of them is extremely ancient."[1]

THE HEAVENLY GUIDE

This is the case especially for that exemplar of mind-altering plants, cannabis. We have already noted that it entered Europe by way of the steppes from its point of origin—wherever that might have been. "There is no concerted agreement among botanists as to where the plant originally grew wild and where its cultivation first began," Hui-Lin Li has observed. "Estimates range within the wide span of temperate Asia from the Caucasus Mountains and the Caspian Sea through western and central Asia to eastern Asia."[2] The first indication of the human use of cannabis favors the last suggestion, however, for in the remains of a ten-thousand-year-old village in Taiwan, pottery fragments have been uncovered that had been most likely impressed with strips of hemp cord. These were found along with elongated rod-shaped tools, similar to those later known to have been used for loosening cannabis fibers from their stems.[3] In Chinese culture, hemp fiber occupied such an important place that mourners wore only hemp-textile clothes out of respect for the dead. The earliest surviving fragments of hemp cloth have been found in ancient Chinese burials. If the use of hemp for fiber was known so long ago, then it is likely that the intoxicating properties of cannabis would also be well known—and, as previously noted, knowledge of intoxication may even have come first. The herbal practices of the legendary Emperor Shen-Nung, said to date to 2737 B.C., recognized both the male and female cannabis plants, and he recommended the exudate of cannabis for "female weakness, gout, rheumatism, malaria, beri-beri, constipation, and absent-mindedness."[4] The fifteenth-century B.C. Chinese text the *Rh-Ya* mentions the herb *ma*, the *Cannabis sativa* plant, specifically referring to its ritualistic or shamanic use. In addition to its eventual passage westward, cannabis found a home at an early date in Persia and India, where its welcome has been sustained. Although it was as highly prized in India as in China for its medicinal virtues, cannabis became deeply rooted in Indian religious life. It became known as the "heavenly guide" and decoctions of cannabis were used before reading holy texts or entering sacred places.[5] Knowledge of the use of cannabis spread on through India and Saudi Arabia, to Africa.

But cannabis is only one of several mind-altering plants of the Old World that can claim great antiquity and influence.

URINE LUCK: THE AMANITA STORY

The fly agaric, *Amanita muscaria*, is perhaps the hallucinogen that is most famously associated with shamanism in the Old World. It is a distinctive mushroom, typically with a bright bloodred cap up to several inches across, flecked with white "warts," the remains of the young mushroom's veil. It is supported by a thick, hollow, tubular white *stipe* or stem, and particularly fine examples can grow up to eight or nine inches tall. It shares a symbiotic relationship with certain trees, especially the birch, and it is no accident that the birch tree was the Siberian shaman's "World Tree," seen as a kind of "cosmic axis" onto which the three flat wheels or planes of the universe were fixed: the underworld, the "middle earth" of everyday existence, and the upper heaven world. This magical tree "at the center of the world" was the means by which the ecstatic shaman could in spirit clamber up to the gods or down to the subterranean realms of the shades. It was the way between the worlds, and is an archetypal image which has manifested in one form or another wherever shamanism held sway.

Amanita muscaria was ritually used as a sacred mushroom by numerous shamanic tribes across the northern reaches of Eurasia, from the Baltic Sea to the easternmost extent of Siberia. Since 1658, various individuals, including prisoners of war, travelers, explorers, and anthropologists, have documented its uses in such Siberian reindeer-herding tribes as the Koryak, the Chukchi, the Ostyak, the Yukagir, and the Kamchadal. Not all Siberian peoples used the mushroom, but those that did held it central to their religious practices. In many tribes its use was limited to the shaman, who might eat a number of mushrooms prior to performing a seánce. In others, such as the Koryak and Chukchi, it could be consumed more generally—though primarily among the men of the tribe. The mushrooms were usually dried and strung together in threes, which was considered the standard dose. Sometimes a less intoxicating soup or liqueur might be made from

Amanita muscaria, but most commonly the dried mushrooms would be shredded and chewed with water or rolled into small pellets and swallowed. The level of intoxication could vary considerably depending on the strength of the mushrooms consumed and the predisposition of the individual taking them.

The first effect of *Amanita muscaria* intoxication was generally a feeling of pleasant invigoration, and the individual would be prone to break out into song, dance, and laughter. This would be accompanied by a marked increase in physical strength. Russian anthropologist Vladimir Bogoras observed a Chukchi tribesman take off his snowshoes after eating some of the mushroom and deliberately walk for hours through the deep snow just for the sheer pleasure of conducting tireless exercise.[6] This early stage of *Amanita muscaria* intoxication is clearly preserved in a Koryak myth, in which their culture hero, Big Raven, found himself unable to carry a heavy bag of provisions. He implored the great deity Vahiyinin ("Existence") to help him, and was told to go to a certain place where he would find spirits called *wapaq* who would give him the strength to complete his task. At the appointed place Vahiyinin spat upon the ground, and where his spittle fell little white plants appeared. They had red hats that the god's saliva had dappled with white. These were the *wapaq*, and Big Raven was told to eat them. On doing so, Big Raven felt charged with strength and energy and was able to lift the bag with ease. Big Raven entreated the *wapaq* to live forever on the earth, instructing his children that they should learn whatever *wapaq* had to teach them.

In the next stage of *Amanita muscaria* intoxication, hallucinations set in. In the 1790s, a Polish soldier named Joseph Kopec unwillingly ate part of a fly agaric for medicinal purposes. He fell into a sleep in which he had visions of fabulous gardens "where only pleasure and beauty seemed to rule." Beautiful white-clad women fed him fruits and berries and offered him flowers. When he awoke he was so distressed to return to mundane reality that he consumed an entire mushroom and fell back into a deep sleep in which new visions carried him to "another world." In another recorded case, on the other hand, a Cossack who took the mushroom had a horrific vision of a fiery chasm into which he was about to be thrown—the very brink of hell itself. *Amanita muscaria* intoxication typically produces macropsia, when one's sense of scale is lost and small objects can look many times their actual size; the complementary effect, micropsia, can also occur. The mushroom taker is likely to hear voices telling him to perform bizarre actions, or the spirits of the mushrooms might appear to the individual and converse with him directly. He might even feel himself turning into a mushroom spirit. The mushroom spirits tend to wear wide hats on heads that sit on stout cylindrical bodies without an intervening neck, and the number seen depends on the number of mushrooms eaten. The bemushroomed person will run after the spirits, who will tell him things as they lead him on a merry chase along interminably intricate paths that often lead past where the dead reside. One map of such paths was drawn by a Chukchi for Bogoras. On that map the paths traced by the legs of the mushroom spirits are winding and convoluted, but *straight lines* have very deliberately been drawn issuing from some of the spirits' heads. This feature is rarely commented upon; it may be an attempt to depict the sensation of out-of-body flight. (As we'll see, straight lines have universally been associated with spirit movement. Similar drawings in Bushman rock art in southern Africa have been identified as expressing the feeling of the spirit leaving through the top of the head.) Eventually, the spirits are likely to take the mushroom eater by the arms and take him to the otherworld. It is then that stage three of the intoxication begins, and the person becomes unconscious of his surroundings.

A Chukchi shamanic drawing of mushroom spirits. *(Collected by W. Borgoras, 1905)*

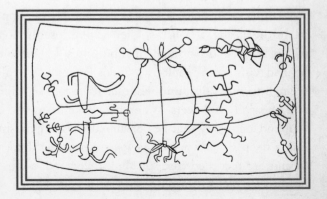

The reindeer of these remote wastes also have a hankering for *Amanita muscaria*. When they eat it they become stupefied and stagger around. If a reindeer is killed while intoxicated, the meat will pass on the effects of the *Amanita muscaria* to the human who eats it. This is merely one part of a strange ménage à trois involving human beings, reindeer, and the mushroom itself. When they dine on certain mosses and lichen, reindeer also develop an insatiable passion for urine, their own *and* that of humans; for them, pee-stained snow is a delicacy. In 1905, Russian anthropologist Waldemar Jochelson reported that men urinating in the open might alert the sensitive sense of smell of reindeer in the vicinity and took a real risk of being run down by animals galloping in from all sides. The Koryak, and doubtless other tribes, made use of this strange fact by carrying sealskin containers they called "the reindeer's nightchamber," in which they collected their own urine. This was used to attract reindeer who they were having trouble gathering into the herd.

But there was another value in human urine: the active constituents in *Amanita muscaria* remain intact even when passed through a person's bladder. "The Koryaks know this by experience, and the urine of persons intoxicated with fly agaric is not wasted. The drinker himself drinks it to prolong the state of hallucination, or offers it to others as a treat," Jochelson observed. "According to the Koryak, the urine of one intoxicated by fly agaric has an intoxicating effect like the fungus,

Dod, the cartoon snail of *The Ley Hunter* journal, encountering an amanita-eating reindeer.

though not to so great a degree."[7] Filip Johann von Strahlenberg, a Swedish prisoner of war in the early eighteenth century, reported seeing Koryak tribespeople waiting outside huts where mushroom sessions were taking place, waiting for people to come out and urinate. When they did, the warm, steaming tawny gold nectar was collected in wooden bowls and greedily gulped down. The *Amanita muscaria* effect could apparently be recycled up to five times in this manner, and was less likely to cause the vomiting often associated with the direct ingestion of the mushroom itself.

"It is hardly surprising that the tribes considered the reindeer to be great spirits," psychologist Rogan Taylor has commented. "What other animal could satisfy simultaneously both hunger and the desire for ecstatic experience?" He speculated that observing the reindeer may have led the tribespeople to learn of the urine secret in the first place.[8] Perhaps this interspecies interaction, involving mushroom, deer, and human being, lies at the heart of an archaic, virtually universal shamanic motif—the shaman wearing a deerskin and deer-antlered headgear.

The active principle of *Amanita muscaria* was thought to be muscarine, but it turned out that this was merely a minor constituent. The important psychoactive compounds were two isoxazoles, ibotenic acid and the alkaloid muscimole. Muscimole is an unsaturated cyclic hydroxamic acid that passes through the kidneys in essentially an unaltered form. This is the secret of *Amanita muscaria*'s remarkable ability to retain its effects in urine. Ibotenic acid converts to muscimole when the mushrooms are dried, the preferred method of preparation by the Siberian tribes. Clearly the pharmacological wisdom of ancient peoples runs deep.

The antiquity of shamanism in Siberia is such that it is considered the classical form of the ecstatic practice. The very word *shaman* derives from the Tungus verb meaning "to know." This antiquity, and the association of the fly agaric mushroom with shamanic practice in the vast Siberian region, was underlined in the 1960s by the discovery of certain petroglyphs (rock art carvings) alongside the Pegtymel River near the northeastern coast of Siberia, in Chukchi country. These small petroglyphs, up to several centimeters in height, depict various animals

Examples of Siberian petroglyphic forms of mushrooms and mushroom people or spirits.

and many mushrooms of the amanita type along with various human-mushroom forms. Some are human figures (primarily female) with mushroom heads or mushrooms growing out of their heads. According to Gordon Wasson, the late, great amateur mushroom expert, or mycologist, the petroglyphs are likely to portray the mushroom spirits.[9] The rock art is dated by Russian archaeologist N. N. Dikov to the Bronze Age. Similar Siberian rock drawings found elsewhere have been dated to the same remote period by other archaeologists.

The use of *Amanita muscaria* was, of course, practiced by certain groups right across northern Eurasia, though most cases are less thoroughly documented than in eastern Siberia. In many Finno-Ugric languages (that is, the family of tribal languages spanning eastern Europe and western Siberia) words meaning "ecstasy," "intoxication," and "drunkenness" can be traced to names meaning fungus or fly agaric.[10] Lapps (Saami) continued to use the sacred mushroom for ecstatic purposes well into the twentieth century.[11] Reid Kaplan has discovered evidence for a Bronze Age mushroom cult in Scandinavia by matching motifs engraved on flat bronze wide-bladed razors found in Bronze Age burials in Denmark with those on rock surfaces in Sweden. One of the recurring motifs engraved on the bronze razors is that of a boat, which seems to contain religious symbols. One of these symbols is often a mushroom-shaped object. Kaplan compared this motif to two rock carvings found in Sweden, which are clearly of the same basic style, and date to the Bronze Age. One of the rock carvings shows the mushroom object being held aloft by a human being displaying a reverential gesture. Explanations that the object is a bush or a depiction of the World Tree have been dismissed. Kaplan suggests that we accept it for precisely what it looks

The "mushroom boat" motif on prehistoric bronze razors (top) compared with that in Swedish petroglyphs. In the case of one of the razors, the motif has been reduced virtually to a curvilinear pattern. *(After Reid W. Kaplan, 1975)*

like—a mushroom. He feels that it portrays *Amanita muscaria,* and points out that the mushroom is abundant in Scandinavia today and likely always has been. Pollen samples show that pine and birch were growing in Scandinavia during the Bronze Age, and *Amanita muscaria* has been found everywhere such trees grow. He also refers to a Swedish custom of throwing a "toadstool" on a bonfire (Balder's balefire) on Saint John's Eve (June 24) to counteract the powers of evil spirits, and suggests that this may be a relic of mushroom veneration.[12]

There is no hard evidence that the fly agaric mushroom was used in northern and western Europe for causing ecstatic experience. (It has been used in various other ways, especially soaked in milk as a folk method to kill flies, and some believe the Berserkers used it to give themselves superhuman strength and fierceness in battle.) Christian Rätsch has indicated that there is some evidence that those who used prehistoric drinking vessels known as "beakers" in Britain took fly agaric "in a cultic context," and remarks that it has been associated in myth with the Germanic god-shaman figure Wotan or Odin.[13] There are also relatively modern hints that suggest a surviving vestige of folk memory concerning ancient magical usage of the mushroom. For example, Gordon Wasson drew attention to some German nursery rhymes that seem to contain unambiguous references:

A manikin stands in the wood
Stock-still and mute

He has of purple pure
A mantle around him.
Say, who may the manikin be
Who stands there on one leg?

An alternative ending exists:

Say, who may the manikin be
Who stands there in the wood alone
With the purple red mantle?

The children are supposed to reply:

Happiness mushroom! Fly agaric! (Glückspilz! Fliegenpilz!)[14]

Wasson also drew attention to the English term "toadstool," which is now used in a general way to mean unpleasant, dangerous fungi, and may derive from the innate Anglo-Saxon tendency to fear and dislike mushrooms. Why such mycophobia? We may perhaps suspect some deep-seated associations implanted many centuries ago to account for this. The toadstool has vague associations with witchcraft and is also typically shown in fairy tales as a red-capped mushroom with white spots. We know the image from our nursery days, and it is an old one: a medieval chapbook, for instance, has a woodcut showing fairies dancing in front of a fairy hill, with the spotted toadstool nearby.

A woodcut from an old English chapbook showing fairies dancing before a fairy hill (with door), with a "fairy toadstool" in the foreground.

"The virtual panic fear

of 'toadstools' by some Europeans may ... derive from pagan times," Weston La Barre observes, "since the use of hallucinogenic *Amanita* mushrooms antedated (and culturally influenced) the Greek and other Indo-European gods originating in northern Eurasia, *Amanita* being thought to be born of divine thunderbolts."[15] According to Rogan Taylor, perhaps the most amusing hint of amanita-based shamanism may well be enshrined, perhaps by accident, in the popular contemporary image of Santa Claus.[16] The figure of Father Christmas evolved over centuries out of pagan traditions, but the modern image of Santa owes most to the elements cobbled together in the 1820s by Professor Clement Clark Moore of Albany, New York, along with illustrators Thomas Nast and Moritz von Schwind, both of Germanic descent. Taylor feels that some traditional elements got drawn into their version, perhaps from the professor's wide reading, or from the illustrators' Old World links—or both. He points out that Santa's robe of red edged with white contains the colors of *Amanita muscaria*, and that the idea of Santa clambering down the chimney evokes the entry via the smoke hole into Siberian yurts during winter. Moreover, the reindeers that pull the sleigh can be seen as a link to the reindeer-herder tribes who took the magic mushroom. And the magic flight of Santa Claus through the midwinter night sky is a superb expression of the basis of all shamanism—ecstasy, or the flight of the spirit.

Finally, it is worth noting that *Amanita muscaria* was not the only mushroom used ritually in Siberia: research early in the twentieth century among the Vogul living near the Upper Lozva River revealed that *pa:nx*, a small mushroom that grows at the base of tree stumps, was dried for consumption by shamans.[17]

SOMA: THE CLASSIC SACRED HALLUCINOGEN

During the second millenium B.C., pastoral peoples ("Aryans") came from a now ill-defined region south and east of the Caspian Sea (the "Greater Iranian area," as some scholars have termed it) into what is today Afghanistan, Pakistan, and northern India, and assimilated the

Dravidian-speaking peoples of the collapsed Indus Valley civilization. Their language was Vedic, of the Indo-European family, closely associated with classical Sanskrit. One of the earliest sacred texts of these people was the Indian *Rig Veda*, written in the first millenium B.C. but deriving from preexisting oral tradition. Of over 1,000 hymns in the *Rig Veda*, 120 are devoted to soma, which was at one and the same time a god, a sacred plant, and a sacramental drink with unsurpassed powers to ecstatically transport the drinker to transcendental realms. It was "the focal point of Vedic religion" as Vedic scholar Wendy Doniger O'Flaherty has stated. In a similar vein, three chapters (*Yasna* 9, 10, 11—the *Hom Yasht*) of the Iranian *Avesta*, a Zoroastrian text dating to the same general period as the *Rig Veda*, and ethnically and etymologically linked to it, refer repeatedly to *Haoma*, etymologically linked with soma.

Whatever it originally was, the Vedic soma was forgotten, perhaps because of difficulties obtaining it in the "new homeland" of the northern Indian area, and a range of substitutes was used for the rite. Most Vedic scholars have never been very interested in determining what the true soma/*Haoma* was, and those suggestions that have been offered have all proved inadequate for one reason or another. In 1963, Gordon Wasson set about trying to determine its nature, and, with the assistance of Wendy Doniger O'Flaherty, published his findings in 1968 in *Soma: Divine Mushroom of Immortality*. Wasson was convinced that the Indo-European invaders of the Indus Valley had brought with them an archaic cult centred on *Amanita muscaria*, of which the Siberian shamanic usage was a vestige. He focused mainly on the *Rig Veda*, teasing out the clues that would indicate the characteristics of the soma plant. As one item of evidence, Wasson picked out a reference that occurs seven times in the ancient text, *Aja Ekapad*, "the Not-Born Single-Foot," as an allusion to a mushroom: "single-foot" and "one-legged" are old, widespread euphemisms for mushrooms (as we saw in the German nursery rhyme), and their sudden seedless generation can reasonably be described as "not-born." Another significant factor is that nowhere in the *Rig Veda* is there a mention of the leaves, branches, blossoms, seeds, or roots of the soma plant, and this reinforces the idea that it was a mushroom.

The father of soma was Parjanya, God of Thunder, and the association between mushrooms and lightning is curiously widespread around the world; in Guatemala, for example, ancient Native Americans referred to fly agaric as the "lightning bolt," while the Mayan *Popol Vuh* refers to the mushroom as "lightning-bolt one-leg." Soma is referred to as "the mainstay of the sky" in the *Rig Veda*, which Wasson took to allude to *Amanita muscaria*'s stout stem supporting the hemispherical cap. (This is also effectively an image of the World Axis. In yet another striking Old World–New World parallel, at Nyarit, Mexico, a two-thousand-year-old ceramic rendering of a fly agaric mushroom as a "World Tree" has been found.)

The *Rig Veda* states that soma was a fragrant liquor crushed from the juice of the plant, and while this may not seem likely to most people with regard to a mushroom, Wasson had, in fact, seen sacred mushrooms ground on metates in Mexico. During fieldwork in Orissa, India, Wasson and colleagues collected a mushroom called *putka*—which even today is considered to be "endowed with soul" in India—that they felt sure was the same as *putika*, which had been the primary substitute for soma. The mushroom theory again makes sense if a mushroom was substituting for what had been a mushroom in the first place.

In his search for allusions to *Amanita muscaria*, Wasson relied heavily on anything he could find regarding urination, hoping to link soma with the fly agaric's distinguishing ability to pass its effects on through the human bladder. He noted one passage in the *Rig Veda* that mentioned "those charged with the office, richly gifted, do full honor to Soma. The swollen men piss the flowing [soma]." In the *Avesta* he found reference to "this urine of drunkeness." In the later Indian text, the *Mahabharata*, Wasson found a powerful piece of evidence. A disciple is offered the urine of an outcast to slake his thirst, but rejects it with disgust. The Lord Krishna then appears to the disciple revealing the outcast to be the god Indra in disguise. Krishna explains that he had instructed Indra to give the man the *amrta* (cognate with the Greek *ambrosia* and certainly a reference to soma) in the form of water. Whereupon Indra complains that "a mortal should not become immortal" and suggests that some other boon be given the fellow.

There are other examples in Indian literature where urine is regarded as an elixir. "In the classic yoga manual *Siva Samhita*, it is said that the yogin can transmute base metals into gold by rubbing them with his own excrement or urine. The Aghori ascetics of contemporary Benares in Northern India . . . describe their urine in their ritual language as *amari pan* . . . meaning 'nectar of immortality,'" Richard Rudgley informs us.[18] He describes the traditional use of cattle urine in secular and sacred cleansing rites in both Iran and India: the bull was a metaphor for soma.

In reviewing Wasson's book, Harvard Sanskrit scholar Daniel H. H. Ingalls cited another verse from the *Rig Veda*:

Like a thirsty stag, come here to drink.
Drink Soma, as much as you want.
Pissing it out day by day, O generous one,
You have assumed your most mighty force.[19]

Despite the circumstantial evidence he amassed, Wasson's efforts met with little enthusiasm from Vedic scholars. It was pointed out that there was no specific claim in the *Rig Veda* that soma was actually drunk as urine. Other perceived weak points in Wasson's ideas included the geographic availability of soma. The sacred plant was said to grow only in the mountains, and in the Indo-Iranian region the mushroom's growth is indeed limited to a few high mountain areas. Yet the Indo-European pastoralists conquered only the valleys and did not have direct access to the growing areas of the mushroom, so how could the *Rig Veda* contain descriptions of the various growing stages of whatever the soma plant was? Wasson had to perform some intellectual gymnastics to get around this difficulty.

In 1989, D. S. Flattery and M. Schwartz published a critique of Wasson's theory and identified soma as the psychoactive *Peganum harmala*, or Syrian rue, a suggestion first made by Sir William Jones in 1794 in *The Laws of Manu*. They pointed out that it is the most abundant psychoactive plant in the Indo-Iranian region, has long been known to have mind-altering powers, and was referred to as sacred in ancient

Iran. Furthermore, in pre-Islamic texts the first use of *Haoma* is attributed to the founding figures of Zoroastrianism, and the plant is said to bring healing, victory, salvation, and protection, as well as being an aphrodisiac; in post-Islamic Persian, Mandaean, and Turkish texts, *Peganum harmala* is said to have first been used by the founders of Shi'a Islam and to have precisely the same range of attributes. However, there are also problems for Flattery's and Schwartz's case because, although the plant's psychoactive effects in contemporary Iranian folk medicine are well known, there seems to be no evidence for the specific use of *Peganum harmala* as a sacred hallucinogen in ancient times. Therefore, in order to drive their case home, Flattery and Schwartz were obliged to refer to the ethnographic data abundantly available on the South American "soul vine," *Banisteriopsis caapi*. The seeds of *Peganum harmala* contain the beta-carboline alkaloids harmine, harmaline, and tetrahydroharmine, among others—the same alkaloids, the two researchers argued, as those contained in *Banisteriopsis caapi*. They cited studies of Amazonian Indian usage of *yagé* (*yajé*) or *ayahuasca*—these are decoctions made from *Banisteriopsis caapi* to which, as a rule, other plant substances, many of them hallucinogenic, are added. But hallucinogen expert and scholar Jonathan Ott considers this to be "an exceedingly weak line of argument," pointing out that "it has been well established that harmaline is [only] a trace constituent in *ayahuasca* brews, and does not contribute significantly to *ayahuasca* pharmacology." He adds that the mind-altering effects of such decoctions "are generally not due to the harmane alkaloids but to DMT, scopolamine, and other active principles" in the substances added to the brews.[20] Ott feels the *Peganum harmala–yagé* link argued by Flattery and Schwartz to be "a specious equivalence." To overcome the chemistry problems, Flattery suggested that DMT-rich plant admixtures were added to *Peganum harmala* to create soma/*Haoma*, but, as Ott observes, there is "absolutely no evidence" of this. Ott considers Flattery to have backed himself into a corner and to be grasping at straws.[21]

Richard Rudgley locates what he considers the "most comprehensive account of the use of an intoxicant in Zoroastrian literature" in the *Book of Arda Wiraz*, that dates to the ninth century A.D., produced from material composed as early as the third century A.D. It describes the visions of the religious figure Arda Wiraz when he took *mang*, which Rudgley feels can be safely identified with the original *Haoma*. In the account, Arda Wiraz is charged with finding out if the prayers and ceremonies being performed in his day were suitable to God. Wiraz washes, puts on fresh clothes, perfumes himself, and lays out a new carpet. He drinks three cups of *mang* and enters a seven-day trance, while priests keep watch over his body. In spirit, Arda Wiraz is taken to both heaven and hell. On awakening, he describes heaven as "the all-glorious light of space, much perfumed with sweet basil, all-bedecked, all-admired, and splendid, full of glory and every joy and every pleasure, with which no one is satiated."

Rudgley acknowledges that there are differences between the imagery of Arda Wiraz's visions and those reported by Indians who take *ayahuasca*, but notes this could be due to the chemistry of secondary ingredients in the Amazon decoctions. He ascribes most of the differences to cultural factors. (As has already been remarked, all visionary or hallucinatory content is profoundly influenced by the set and setting of the individual experiencing it.) Nevertheless, he feels the resemblance between the Iranian and Amazonian traditions to be "striking," citing in particular the sensation of spirit or soul flight so clearly expressed in the Wiraz account and in *ayahuasca* experiences. But this is a primary effect of numerous hallucinogens, and cannot be used to make any specific correlations. However, Rudgley does make two intriguing points. He suggests that the seeds of *Peganum harmala*, which produce a rich red dye, might have been used not only to color Persian carpets, but also, through their psychoactivity, to provide the "blueprints" for the symmetrical, geometric patterns that are characteristic not just of Persian carpets but of hallucinogenic trance itself. Secondly, Rudgley wonders whether the hallucinogenically generated sensation of flight accounts for the legends concerning magic "flying carpets."[22]

Terence McKenna, ethnopharmacologist and philosopher of the contemporary psychedelic scene, has argued against identifying soma/*Haoma* with *Amanita muscaria*. He does so largely on the grounds that the mushroom did not provide him with visionary experience on the two occasions he took it himself, and because a few other people, including Wasson, have similarly reported experiences that were not truly psychedelic. "In short, *Amanita muscaria* is doubtless an effective shamanic vehicle in the floristically limited Arctic environment in which it has been traditionally utilized as a psychoactive agent," McKenna concludes. "But the rapturous visionary ecstasy that inspired the Vedas and was the central mystery of the Indo-European peoples as they moved across the Iranian plateau could not possibly have been caused by *Amanita muscaria*."[23] But Ott lambasts McKenna, claiming that his "soundings of the literature have been cursory."[24] Ott goes on to cite a rich body of study reports, including his own, which demonstrate that the effects of fly agaric mushroom can be powerful indeed (though the variability in the mushroom's effects have been widely noted—it is this that might lead to such differing conclusions). Ott demonstrates conclusively that on effectiveness grounds alone, *Amanita muscaria* cannot be ruled out as a candidate for soma, and would produce a far more powerful experience than *Peganum harmala* seeds, which are "a *Valium*-like drug."

McKenna suggests that the psilocybin-rich *Stropharia cubensis* mushroom is soma. He states that Wasson ignored "ample evidence" that seems to indicate this answer to the ages-old question. McKenna contends that *Stropharia cubensis* or a closely related species was likely to have been present on the Iranian plateau thousands of years before the Indo-Europeans arrived. He contends that it may even have been used in conjunction with *Peganum harmala*, which, he notes, "would synergize and enhance the effects of psilocybin."[25] Ott admits that the religious role of urine would fit with psilocybin mushrooms just as well as with *Amanita muscaria*, as psilocybin in the body converts to psilocine, a good proportion of which is excreted in the urine. He notes that the first suggestion that psilocybin mushrooms might have been soma was made by two mycologists, R. F. Schroeder and G. Guzmán, in 1981.[26]

It is clear from all of this that much controversy still surrounds the identity of soma, the legendary juice that is the classic, most famous, and most ancient religious hallucinogen in the world. It may well be, as Wendy Doniger O'Flaherty has suggested, that the quest for an original soma may be misguided, that all later substitutes were surrogates for a mythical plant, or a mythical concept of an ultimate sacred plant. Richard Rudgley protests that we cannot "conjur away" soma like this.[27] What if we restate this idea slightly, and suggest that "soma" is a sort of archetypal concept that stands for the psychoactive, sacred experience that can be found in the plant kingdom?

This approach is supported by archaeology and the work of Andrew Sherratt, who demonstrated how the "smoking complex"—the ancient practice of taking in aromatic and psychoactive substances by smoke, *par fume*—preceded the later, Bronze Age "drinking complex." To some extent these complexes still distinguish the modern Judeo-Christian West and the Islamic world. In a 1995 paper, Sherratt describes the desert plateau of Iran and its borderlands during the second millennium B.C. as being a "contact zone" between the new "drinking complex" homeland of the eastern Mediterranean area and the old "smoking complex" region of the central Asian steppes. Substances that were formerly burned or chewed, he argues, were adapted to the drinking mode used for alcohol. He then provides crucially important new information:

> In the oases of the upper Oxus and adjacent northward-flowing rivers in Turkmenistan and Tadjikistan, at the western end of the later Silk Route, a series of fortified citadel-like sites, built of mud-brick and dating to the second millennium, has been excavated by Russian and local archaeologists. Many . . . enclose temple complexes that include both ash repositories from sacred fires, and preparation rooms where vats and strainers for liquid were found. Pollen analysis of their contents has identified traces of *Ephedra*, *Cannabis* and *Papaver* . . . well known as euphoriants. Some of these were prepared by grating with stone graters and pounding with distinctive fine imported stone pestles, and the products were consumed as liquids (perhaps through decorated bone pipes, showing wide-eyed faces). Cylinder seals show animal-masked figures, playing a drum or leaping over a pole. The association of fire shrines and the consumption of psychoactive drinks suggested to the excavator that this is the origin of the tradition of Iranian fire rituals, which was reformed by the prophet

Zarathustra [Zoroaster] in the early first millennium B.C. The genesis of the tradition which gave rise to Zoroastrianism would thus have taken place in the context of interaction between oasis communities—probably familiar with alcohol, since wine had been prepared in western Iran since the fourth millennium—and steppe and desert tribes. . . . The ritual plant products traditionally consumed on the steppes in braziers would now have been prepared as euphoriant or inebriating drinks.[28]

It was from this area that the Indo-European groups descended upon the Indus Valley people. "It seems likely, therefore," Sherratt writes, "that the drink described as *soma* involved the infusion of various plant products known earlier on the steppes, and that there is no single answer to the *soma* question."[29] He mentions that *Peganum harmala* could have been one of these plants, as it is known to have been burned in central Asia as an intoxicant, but cautions that many psychoactive substances used by the Eurasians may have since been forgotten, and "it may be a mistake to attribute all possible indications to the famous ones."[30]

And so soma/*Haoma* may well be an expression of the godlike gift of expanded consciousness that the plant world bestows on human beings. In that context, the sacred soma is the symbol of all plant hallucinogens.

TEMPLES OF MYSTERY

Two famous Greek temples also prove difficult for scholars trying to determine the nature of the hallucinogens used there. The problem they encounter is central to understanding Eleusis, the focus of a Mystery cult that lasted for nearly two thousand years. Today the temple complex lies in picturesque ruins hemmed in by dusty cement factories and housing about twelve miles west of Athens. Because of its unfortunate modern surroundings, the old temple of the Mysteries lies somewhat off the tourist route, but it is well worth visiting on our long trip, for the ruins still exude an enchantment that speaks of profound events.

Eleusis is where Persephone (Kore) was abducted by Hades, the king of the Underworld. Persephone's mother, Demeter, wandered the Earth looking for her daughter and vowed never to return to Olympus nor to allow crops to grow on the Earth until Persephone was returned to her. Eventually, Zeus sent his messenger Hermes to the Underworld to retrieve Persephone. Before she escaped, however, Hades tricked her into eating pomegranate seeds, which meant that she would have to return to his realm for a third of each year. Thus was the cycle of the seasons established. Reunited with her daughter, Demeter gave Triptolemos, the son of a nearby king, seeds of wheat and a magical chariot in which he could roam around the world teaching agriculture and the use of the plow. Demeter taught humans the rites that were to be carried out at Eleusis. The mythic geography surrounding the temple includes Mount Kerata ("Horns"), with its pronounced cleft peak. Such distinctive, twin-peaked mountains overlook numerous other Greek temples, and to the ancient Greek mind they represented the Great Earth Goddess, of which the Demeter/Persephone complex is of course a reflection.[31, 32]

A settlement arose at Eleusis between 1580 and 1500 B.C., but the area now occupied by the ruins of the Eleusinian precinct was left empty even at that time, suggesting that an early form of the Mysteries may have been in operation even at this early date.[33] The first stone structure on the site is what archaeologists call Megaron B, from the fifteenth century B.C. Over the following thousand years, various structures were built and destroyed, buildings enlarged and added. The Mysteries themselves were a ten-day ritual event held in September each year, and were open to almost anyone. The climax was the procession from Athens to the temple for the Mystery Night, where the revelation of the Mystery, the *epopteia*, to the initiatory candidates, the *mystai*, would take place. After initial preparation, involving a period of fasting, the *mystai* were led by the *mystagogos* in joyful procession along the Sacred Way from Athens to Eleusis. The journey lasted all day because observances were made at various shrines along the route.

Along the way they also partook of a sacred drink, the *kykeon*. The nature of the drink, like the details of the Mystery, was locked in secrecy, and has so remained through the ages (though there were a few scandals in which certain individuals were accused of revealing aspects of the secrets). We know that the beverage was carried in metal or pottery containers, some of them fixed to the heads of priestesses and initiatory candidates by cords or thin straps. But what was the *kykeon* made from? It certainly wasn't wine, for wine was not permitted.[34] Ingredients of the potion, of which a specific dose had to be taken, were said to have been water, barley, and fresh leaves of some variety of pennyroyal—probably the mint *Mentha pulegium*. Nothing hallucinogenic here—or is there? The principle constituent of pennyroyal is poley oil (*Oleum pulegii*), large doses of which can induce delirium, unconsciousness, and convulsions. Carl Kerènyi noted that a plant of the same family, *Salvia divinorum*, was found in use among the Mazatec Indians of Mexico in a divinatory context, and may have been the Aztec magic plant *pipiltzintzintli*. Christian Rätsch assures us that it contains nonalkaloidal constituents called Divinorin A and Divinorin B, whose psychoactive effects have been experimentally verified.[35] Kerènyi implied that this may indicate a psychoactive quality to the *kykeon*,[36] but Albert Hofmann later felt that Kerènyi had "overstated" the possibility.[37] Instead, Hofmann joined with Gordon Wasson and Carl Ruck, who had their eyes on the barley. They pointed out that a water solution of *Claviceps purpurae*, or ergot, a parasitic fungus found on wheat and barley, or its less toxic variety parasitic on *Paspalum distichum*, a grass growing around the Mediterranean, could easily have been made. As we will recall from the introductory chapter, ergot contains alkaloids from which LSD can be produced. This possibility of the *kykeon* having been a hallucinogenic, ergotized beer is supported by the fact that Demeter was sometimes referred to as *Erysibe*, "ergot," and her symbolic color was purple, the color of ergot at certain stages of its growth cycle (hence *purpurea*).

This theory vindicated a prediction Wasson had made in 1957 that "the secret of the Mysteries will be found in the indoles, whether derived from mushrooms or from higher plants or . . . from both."[38] The research team of Hofmann, Wasson, and Ruck presented their findings at a conference and, later, in a book, *The Road to Eleusis* (1978). Their theory remains

The ruins of the Plouton temple are seen in front of the cave at Eleusis, the entrance to the underworld. *(Paul Devereux)*

the most convincing, though Terence McKenna has revived a 1964 suggestion by poet-scholar Robert Graves that hallucinogenic mushrooms were involved with the Eleusinian Mysteries. McKenna speculates that perhaps *Stropharia cubensis* "or some other psilocybin-containing musroom" was at the core of the Eleusinian ritual.[39]

In flickering torchlight, the *mystai* arrived at Eleusis by nightfall. They danced and conducted rites at various points around and within the temple complex, including the eerie Plouton, a temple considered to be an entrance to the Underworld. Eventually, the *mystai* assembled at the Telesterion (from *teleo*, "to initiate"), a vast building unlike other Greek temple architecture in that it had a plain exterior. Inside there was a forest of columns and an inner enclosure known as the Anaktoron. Although the Telesterion had been rebuilt and enlarged numerous times, this central structure remained. In the great, final revelation of the Mysteries, and under the control of the hierophant ("he who makes the holy things appear"), flames erupted from the only door in the Anaktoron, and Persephone manifested herself. Exactly what this was no one has been able to determine, for it was kept secret on pain of death or banishment, but those who saw it—and this included many notable names of ancient and classical Greece, such as Plato, Aristotle, and Sophocles—felt their lives had been changed by the experience; it was said that afterward, death could hold no more fears. The revelation seems to have been some kind of powerful theatrical event unleashed on the hallucinogenically charged perceptions of the *mystai* in a highly programmed set and setting. The flames, the "Great Fire," could be seen issuing out of a spe-

The remains of the Anaktoron, the very heart of the Eleusian Mysteries, within the vast ruins of the Telesterion.
(Paul Devereux)

cial opening in the roof of the Telesterion, a signal to those outside that the *epopteia* had taken place. The hierophant closed the event with a Zenlike act: he wordlessly showed an ear of corn to the congregation within the Telesterion.

The Temple of Delphi, another important and famous ancient Greek temple complex, stands on the lower slopes of Mount Parnassus, seventy miles or so northwest of Eleusis. Legend has it that a herdsman named Koretas discovered a chasm or fissure at the site of what became the temple. Fumes issuing from the fissure put Koretas into a trance in which he saw visions of the future. A timber oracle house dedicated to the Earth Goddess Gaea was built there. Another legend states that when the young god Apollo came across the place, then called Pytho, he encountered and killed the she-dragon, the Python, that dwelled there. The Pythian games were instituted to commemorate this mythic event, which seems to encode the memory of the usurpation of a Bronze Age goddess shrine by the later Apollo cult. The Oracle of Delphi was active for over a thousand years and was the most famous oracle of its day. Kings, soldiers, and regular folk came from far and wide to consult it.

The prophetess or *Pythia*, who issued the oracular pronouncements, was situated in the Temple of Apollo: the ruins standing there today date from the fourth century B.C., and supplanted earlier stone and timber shrines. The Delphi prophetesses were originally young peasant women, but after one of them had been abducted and raped, older women assumed the role. The prophetess would purify herself

The Temple of Apollo, Delphi. *(Paul Devereux)*

before an oracular session by bathing in and drinking from the Castalian spring at the foot of the mountain. She would also drink the waters from the Kassotis spring, which ran into the temple itself. The *Pythia* would then burn laurel leaves (as tradition has it) with barley on an altar before entering the oracle chamber, the *manteion*, where she was attended by priests. No other woman was allowed there.

The person seeking an answer would go into a room adjoining the oracle chamber. There the question would be written on a lead tablet. In the oracle chamber, the *Pythia* would be seated on a tripod—a tall, three-legged metal stool with a bowl-like seat—and in one hand held a laurel leaf, which she occasionally shook. She would go into trance and utter the oracular response to the question asked.

It had long been assumed that the Temple of Apollo was situated over the fuming fissure that Koretas had originally discovered, and that the tripod was to suspend the prophetess over it in order that she would be able to breathe in the fumes that sent her into the prophetic trance. But scholar Joseph Fontenrose spent some forty years investigating this idea, combining site visits with the most thorough appraisal of all the available literature.[40] He found that no archaeological investigation had ever revealed a fissure and that the original references to it

An ancient Greek design showing the Pythia Themis on her tripod divining for King Aigeus. *(From the Vulci Cup, fourth century A.D.)*

were confused and misinterpreted, and he concluded that the whole concept of a toxic vapor was a romantic myth without any factual foundation.

Another theory was that the *Pythia* became intoxicated from the laurel leaves she burned (and was also said to have chewed). It had been supposed that this laurel smoke might have been psychoactive, but Albert Hofmann has confirmed analytically that the plant contains no chemically active principles that could induce prophetic trance.[41] This conclusion has been supported in self-experimentation by psychologist Julian Jaynes, who "crushed laurel leaves and smoked quantities of them in a pipe and felt somewhat sick but no more inspired than usual."[42]

Other plant sources for the (assumed) trance-inducing smoke at Delphi have been suggested. The strongest contender is the psychoactive herb henbane (*Hyoscyamus niger*), which contains the tropane alkaloids hyoscyamine, scopolamine, and atropine. This theory is championed by Christian Rätsch.[43, 44] The Greeks consecrated the plant to Apollo, which would certainly have made it appropriate for the Temple of Apollo at Delphi, and it was used for trance induction or for its medicinal properties from ancient times in Sumeria up until medieval times in western Europe. The German toxicologist Gustav

Schenk, writing in 1955, gave an account of an experiment in which he inhaled the fumes from a handful of henbane seeds thrown on a hot iron plate. He found that the psychoactive smoke obliterated his memory so that he only recalled vivid but disconnected images afterward, but these nevertheless contained the memory of "tremendous imaginings" and "powerful and sinister pictures":

> There were animals, which looked at me keenly with contorted grimaces and staring, terrified eyes; there were flying stones and clouds of mist, all sweeping along in the same direction. They carried me irresistibly with them. . . . They were enveloped in a vague gray light which emitted a dull glow and rolled onward and upward into a black and smoky sky. . . . Above my head water was flowing, dark and blood-red. The sky was filled with whole herds of animals. Fluid, formless creatures emerged from the darkness. . . .
>
> My teeth were clenched and a dizzy rage took possession of me. I know that I trembled with horror; but I also know that I was permeated by a peculiar sense of well-being connected with the crazy sensation that my feet were growing lighter, expanding and breaking loose from my body. This sensation of gradual bodily dissolution is typical of henbane poisoning. . . . I was seized with the fear that I was falling apart. At the same time I experienced an intoxicating sensation of flying.
>
> . . . I soared where my hallucinations—the clouds, the lowering sky, herds of beasts, falling leaves which were quite unlike any ordinary leaves, billowing streamers of steam and rivers of molten metal—were swirling along.[45]

Another "witch herb" suggested as a source for the smoke of Delphi was mentioned in the eighteenth century by Baron Ernst von Bibra, who claimed that "priests at the oracle of Delphi administered the prepared seeds of the thorn apple to their seers to put them in the desired prophetic ecstasy."[46] Schenk also cites a seventeenth-century report of thorn apple poisoning, in which seeds of thorn apple had accidentally got into a dish of lentils served to the servants of a large household:

Afterwards they all became foolish. The lacemaker worked with unusual diligence . . . but getting everything into a frightful muddle. The chambermaid came into the room shouting at the top of her voice: "Look, all the devils from hell are coming in!" One servant carried the wood piece by piece into the secret chamber, announcing that he must burn brandy there. Another stuck two hatchets of wood axes together, saying he had to chop up wood. Another crawled about on all fours scratching up grass and earth with his mouth and grubbing around in it like a pig with its snout. Yet another imagined himself a cartwright and wanted to bore holes in every piece of wood he could lay hands on. . . . The next day none of them knew what ludicrous antics they had got up to.[47]

The two Old World psychedelic standbys, cannabis and *Amanita muscaria*, have also been touted as candidates for supercharging the *Pythia's* incense, but with little supporting evidence. In the end, we cannot know for sure just what the *Pythia* did inhale, for it is simply not documented. On balance, however, Rätsch's ideas concerning henbane seem the most likely answer.

THE DARK CONTINENT

The use of hallucinogens in Africa seems to have been limited and fragmentary—or, perhaps more accurately, our knowledge of it is. In regard to the West's knowledge and documentation of its hallucinogenic traditions, it is as much a terra incognita as it was in terms of its vast unknown geography when the first European explorers arrived.

The blue water lily (*Nymphaea caerula*) is known to have been used ritually as part of the Osiris cult in dynastic Egypt. The lily was the form in which Isis restored the murdered Osiris, and was thus a symbol for him. It was also a symbol of divination and was often portrayed together with mandrake, poppy capsules, and the toad.[48] Rätsch notes that the *Egyptian Book of the Dead* contains a text known as the "Transformation of the Water Lily," which describes a shamanic or alchemical transformation: "I am the sacred water lily, which came out of the light, which belongs to the nostrils of Ra and to the head of Hathor. I am the pure water lily, which came from the field of Ra".[49] Buds of *Nymphaea caerula* have been experimentally shown to have hypnotic effects, but the chemistry of the plant still requires investigation.

Opium was also known in ancient Egypt, as was khat (or *qat*), which means "the shrub" or "the tree" in old Egyptian.[50] The word was known also in Nubia and in Kenya, and the bush was known by other names elsewhere in Africa. The shrub, which can reach a height of up to ten feet, is known as *Catha edulis* in Western botany, and contains the euphoriant norpseudoephedrine and the stimulant ephedrine. It is said to have dream-inducing effects, among others. Its use today is centered in Yemen.

In northeast Africa, Kunama magicians use plant mixtures thought to contain *Datura* species to induce trance during rituals in which women become possessed by the spirits of the dead, but this practice may or may not have roots in antiquity.

Evidence for very ancient hallucinogen use in Africa is preserved in the rock paintings of the Tassili n'Ajjer Plateau in the Sahara Desert of southern Algeria. Here, eroded rock escarpments have been sculpted into a vertible labyrinth of steep, rocky passageways, presenting an extraordinary spectacle. Among these weathered rock features are secreted rock shelters embellished with mysterious paintings dating back thousands of years, produced by an unknown people. Some of the rock art seems to offer visual evidence of a lost religion based on hallucinogenic mushrooms: there are depictions of figures sprouting mushrooms all over their bodies, others holding mushrooms in their hands, and still other figures that are hybrids of mushrooms and humans. Frank Elgar's *The Rock Paintings of Tassili* shows a variety or remarkable images. One depicts a shaman in antler headgear with a bee's face, clutching fistfuls of mushrooms. In another panel what seem to be mushroom spirits run along in impish glee, their heads mushroom-shaped, their hands holding mushrooms aloft, surrounded by dots and geometrical patterns that are the signatures of trance—the "entoptic" imagery involuntarily produced by the human brain in trance and hallucinogenic states. It may seem strange to find these enigmatic artifacts

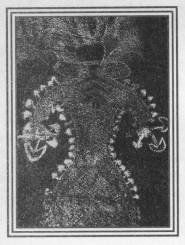

Tassili rock art image of a supernatural being or a shaman figure sprouting and clasping what seem to be mushrooms. *(Author's drawing)*

Playful-looking mushroom men or spirits with entoptic imagery at Tassili. *(Author's drawing)*

in such an arid zone, but we must remember that the Sahara once had rivers flowing through it, as satellite photography has revealed. It may well have harbored civilizations older than ancient Egypt.

Various religious artifacts in Nigeria—such as *panka*, the wooden boards used as protective covers for the Koran—display features that seem to be mushroom representations. Psilocybin mushrooms are known in Kenya.

Nutmeg (*Myristica fragrans*), native to the Banda (Nutmeg) Islands in Indonesia, is psychoactive.

Nutmeg's properties have been known since ancient times in India. It has recently been reported that the indigenous peoples of the Bassa region of Cameroon in west-central Africa use *Myristica fragrans* to induce contact with water spirits.[51] The antiquity of the practice isn't yet known. Its oil is composed of myristicine and safrole; myristicine aminates in the body, resulting in the production of the amphetamine derivative MDA, and safrole chemically changes to MDMA (better known as "Ecstasy" today). In high dosages nutmeg can be physically harmful, with unpleasant side effects. Nevertheless, it can also produce psychedelic effects, and, more particularly, can enhance dreaming when taken occasionally in modest amounts—say, a level teaspoonful, or even when used generously in food—prior to sleep. Experimenting with nutmeg, I had my first full, lucid dream. A lucid dream is a state of consciousness in which the dreamer achieves full awareness within a dream without awakening from sleep, causing the dream to take on such vivid realism that it becomes virtually indistinguishable in clarity and detail to the perception of normal, waking reality. In my nutmeg-inspired experience I "awoke" in a dream to find myself flying through a clear azure sky over a sun-drenched countryside of rolling hills and fields. I saw houses, people in one-piece greenish tunics, and unusually engineered tricycles, and was able to feel the waxy texture of leaves on trees as I floated by.[52]

Tabernanthe iboga is a powerful hallucinogen widely used by many native peoples in the tropical rain forest area of west-central Africa, mainly Gabon, Zaire, and the Congo region. Called *eboka* by the Fang people, *Tabernanthe iboga* is a member of the dogbane family. It grows wild and is also cultivated in some native villages. It is used today primarily in the MBieri curing cult, and in the Bwiti ancestor religion, which has managed to strongly resist the intrusions of Western, Christian, and Islamic influences. Europeans reported the use of *Tabernanthe iboga* in the 1800s. Although today some branches of the Bwiti "religion of the trees" have a Christian veneer, the history (or prehistory, rather) of *Tabernanthe iboga* usage in some form or another is likely to be long. The Fang people, who migrated to the tropical forest from the savannahs to the north, credit its original use to the pygmies who inhabited the forest long before them. A Fang myth tells how the pygmy Bitumi died in an accident and the creator god Zame ye Mebege cut off his little fingers and toes and planted them in various parts of the forest. These digits grew into *eboka* plants.

Tabernanthe iboga contains at least twelve indole alkaloids, the principle one being ibogaine, which is found throughout the entire plant but is mainly concentrated in the bark. Ibogaine's hallucinogenic effects are accompanied by strong stimulation of the central nervous system, and it formed the basis of Western medicine's first antidepressant drug early in the twentieth century. In the Bwiti religion shavings taken from the bark are powdered or soaked in water and drunk as an infusion. It is said that one can't be a member of the religion unless one has seen the god Bwiti, symbolized by a sculptured post, and the only way to see him is to take *eboka*.

There are two ranges of dosage. The usual one is relatively small—two to three teaspoonfuls for women, three to five for men. This brings on a dream state that promotes out-of-body sensations and travel to the spirit worlds. Initiates, however, are given massive doses—forty to sixty times the threshold dose—in order to "break open the head" and allow the initiate to have deep contact with the ancestors. *Tabernanthe iboga* is toxic in very high doses, and occasional deaths do occur. The drug can be used on its own, or with admixtures, none of which are known to be hallucinogenic. Other hallucinogens are employed in a secondary role. One of these, *Alchornea floribunda*, known as *alan*, produces a state that is known as "passing over the land of the ancestors." The milky juice of another, *Elaeophorbia drupifera*, is mixed with oil to produce eyedrops that affect the optic nerves, producing bizarre visual effects.[53]

Eboka is used for a number of purposes, such as divination, enhancing physical endurance, discovering "places of power," and establishing contact with the spirits of the trees, springs, and rocks. However, within the Bwiti cult its main function is to promote access to the realm of the ancestors, which is referred to in a generalized sense by the term "the Bwiti."[54] One initiate gave this description of his experience:

I found myself taken up by a long road in a deep forest until I came to a barrier of black iron. . . . In the distance beyond the barrier it was very bright, I could see many colors in the air but . . . could not pass. Suddenly my father descended from above in the form of a bird. He gave to me then my *eboka* name, Onwan Misengue, and enabled me to fly after him over the barrier of iron. As we proceeded the bird who was my father changed from black to white—first his tail feathers, then all his plumage. We then came to a river of blood in the midst of which was a great snake of three colors—

blue, black and red. . . . On the other side there was a crowd of people all in white. We passed through them and they shouted at us words of recognition until we arrived at another river—all white. This we crossed by means of a giant chain of gold. On the other side there were no trees but only a grassy upland. On the top of the hill was a round house made entirely of glass and built upon one post only. Within I saw a man, the hair on his head piled up in the form of a Bishop's hat. He had a star on his breast but on coming closer I saw that it was his heart in his chest beating.[55]

A spirit guide of some kind appears in many reported experiences, as do rainbow colors, long roads, and white figures—white being symbolic of death. Initiates often have their bodies painted. A sense of a great passing of time while in the spirit world is often experienced, and Peter Stafford notes that the *eboka* taker often "meets the ancestors in order of descent, going further and further back in lineage."[56] The imagery confronting the initiate can be gruesome, such as the guiding phantom taking him or her by the hand past a procession of skeletons and pale cadavers, who gesticulate and give off insufferable odors. Bwiti himself can present an even more horrible visage.[57]

There are some instances of Westerners experimenting with ibogaine, which seems to be remarkably successful in curing drug addicts—numerous reports suggest that it is able to interrupt and "reset" habitual mental patterns.[58] It is interesting that without the tradition of ancestor worship that informs the African users of *eboka*, one American subject described an experience that seems essentially similar. As he put it, the "subconscious comes forth, and you're able to view it in a totally impartial way," and he found himself able to gain information from what he called his "individual hereditary archive."[59] A common report from Western subjects is that previously buried memories can be vividly reconstructed as intense lucid dreams.

In southern Africa, we have evidence of the use of various plants by indigenous peoples. The !Kung of the Kalahari claim to have used the roots of *gaise noru noru* (*Ferraria glutinosa*) to help enter *kia*, an altered state of consciousness, in their trance dances.[60] The roots are made into a drink, and given to everyone taking part in the dance, though those who have never experienced *kia* before are encouraged to drink larger amounts. The psychoactive principles in the roots have not yet been identified by modern analysis. The use of *gaise noru noru* seems to be the continuation of an ancient Bushman tradition.

The Bushman peoples are also said to use *kwashi* bulbs (*Pancratium trianthum*) both to obtain visions and as a medicine. There are fifteen species of *kwashi*, and all contain highly toxic alkaloids.

The Bushman-related Hottentot smoke the roots and leaves of the strong intoxicant *kanna* (*Mesembryanthemum expansum*) today as they did two centuries ago when Dutch explorers reported the practice. *Kanna* contains the psychoactive alkaloids mesembrine and mesembrenine but is not now used hallucinogenically; Schultes and Hofmann nevertheless suspect that it was probably "once used as a vision-inducing hallucinogen."[61]

Zulu healers inhale straw flower (*Helichrysum foetidum*) to induce trances. The antiquity of the practice does not seem to be known, but it is likely to have a long history.

Cannabis is occasionally smoked by the Bushmen, but it is not known how old that practice is, and the !Kung seem to consider it an inferior way to achieve altered states. Brian M. du Toit has reckoned that cannabis was likely to have been known in southern Africa "in pre-Portugese times, i.e., before A.D. 1500."[62] This does not, of course, tell us how far back cannabis usage goes in Africa, though du Toit does note that it has been grown in Egypt for a thousand years.

The Shagana-Tsonga of the northern Transvaal are said to use *Datura fatuosa* during female initiation at puberty. It can produce eagerly sought auditory effects—which are interpreted as ancestral voices, which bestow fertility—and *mavalavala*, visual phenomena in blue-green hues.

VISIONS IN PARADISE

We do not have a great deal of information regarding traditional or ancient hallucinogen use in the vast section of the globe encompassed by

Australasia, Southwest Asia, and Oceania. As with the dearth of knowledge regarding African traditions, this is probably due to incomplete research. Although there doesn't seem to be a wide variety of traditional hallucinogens reported in this area, those we know about seem to be used by many of the various peoples inhabiting this huge geographical zone.

The Aborigines of Australia appear to have chewed the dried leaves of a species of tobacco "for their narcotic effect" prior to contact with the outside world.[63] Though probably originating in South America, varieties of tobacco have in fact been present in Australia for millions of years. Not commonly regarded as a psychedelic, tobacco can be quite mind-altering, as we shall see.

The Aborigines also made use of another nicotine-containing plant, *Duboisia hopwoodii*, known as *pituri* or *pitcheri*, which was also chewed. It was used for various purposes, including magico-religious activities such as prophecy.[64] Extensive trade networks, referred to as *"pituri* roads," existed over the outback.

In many parts of Southeast Asia, an important psychoactive plant is the areca or betel nut (*Areca catechu*). This is traditionally chewed, mixed with lime and a leaf from the vine *Piper betel*, remains of which have been found in Spirit Cave, Thailand, and dated to 6000 B.C. *P. betel* and areca dating to 3000 B.C. have also been found in Timor. The mixture is not hallucinogenic, but Alfred Gell's observations in Papua New Guinea led him to describe the effects as "mild dissociation . . . feeling of reduced gravity . . . a 'marginal' state of consciousness."[65] It was always used by participants in rituals, and betel-spit was used to impart magical power to ritual masks and similar objects. It is also now widely used as a mundane stimulant in daily routine.

The Kuma of the western highlands of New Guinea also use a range of other psychoactive plants, especially mushrooms: *Nonda*, *Nonda Mbolbe*, and *Nonda-mos* (*Boletus* spp., *Heimiella* spp. and *Russula* spp., respectively). These seem to be implicated in what has been called "mushroom madness" among the Kuma. This is a kind of group frenzy, in which, contrary to their normal behavior, men become violent to kin, and women become lascivious. Similar reactions are noted among another New Guinea tribe, the Kiambi, and both the Kuma and the Kiambi say the mushrooms cause their altered states. Little is known about the chemical makeup of these mushrooms, though Ibotenic acid-muscimole, similar to *Amanita muscaria,* has been found in *Russula* species.

It has been noted that the Bimin-Kuskusmin people of the West Sepik region of New Guinea display a "highly systemic use of intoxicants."[66] They have complex male initiation procedures that involve sacred plants, called *waraang,* meaning "heart palpitations," a reference to their physiological effects. In the course of these initiations, the spirit leaves the body and, assisted by a guardian ancestor spirit, is taken to the ancestral underworld. Mushrooms are among the *waraang* employed in the procedures, two of which can be used only by the adept, as they are considered so powerful and dangerous.

What may be the unusual relics of a mushroom cult have been reported by researcher Chris Ashton at three remote, uninhabited villages in southern Nias, an island off the west coast of Sumatra. After a tortuous journey, he came to the first village, positioned on an artificially flattened hilltop, where he saw a number of tall standing stones and a tablelike stone with dragon-head carvings. "The most intriguing feature of the site, though, was the abundance of three-foot-high stone mushrooms," Ashton remarks. "They were about a yard in diameter with flat tops and had a slight ring to them when given a sharp rap with one's knuckles. The odd thing about them was that they had intricate and delicate carvings on their undersides depicting flowing geometric lines. I found these stone mushrooms at the three uninhabited sites that I visited but none at the inhabited megalithic villages on the island."[67]

It has recently been reported that the Igorot, the aboriginal Malayan inhabitants of the Philippine island of Luzon, have maintained a traditional *Amanita muscaria* cult. They call the mushroom *ampacao.* Six mushrooms are brewed into a hallucinogenic drink, which is taken during rites of passage.[68]

By far the most popular psychoactive plant among the Pacific islands is *kava-kava (Piper methysticum).* It belongs to the pepper family, contains methysticin and several other active pyrones, and is made into a drink. It was first noted by Europeans when Captain Cook visited the Sandwich Islands (Hawaii) in 1768. It is used socially, for inebriation, or to welcome guests and visitors, as an aphrodisiac, as an offering to the gods, as well as in healing, magic, and religion—though religious usage seems to have been its oldest function. It is used in Hawaiian Huna magic (*kahuna*) also. When prepared for communal rituals, fresh *kava-kava* roots were traditionally chewed by young men or women, and the resulting saliva mixture spat out into a ceremonial pot filled with water. After several hours the saliva fermented the mixture, and the drink was "ripe." This method is still followed in a few Pacific islands, but elsewhere the roots are pulverized, even though this is said to produce a less potent drink.

Kava-kava is a euphoriant rather than a hallucinogen, and can cause a mild sensation of dissociation, and sometimes, in appropriate dosages and conditions, a full out-of-body experience. It was traditionally thought to enhance the psychic powers of mediums and seers, to aid contemplation, and to increase inspiration. Although it isn't truly a hallucinogen, visual distortions can sometimes be experienced, and there have been a few reports of visual hallucinations. Taken prior to sleep it can promote strong dreams, and, occasionally, lucid dreams as well. Auditory hallucinations can also occur, usually in the form of music. *Kava-kava* tends to give the individual a sense of relaxation and well-being. There are no negative side effects provided that high and frequent dosages are avoided, as it can then cause skin rashes.

WITCHES' BREWS (CATCHING THE LAST FLIGHTS IN MEDIEVAL EUROPE)

The magical and medicinal plant lore of the rural "wise woman" (or man) in Anglo-Saxon, medieval, and immediately postmedieval Europe may not occupy a period we can properly call prehistory, but we can say that it was *outside* history in that it was a living knowledge largely overlooked or dismissed by the ruling classes and the sophisticates, or discouraged and repressed by the Church. The Church-orchestrated witch persecutions of the late Middle Ages and the century immedi-

ately after the medieval era transformed what was in fact a quietly surviving country tradition into what was hysterically and neurotically
seen as a satanic activity. This distortion fed the needs of the Church.
The remnants of these ancient traditions of plant lore survived in frag-
mented form and endure in isolated pockets to this day, especially in
eastern Europe and the western Celtic fringe of the continent.

One of the key elements of what became known as "witch lore"
was that witches were able to fly on broomsticks, rods, or other instruments to their sabbats and other nighttime gatherings, held in the dark
woods beyond the pale of the town. "Flying ointments" were often
used, either smeared on the person's body or flying implements. Long
before the Church contextualized this "flying out" to the wilderness as
a diabolic practice, however, it was simply a part of the practice of
women and men wise in the rural magic arts and healing based on arcane plant knowledge. The people who became identified as "witches"
by the Church were in actuality simply the practitioners of an ancient
tradition—"night travelers."[69] In northern Europe they were called
qveldriga, "night rider," or myrkrida, "rider in the dark." In Scandinavia,
there was the tradition of seidhr, in which a prophetess or seidhonka
would travel to farmsteads and hamlets with a group of girls to give
divinatory trance sessions. She wore a ritual costume and carried a
staff. The goddess Freya, who taught Odin the secrets of magical
flight, was the patron of seidhr, and is shown in a twelfth-century mural
in Schleswig cathedral, Germany, in the cloak of a seidhonka flying on a
distaff. Her sister, or alternate aspect, Frigg, accompanies her, flying on
a large striped cat. "Night travellers and the later witches are carelessly
lumped together," Hans Peter Duerr warns.[70]

Depending on the time or place in Europe they operated, the
night travelers might join the flying hosts of Diana, or Frau Holda–
Mother Holle, the Old Norse Hela—the veiled goddess of the underworld, whose sacred bird was the migrant snow goose.* She is

*The winter snows were said to be feathers falling from these birds' wings. (The
goose or gander was a widespread symbol of shamanic spirit flight, ranging from the
iconography of Siberian shamans to the literature of Vedic India to archaeological
finds of geese effigies in the graves of Inuit—Eskimo—shamans.)

Freya flying on her distaff. *(Author's drawing of a twelfth-century mural, Schleswsig Cathedral)*

remembered in the nursery-rhyme image of Old Mother Goose, who, when she wanted to wander, we will recall, would fly through the air on a very fine gander. Researcher Nigel Jackson has noted:

> Celtic iconography from the Dauphine shows the goddess Epona riding upon a goose in flight. The high calls of the migrant geese on winter nights were poetically perceived as the baying of the spectral hounds by folk in the north of Europe and are closely linked with the flight of the Wild Hunt in Celtic and Germanic regions. The German witch Agnes Gerhardt said at her trial in 1596 that she and her companions transformed themselves into snow-geese in order to fly to the sabbat.[71]

Medieval "witches" sometimes rubbed themselves with goose grease, perhaps enriched with hallucinogenic herbs, as a symbolic gesture of supernatural flight. Duerr remarks that the night flights were known as "grease flights" and the night travelers themselves were called "grease birds" or "lard wings."

The antiquity of the image of the night-flying woman is shown by such instances as the scene in *The Golden Ass*, written by Lucius Apuleius in the second century A.D., in which a woman is seen smearing herself all over with an ointment, muttering a charm, turning into an owl, and flying off over the rooftops. The night traveler and later the "witch" surely represented the vestiges of archaic Indo-European shamanism: she is the last echo of traditional ecstatic experience in Europe, an echo the church effectively silenced by intimidation, widespread persecution, and sheer murder.

The boundary between the town or village ("civilization") and the wilderness beyond was freighted with dark meaning in medieval Europe. Jackson points out that Saxon tribes referred to the night traveler as *baegtessa*, the "hedge rider," for she could traverse the mysterious "hedge" (boundary) that divided the worlds of the living and the dead. "Very early, women undertaking 'night travels' and fence demons are mentioned in the same breath," Duerr informs.[72] The stick on which the woman rode was known as a "fence switch." The idea of the hedge-hopping night traveler or witch took on literal meaning in the minds of the ordinary people, and plants such as juniper, thought to ward off witches, were woven into real, physical hedges. Certain places along hedgerows were thought to be where witches were able to breach the boundary. The front doors of houses would be protected by such devices as "witch bottles," tangled threads inside a bottle that would ensnare the spirit of any night-traveling witch who might happen to gain entry.

The real boundary was that between the conscious, waking mind— "civilization"—and the dark, fearsome, and unknown regions of the unconscious—"wilderness." It was simply literalized and projected onto the physical environment. In reality, the night traveler's flight into the wilderness was, of course, a trance "journey" into the deep reaches of the unconscious mind, a "spirit flight" caused, usually, by hallucinogens in the flying ointments. The woman herself might even think of it as being a literal flight: John Cotta in *The Trial of Witchcraft* (1616) refers to an Italian case in which a woman who had rubbed flying ointment on her body fell into a trance from which she could not be roused. When she finally came around of her own accord, she declared that she had been flying over seas and mountains, and could not be convinced otherwise even though others had witnessed her body lying in an entranced state. Commentators over the years remained divided over whether the witches actually flew or only flew mentally, but Francis Bacon had the measure of the matter in

1608 when he wrote in *Sylva Sylvarum* "I suppose that the soporiferous medicines [in the ointments] are likest to do it."

Interestingly, there is little evidence in the confessions of witches that they used flying ointments. Duerr points out that it was in the interest of the Church to downplay the hallucinogenic nature of the flying ointments. If their role was recognized, then the "Devil would then have been left with only a very modest significance, or none at all."[73] But there *are* some records. A Belgian witch called Claire Goessen confessed in 1603 that she had flown to sabbats several times on a staff smeared with an unguent. In northern France in 1460, five women confessed to receiving a salve from the devil himself, which they rubbed on their hands and on a small wooden rod they placed between their legs and flew upon "above good towns and woods and waters." Swedish witches in 1669 rode "over churches and high walls" on a beast given to them by the devil, who also gave them a horn containing a salve with which they anointed themselves. Members of Somerset covens admitted to smearing their foreheads and wrists with a greenish ointment "which smells raw" before their meetings. It may well have been that under the hysteria of the times and the intimidation of the Church authorities, some of those who confessed falsely admitted to the use of ointments—as they clearly bowed to the pressure to say that the ointments were obtained from the devil. But even if this were the case, the idea of ointments itself was a reference to traditional practices that were still known among the rural classes at the time, and that had probably been around for untold generations.

It is known that some of these ointments were actual because certain European writers of the sixteenth and seventeenth centuries recorded recipes for them. Along with animal fat, the blood of bats or lapwings, toads, and other weird and disgusting ingredients, the most commonly listed plants were aconite, hemlock, deadly nightshade, henbane, poppy, and mandrake. We have already noted the effects of opium in the previous chapter, and of henbane in Schenk's account earlier this chapter—especially the sensation of the body feeling light followed by the sensation of flying. Both aconite (*Aconitum* spp.) and hemlock (*Conium maculatum*) were sacred to Hecate, goddess of the

A fanciful sixteenth-century rendering of a mandrake root.

earth and the underworld, and both are very poisonous. In German tradition, hemlock (*Conium* means "stimulating dizziness") was home to a toad, which lived beneath it and sucked up its poisons.[74] (Certain toads do have hallucinogenic chemicals in or on their bodies and this might explain their association with witches' brews.) Both plants in nonlethal doses can elicit feelings of flying. Mandrake (*Mandragora officinarum*) owes its enormous importance in magical lore, in part, to the fact that its roots can sometimes look like a human figure, and there were specific folk traditions surrounding its gathering and uprooting. But it also is psychoactive.

Deadly nightshade or belladonna (*Atropa belladonna*) is the classic witchcraft plant. It was known in Old English as *dwayberry*, which derives from the Danish *dvaleboer*, meaning "trance berry," confirming the knowledge of its poisonous and hallucinogenic effects. Belladonna, mandrake, and henbane are members of the *Solanaceae* or nightshade family, as are species of *Datura*, which are or were widely used for ritual hallucinogenic purposes in the Americas and elsewhere. (In fact, thorn apple—*Datura stramonium, Datura* spp.—was introduced into Europe from the New World in time to establish itself and become included in witches' brews.) They contain tropane alkaloids, especially hyoscyamine, "a powerful hallucinogen, which gives the sensation of flying through the air . . . among other effects."[75] Michael Harner has observed that atropine is absorbable even through intact skin,[76] so the act of rubbing ointments made from atropine-containing solanaceous plants would be an extremely effective way to become intoxicated. This has been confirmed in recent—and clearly dangerous—experiments. Folklorist Dr. Will-Erich Peuckert of Göttingen, for example, mixed an ointment made up of belladonna, henbane, and datura from a seventeenth-century formula and rubbed it on his forehead and armpits. A number of colleagues did the same. They all fell into a twenty-four-hour sleep.[77] "We had wild dreams. Faces danced before my eyes which were at first terrible. Then I suddenly had the sensation of flying for miles through the air. The flight was repeatedly interrupted by great falls. Finally, in the last phase, an image of an orgiastic feast with grotesque sensual excess," Peuckert reported.[78] Harner emphasizes the importance of the greased broomstick or similar flying implement, which he suggests served as "an applicator for the atropine-containing plant to the sensitive vaginal membranes as well as providing the suggestion of riding on a steed, a typical illusion of the witches' ride to the Sabbat."[79]

"A characteristic feature of solanaceae psychosis is furthermore that the intoxicated person imagines himself to have been changed into some animal, and the hallucinosis is completed by the sensation of the growing of feathers and hair, due probably to main paraethesic," Erich Hesse claimed in 1946.[80] In 1658, Giovanni Battista Porta wrote that a potion made from henbane, mandrake, thorn apple, and belladonna would make a person "believe he was changed into a Bird or Beast." He might "believe himself turned into a Goose, and would eat Grass, and beat the Ground with his Teeth, like a Goose: now and then sing, and endeavor to clap his Wings." Animal transformation is a primary aspect of the hallucinogenic experience, whether it is a shaman in the Amazon turning into a jaguar, or a Western subject in a psychological experiment. Take this example of the latter, from a series of studies of the effect of harmaline, conducted by psychologist Claudio Naranjo in the 1960s. The subject had felt like a huge bird, then a fish, but then:

> I wasn't a fish anymore, but a big cat, a tiger. I walked, though, feeling the same freedom I had experienced as a bird and a fish, freedom of movement, flexibility, grace. I moved as a tiger in the jungle, joyously, feeling the ground under my feet, feeling my power; my chest grew larger. I then approached an animal, any animal. I only saw its neck, and then experienced what a tiger feels when looking at its prey.[81]

Witches flying on a pitchfork while transforming into animals. Sensations of flight and body-image change are typical of datura intoxication. *(Ulrich Molitor, De Lamiis et phitonicus mulieribus, fifteenth century)*

The night travelers and "witches" often thought of themselves as flying animals—owls, farmyard beasts, and, quite often, wolves. Harner has commented that perhaps the ancient and widespread European belief concerning humans turning into wolves—lycanthropy—resulted from hallucinogenic experience, and suggests that the inclusion of animal fat, blood, and body parts in witches' ointments may have been for the purposes of creating the suggestion of becoming an animal.

We can see from this wide-ranging survey that the psychedelic experience was deeply insinuated into the beliefs and practices of the Old World, at least in its ritual and magical aspects—and to a limited extent, in its religious life too. Just how extensive this influence was in the development of Western culture awaits further investigative scholarship, which in turn relies in good measure on the willingness of modern Europeans to be prepared to accept that the emergence of their culture was accompanied by the sort of ceremonial drug practices still surviving in traditional societies such as those to be found in the Americas.

three

Tribal Tripping in the Americas

High Old Times in the New World

Perhaps the greatest mystery about ancient and traditional hallucinogen use in the Americas is simply that there is so much of it, compared to the Old World. The recognized authority on New World hallucinogens, Richard Evans Schultes, originally made this observation back in 1963. Over thirty years later, this imbalance seems even more marked, as an increasing number of native American hallucinogens have since been discovered—many by Schultes himself thorough his heroic fieldwork. By the end of the 1970s, Schultes could write: "Of the probable half-million species in the world's flora, only about 150 are known to be employed for their hallucinatory properties. . . . Nearly 130 species are known to be used in the Western Hemisphere, whereas in the Eastern Hemisphere, the number hardly reaches 20."[1] Despite the fact that only a modest number of different species comprise the flora of Mexico, and some hallucinogenic substances referred to by their Indian names in the Spanish chronicles still haven't been identified, that country "represents without a doubt the world's richest area in diversity and use of hallucinogens in aboriginal societies."[2]

Anthropologist Weston La Barre agreed with Schultes, and referred to a "New World narcotic complex" (using the term "narcotic" to cover substances whose prime action is hallucinogenic) that extends from a mid–United States latitude southward to include much of South America.[3] La Barre was himself staggered at "the enormous number of psychotropic drugs that were used ritually—narcotic mushrooms, cacti, beans, seeds, leaves, barks and vines, and in Amazonia even a narcotic bamboo-grub."[4] The Old World has a far greater landmass than the New. Its people have been present for far longer than those in the Americas and had more time to discover the hallucinogenic properties of its equally rich flora. So why the disparity? Both Schultes and La Barre sought a cultural explanation, and that brings us to the question of the origin of the Native Americans.

ANCIENT ORIGINS

Although there is tentative evidence that people from the Pacific may have come to some parts of the Americas, most authorities currently agree that most, if not all, ancestors of the Native Americans came originally from Asia. Siberia and Alaska were once connected by a low-lying landmass known to geologists as "Beringia"—the famous "land bridge" between the Old and New Worlds. This had been free of ice from about seventy-five to forty-five thousand years ago, at which point a warmer climate raised sea levels and reduced the land bridge to a periodically flooded isthmus. Around twenty-five thousand years ago another period of bitter cold ensued, and the sea levels again fell. This time the land bridge lasted until around fourteen thousand years ago, when the rapid postglacial warming began, and the modern Siberian and Alaskan coastlines took shape. The people who crossed the land bridge from Siberia, following big game, might have gradually filtered their way down into the warmer reaches of what is today the United States and points south, along the Pacific Coast or through corridors in the retreating glacial ice masses. There is still debate as to how exactly the migration proceeded southward at the end of the Ice Age. Archaeologists admit that the actual time when human beings set foot on the land bridge is "a complete mystery."[5] Estimates for when people first began to migrate into North America range wildly, from fifty thousand to twelve thousand years ago. But come they did, and remains of early human activity scattered through the Americas have been archaeologically investigated. In some cases remarkably early dates have been announced: radiocarbon dates reaching back nearly twenty thousand years were obtained at the Meadowcroft Rockshelter in Pennsylvania, for instance. But these older dates have all been the subject of challenge and controversy. More accurate chronological dating is possible with what archaeologists call the "Clovis culture" of around eleven and a half thousand years ago. At this point widespread and repeated evidence of human presence appears in the archaeological record—"a veritable explosion in the number of archaeological sites throughout North America, from the California deserts to the Eastern Woodlands," as archaeologist Brian Fagan puts it.[6]

Archaeological evidence confirms the use of hallucinogens in fairly distant times. The best example is the so-called red bean or mescal bean, in reality the seed of *Sophora secundiflora*, an evergreen shrub or small tree native to Texas and northern Mexico (and not related to mescal, a distilled Mexican liquor, or to peyote). Red bean causes nausea and convulsions, and can be fatal in high doses. It is not strictly hallucinogenic, and it is thought that its visionary effects are created by a kind of delirium.[7] It was used by Indians of the American Southwest up until the nineteenth century. About a dozen or so finds have uncovered seeds in caves and rock shelters in Trans-Pecos Texas (the region west of the Pecos River and south of the New Mexico state line) and in northern Mexico. Bonfire Shelter is an archaeological site where the bone beds of an extinct species of bison hunted by early Native Americans have been uncovered. Red bean seeds have been found at the lowest strata of human occupation, and radiocarbon-dated to between 8440 and 8120 B.C. At another site, Frightful Cave, seeds were discovered—in association with signs of long-term human activity—that radiocarbon dated to 7265 B.C. At Fate Bell Shelter in the Amistad Reservoir area of Trans-Pecos Texas, *Sophora secundiflora* seeds have been unearthed that date to 7000 B.C. These seeds were found in association with the seeds of another shrub, *Ugnadia speciosa*, known as Texas (or Mexican) buckeye. Texas buckeye seeds are genuinely hallucinogenic and have been found with *Sophora secundiflora* seeds in other, similar archaeological contexts, and also with finds of peyote (*Lophophora Williamsii*) dating to 5000 B.C. in one rock shelter. Peter Furst has long noted that the area of the Fate Bell Shelter is rich in ancient shamanistic rock paintings, another telltale sign of hallucinogen usage.[8] Other native American hallucinogens have been securely identified through the archaeological record, as we shall see.

Although religious historian Mircea Eliade referred to the use of hallucinogens as "a decadent form of shamanism," Furst reports that shortly before his death Eliade confided in him that these ancient American dates for hallucinogenic usage forced him to change his mind on this issue, and that he had come to accept that there was no essential difference between ecstasy achieved by plant hallucinogens and that obtained by other archaic techniques.[9]

The tradition of using plant hallucinogens in ritual context is well established in the Americas, seemingly, for as long as American Indians have been here. This gives strong support to the cultural explanation for the "New World narcotic complex" offered by La Barre. He observes that evidence for the Siberian-Asiatic origin of the American Indians is "overwhelming," and notes the many shared traits between Siberians and Native Americans, such as tone languages, the use of the bow and arrow, skin-covered tepees, bark-covered wigwams, the birch-bark canoe, slit-eyed snow goggles, the practice of scalping, and so on.[10] Most importantly, he suggests that shamanism is a key trait the Paleo-Indians brought with them out of Northeast Asia. "Shamanism of a specifically Eurasiatic type is distributed from ancient Scandinavia to eastern Siberia, and continues from Alaska eastward to Greenland and southward to Patagonia in the New World."[11] Shamanism, he points out, is deeply rooted in ecstatic, visionary experience, well manifested in the Native American vision quest, known also to the Paleo-Siberians, in which a young man goes out into the wilderness seeking a meaningful vision or dream. The goal of such a quest was achieving supernatural power. La Barre argues that hallucinogens have a relationship to this primal motivation, and that "ecstatic-visionary shamanism is, so to speak, *culturally programmed for an interest in hallucinogens and other psychotropic drugs*" (La Barre's emphasis).[12] The ritual use of hallucinogens therefore harks back to Paleolithic and Mesolithic shamanism, which lingered in the form of fly agaric usage in various parts of Eur-asia into the twentieth century. In this chapter we will be seeing vestiges even of that specific mushroom tradition in the Americas. The plant hallucinogens themselves represented, manifested, and conferred supernatural power—and fed the visionary hunger of the Paleo-peoples for otherworldly encounter. La Barre speaks of "the Sibero-American ur-culture" that underpinned this search for and exploitation of plant hallu-cinogens. Native American shamanism and vision questing provided "a cultural preoccupation with finding plant hallucinogens. . . . The Indian inhabitants of the New World have *discovered more*, both relatively and ab-solutely, of such hallucinogens."[13] La Barre noted "the traditional high value placed on abnormal 'psychedelic' states" by Native Americans.[14]

In his studies, La Barre has made the important point that the New World is "flatter, simpler in its time depth" than the Old World. Be-cause the Americas have not been subjected to the same cultural se-quences, invasions, influences and overlays, migrations, and all the myriad sociocultural complexities of the Old World, they represent a kind of "Mesolithic fossil," culturally speaking. Through the study of the lifeways and practices of ancient American societies, "one can creep up on Eurasiatic history and protohistory so to speak from the flank, and along an immense time depth."[15] Native American shaman-ism provides us with an echo of the Eurasian spiritual impulse that has reverberated down the long corridors of time. At this point its cultural remains are clearer and stronger in the New World than in most of the Old. This fact is important for understanding the antiquity and context of plant hallucinogen use, and also is a factor in exploring (as we will) its most overlooked remnant: the physical marks it left on the land.

The range of hallucinogens ritually employed and exploited by an-cient Native Americans is vast. We will briefly review the more impor-tant substances, mentioning just a few lesser-known hallucinogens to indicate the remarkable scope and effects of New World hallucinogens.

THE GREAT MUSHROOM HUNT

The use of "sacred" mushrooms is one of the strongest Native Ameri-can hallucinogenic traditions. The antiquity of their ritual use is strongly hinted at by curious "mushroom stones," about three hundred of which have been found in highland Guatemala, southern and west-

A mushroom stone depicting a girl or goddess emerging from the stipe, holding a metate or grinding stone. *(Author's drawing)*

ern Mexico, Honduras, and El Salvador. They integrate various mushroom shapes with a face or other figurative element, and occasionally with the indication of a metate or grinding stone—it is this detail that signifies the association with mushroom preparation and practices. Most of the stones are between twelve and fifteen inches in height, and date from the first millennium B.C. until about the time when the Spanish arrived. The chronicle of the Spanish priest Bernardo Sahagún in the late sixteenth century tells of the sacred mushrooms of the Aztecs. They called them *teonanacatl*, "flesh of the gods."

Despite such early documentation, the significance of the mushroom stones was not fully recognized until the 1950s. The major American botanist William A. Safford, who had denounced the idea of *ololiuhqui*, was equally certain that there was no such thing as a native mushroom cult. He held that the *teonanacatl* referred to by Sahagún was the peyote cactus. Ethnobotanist Blas Pablo Reko was working in Mexico and was aware that there was indeed a surviving mushroom cult, but was unable to make his academic peers listen. In 1936, ethnologist R. J. Weitlaner actually collected some samples from Mazatec Indians in Oaxaca, Mexico, but by the time they arrived at the Botanical Museum of Harvard University they were too badly deteriorated to be identified. In 1938, Weitlaner, Jean Bassett Johnson, and colleagues were the first outsiders since the Spanish conquerors to witness an Indian all-night curing ritual. It took place at the remote village of Huautla de Jiménez, in Oaxaca, and involved the eating of psychoactive mushrooms by a Mazatec shaman. Writing about this unique experience in 1939, Johnson pointed out that several kinds of hallucinogenic mushrooms were known to the Indians. Only a month after this session, Reko and Schultes started research in the same region and secured samples of the mushrooms used ritually in Huautla de Jiménez, one of which was later identified as *Stropharia cubensis*. In 1939, Schultes's paper on the sacred mushrooms of Oaxaca was published.

But the process of bringing expanded knowledge of the ancient Native American usage of mind-altering mushrooms to the world revolved largely around the work of the retired banker and amateur mycologist Gordon Wasson and his wife, Valentina. "In the fall of 1952," Gordon Wasson recalled, "we learned that the 16th century writers . . . had recorded that certain mushrooms played a divinatory role in the religion of the natives. Simultaneously we learned that certain pre-Columbian stone artifacts resembling mushrooms . . . had been turning up, usually in the highlands of Guatemala, in increasing numbers. . . . Like the child in the Emperor's New Clothes, we spoke up, declaring that the so-called 'mushroom stones' really represented mushrooms, and that they were the symbol of a religion."[16] The Wassons set off to find what kinds of mushrooms had been worshiped in Central America, and why. They studied the work of Reko, Weitlaner, Schultes, and others, and saw that all needles pointed to Oaxaca, so they made repeated visits there, beginning in 1953. In 1955, having established sufficient trust with their Indian hosts, especially and crucially with Maria Sabina, an important *curandera* in Huautla de Jiménez, Gordon Wasson and his "friend and photographer" Allan Richardson were the first white outsiders to actually take part in a Mazatec mushroom vigil or *velada*. The two men were offered portions of mushrooms to eat, and Maria Sabina sang "not loud, but with authority . . . infinitely tender and sweet" as Wasson described it. Her voice hovered around the hut, sounding at times as if it were passing beneath them. She struck various parts of her body at the same time, producing differing percussive beats. Wasson and Richardson lay on their mats as the mushrooms took effect. Wasson has left us a classic, beautiful description of his experience:

> Your body lies in the darkness, heavy as lead, but your spirit seems to soar and leave the hut, and with the speed of thought to travel where it listeth, in time and space, accompanied by the shaman's singing and by the ejaculations of her percussive chant. What you are seeing and what you are hearing appear as one: the music assumes harmonious shapes, giving visual form to its harmonies, and what you are seeing takes on the modalities of music—the music of the spheres. . . . All your senses are similarly affected. . . . The bemushroomed person is poised in space, a disembodied eye, invisible, incorporeal, seeing but not seen. In truth, he is the five senses disembodied, all of them keyed to the height of sensitivity and awareness, all of them blending into one another most strangely, until the person, utterly passive, becomes a pure receptor, infinitely delicate, of sensations. (You, being a stranger, are perforce only a receptor. But the Mazatec communicants are also participants with the *curandera* in an extempore religious colloquy. . . .) . . . As your body lies there in its sleeping bag, your soul is free, loses all sense of time, alert as it never was before, living an eternity in a night, seeing infinity in a grain of sand. . . . At last you know what the ineffable is, and what ecstasy means. Ecstasy! The mind harks back to the origins of that word. For the Greeks ekstasis meant the flight of the soul from the body. Can you find a better word than that to describe the bemushroomed state? In common parlance, among the many who have not experienced ecstasy, ecstasy is fun, and I am frequently asked why I do not reach for mushrooms every night. But ecstasy is not fun. Your very soul is seized and shaken until it tingles. After all, who will choose to feel undiluted awe, or to float through that door yonder into the Divine Presence?[17]

Richardson, meanwhile, was having "visions . . . of Chinese motifs, like *Kubla Khan*—palaces, oriental designs and so forth. After that, I saw the vision of a beautiful mantlepiece with the portrait of a Spanish caballero over it, which I happen to remember very well."[18] Richardson remembered it well because of what happened upon their return to Mexico City. He and Wasson were invited to a hacienda where they had never been before. "When we walked into the drawing room, there was the portrait I had seen in my vision. I don't yet know what to make of that," he puzzled, fully thirty-five years later.

A few days after this historic session, Wasson took mushrooms with his wife and daughter, and they became "so far as is known, the first white people to eat 'magic mushrooms' experimentally—removed from the native ceremonial setting."[19]

Wasson continued to visit Mexico, taking the mushrooms again on numerous occasions, and confirming that their use was widespread among certain groups of Mexican Indians, and wasn't confined solely to the Mazatecs. Among various specialists and experts who accompanied him on his expeditions was mycologist Roger Heim of Paris, who conducted botanical identification of the sacred mushrooms. He found that they were from the family *Strophariaceae*, roughly a dozen different species that had not previously been scientifically identified, most of them belonging to the genus *Psilocybe*. Heim had heard of Albert Hofmann's work with LSD at Sandoz. "Thus it was LSD that showed *teonanacatl* the way into our laboratory," Hofmann has remarked.[20] Heim had cultivated a sample of *Psilocybe mexicana* and it was this that Hofmann chemically analyzed. To test if these samples were psychoactive, Hofmann experimented on himself, taking thirty-two mushrooms. He found the effects to be powerful:

> Thirty minutes after taking the mushrooms, the exterior world began to undergo a strange transformation. Everything assumed a Mexican character. As I was perfectly well aware that my knowledge of the Mexican origin of the mushroom would lead me to imagine only Mexican scenery, I tried deliberately to look on my environment as I knew it normally. But all voluntary efforts to look at things in their

customary forms and colors proved ineffective. Whether my eyes were closed or open, I saw only Mexican motifs and colors. When the doctor supervising the experiment bent over me to check my blood pressure, he was transformed into an Aztec priest and I would not have been astonished if he had drawn an obsidian knife. In spite of the seriousness of the situation, it amused me to see how the Germanic face of my colleague had acquired a purely Indian expression. At the peak of the intoxication . . . the rush of interior pictures, mostly abstract motifs rapidly changing in shape and color, reached such an alarming degree that I feared that I would be torn into this whirlpool of form and color and would dissolve. . . . I felt my return to everyday reality to be a happy return from a strange, fantastic but quite real world to an old andfamiliar home.[21]

Hofmann's analysis, published in 1958, revealed two new indole compounds, which he called psilocybin and psilocine, closely related in their structure as well as in their effects to LSD. They also possess a chemical structure very similar to the neurotransmitter serotonin in the human brain. Hofmann observed that it was possible to synthesize the new substances without the aid of mushrooms. (It was synthesized psilocybin tablets that subsequently were used in Timothy Leary's first experiments at Harvard.) "Essentially, when all is said and done," Hofmann observed with characteristic clarity, "we can only say that the mystery of the wondrous effects of *teonanacatl* was reduced to the mystery of the effects of two crystalline substances—since these effects cannot be explained by science either, but can only be described."[22]

Hofmann accompanied Wasson on one of his future forays into native Mexico, looking for other ritual hallucinogens. But scientific colleagues weren't the only ones interested in joining Wasson on his expeditions. He had been approached by the CIA and asked if he would work with them. Wasson refused. Subsequently, James Moore, a chemist from the University of Delaware, made funding possible for Wasson's 1956 expedition on the condition that he be allowed to take part in it personally. Unknown to Wasson, Moore was a CIA operative. "At the time, all we knew was that we didn't like Jim. Something was wrong with him," Allan Richardson dryly remarked many years later.[23]

In 1957, Wasson reported his experiences at Huautla de Jimenéz for *Life* magazine. The centuries-old secret of the Indian mushroom ritual had been revealed. Over subsequent years a flood of thrill seekers went to Oaxaca. They showed lack of respect for the Indian traditions and for the mushrooms, Maria Sabina's "saint children." The remote village was disrupted, and the saintly *curandera* felt the mushrooms were losing their power as a result of the influx of outsiders: "From the moment the foreigners arrived, the 'saint children' lost their purity. They lost their force; the foreigners spoiled them. From now on they won't be any good. There is no remedy for it."[24]

Living traditions of sacred mushroom use have now been discovered among Mayan-speaking peoples in southern Mexico. Peter Furst has identified a number of ceramic mushrooms representing the species *Psilocybe* in two-thousand-year-old tomb art in western Mexico.[25] Native American ritual use of hallucinogenic mushrooms outside of Mexico is indicated by the mushroom stones and by pre-Columbian gold pectorals from Colombia, which clearly display mushroom forms. Some of the Guatemalan mushroom stones resemble that old mushroom of Eurasian shamanism, *Amanita muscaria*, the fly agaric. This is thought to have been used ritually in the Americas as well, though the extent of its usage is mainly inferred from secondary evidence rather than direct ethnological information. The red-capped variety of *Amanita muscaria* grows naturally in British Columbia, in the northwestern United States, in southern upland areas of Mexico, and in highland Guatemala, with a yellow-capped strain growing in more easterly areas of North America. Use of the mushroom has been discovered among the Dogrib Athabascan peoples in the Mackenzie Mountains in northwestern Canada, where it is used sacramentally in shamanism. One neophyte reported that in his initiatory seánce he couldn't eat or sleep, and didn't even think. "I wasn't in my body any longer." At a later session he recorded that he was "ripe for vision" and had "sung the note that shatters structure. And the note that shatters chaos. . . . I have been with the dead and attempted the labyrinth."[26]

Anthropologists have noted that the Coast Salish of the American

Northwest, and also the Alaskan Inuit (Eskimos), carefully preserved their urine, which was thought to have magical and curative properties,[27] and, as late as 1886, were seen to offer urine for drinking.[28] This strongly hints at a continuation of the Siberian tradition of using urine

Pre-Columbian gold pectoral from Colombia, showing a figure holding mushrooms. *(Peter T. Furst)*

for recycled *Amanita muscaria* effects. Anthropologist Claude Lévi-Strauss noted that certain Inuit and Athabascan groups chew the ashes of a fungus that grows on birch trees (the host of *Amanita muscaria*), sometimes in conjunction with tobacco.[29] It has also been discovered that the Ojibwa of Michigan used *Amanita muscaria* as a sacred hallucinogen in an ancient annual ceremony. The mushroom in the Ojibwa language is called *Wajashk-wedo*, "red-top mushroom." Moreover, red mushrooms figure in Ojibwa legends. In Ohio, an intriguing find was made in a major necropolis of the powerful, shamanic Hopewell culture, which flourished around two thousand years ago. In what was

clearly a shaman's mound in the necropolis ("Mound City," Chillicothe) the effigy of an apparently amanita-type mushroom was uncovered. About a foot long, it was fashioned from wood and had been
covered with copper. Various other types of Hopewell shamanic arti-

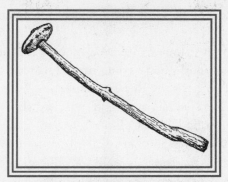

A drawing of the Hopewell Indian mushroom effigy found in a shaman's mound at
Chillicothe, Ohio.

facts have also been found, including many clay pipes shaped as birds,
ritual masks and deer-antler headgear, clay figurines depicting men apparently in trance, and bird claws and swastika designs cut out of mica,
designed for hanging on ceremonial costumes. Wasson felt that the
swastika designs derived from geometric "entoptic" patterns seen in
trance states, and especially hallucinogen-induced trance states.[30]

In Mesoamerica, a miniature clay sculpture from Nyarit, thought to
date to about A.D. 100, shows what clearly seems to be *Amanita muscaria*,
with a figure, apparently a shaman, sitting beneath it.

In Native American ritual use of *Amanita muscaria* we may have the
most profound New World vestige of Eurasian shamanism.

DATURA

As we have seen, species of datura, belonging to the nightshade family,
played a role in witchcraft and other magico-religious activities in the
Old World. However, the genus has had an even wider ceremonial ap-

plication in the Americas, where it has been used for prophecy, divination, diagnosing illness (by providing access to spirit knowledge), medicine (to relieve swellings and to ease the pains of childbirth and rheumatism), in puberty initiation rites, and for the production of visionary states, as it characteristically tends to generate the classic shamanic experiences of spirit flight and transformation into animal form.

In eastern North America, the Algonquian Indians issued a ritual drink, *wysoccan*, to youths undergoing rites of passage in the *Huskanawing* ceremony. The basis of this beverage was *Datura stramonium*, or jimson weed. *Datura inoxid* was—and perhaps still is—used in the Southwest, notably Southern California, Arizona, and New Mexico. The Chumash of coastal Southern California used this hallucinogen, and possibly *Datura stramonium* as well, for puberty rites and shamanic purposes. Its visionary effects are reflected in the imagery in their rock art. Datura was ceremonially employed also by the Miwok of the California Sierras, who left behind mysterious straight tracks through the mountains, and by the Mojave, Yokuts, Cahuilla, and numerous other Californian tribes.[31] The Hopi and Navajo of Arizona are notable among the peoples there who used datura. The Navajo word for it is *ch'ohojilyeèh*. They used it for magic-oriented work, and visions seen under its influence were thought to show causes of disease and identify animals possessing special significance.[32] Ethnological references indicate that datura was still being used for these purposes until recent decades, but the present status of *ch'ohojilyeèh* is not clear—it may be that it is no longer used. The Zuni Indians of present-day New Mexico call datura *inoxia a-neg-la-kya* and have used it both ritually and medicinally. It could only be collected by rain priests or shamans, who applied the powdered root to their eyes, enabling them to see at night, to perceive spirits, and to commune with birds.[33] In the Zuni Kuaua kiva, near Albuquerque, there is a rare pre-Columbian mural depicting a shaman holding a species of datura, which attests to the antiquity of this ritual usage.

The Mexican Indians call the hallucinogen *toloache*, from the Aztec *toaloatzin*. The Aztecs presumably used it the same way that the modern

Kuaua kiva, New Mexico. Reconstructed pre-Columbian wall paintings can be seen. The one at the center left behind the ladder
shows a shaman holding a species of datura. *(Paul Devereux)*

Tarahumara do. A powerfully toxic and very distinct species of datura,
called *Datura ceratocaula*, known as "maddening plant," also grows in the
marshes or shallow water of Mexico, and was used in ancient times
there.

In South America, there are varieties of *Brugmansia*, so-called tree
daturas. These are now recognized as a separate genus, but they contain the same tropane alkaloids as datura, namely scopolamine,
hyoscyamine, and atropine. *Brugmansia* is biologically very complex,
and it is thought that its species may all be cultigens—unknown in the
wild.[34] The leaves, flowers, and seeds of all species of *Brugmansia* have
been used as hallucinogens for thousands of years, either alone or
mixed with other plant substances, in the Andes, from Colombia to
Chile, and along the Pacific Coast. They were of extreme importance
to ancient Indians such as the Inca and Chibcha, and are still used for
divinatory rites by various remote Indian tribes in isolated areas of
Colombia, Ecuador, and Peru. Such Indians include the Shuar (Jívaro)
of Ecuador, and the Kamsá and Ingano Indians (who Schultes considers
may possess "the most intricate narcotic consciousness of any peoples
in the New World") in the Valley of Sibundoy in Andean Colombia.

For centuries these Indians have manipulated *Brugmansia aurea* so that numerous aberrant forms now exist in Sibundoy, each "owned" by a shaman and considered to have special virtues.[35] The shamans or *payés* distinguish differing characteristics of the intoxication provided by the different strains, preferring the less powerful ones for use in divination and prophecy. This makes sense, as the effects of *Brugmansia* can be very disorienting: typically, a person who has just taken a substantial dose may become so violent and agitated that he has to be restrained, until he falls into a deep and disturbed sleep filled with visions.

In 1990, while in the Ecuadorian rain forest, psychologist Ralph Metzner had two experiences with *Brugmansia aurea*. In each case he took a small dose of the green juice prepared by squeezing the inner pulp or pith from the stem. Metzner lay down in bed, entering a "twilight sleep." His body felt relaxed, and he experienced floating sensations, with a feeling of expanding into the immediate environment, and became keenly aware of people in it who were out of his sight and earshot. In his first session, he fell asleep for several hours, and in the morning had two dreams, one about a disagreement with his wife, the other about a dispute with someone with whom he planned a collaborative project. Later, he did indeed have a specifically similar conflict with his wife, and found out information about his potential colleague that confirmed his intuitive decision not to proceed with the collaborative venture. His second session also yielded a dream, in which he saw a petite, dark-haired Spanish-speaking woman giving a lecture to the research group Metzner was part of. The next day, a woman fitting precisely this description and whom he had not seen previously arrived to speak to the group. Metzner concluded from his limited experimentation that *Brugmansia* "does indeed have the potential for producing divinations, in this case verifiable precognitive dreams; possibly the precognitions are anticipatory warnings of personal conflicts."[36]

Recently an intriguing suggestion has been made, relating to a mysterious, prehistoric ground drawing (geoglyph) etched up to three feet deep into a slope overlooking the Bay of Paracas on the Peruvian coast, about a hundred miles north of the equally mysterious desert lines at Nazca. The figure is so large—some six hundred feet long, and nearly two hundred feet across—that it can be seen from many miles out to sea. Pottery fragments found near it have been dated to around 200 B.C. Because of its symmetrical, somewhat treelike design, the three-pronged geoglyph is often referred to as "the Candelabra of the Andes" or "the Trident of Paracas." It is not a motif met with elsewhere in studies of ancient South American art, and there are details in the design that argue against it depicting a trident (as unlikely as that would be in any case). It acts as a landmark, but what is it? It may have been a religious symbol,[37] but that does not explain what it depicts. Now Frank Joseph has suggested that it is a stylized rendering of jimson weed. He has found a small version of the same design on a rock in California's Cleveland National Park, and proposes that the ancient people of Paracas voyaged up the Pacific coast to California to collect this particular species of datura.[38]

VINE OF THE SOUL: "A DRUG FOR FLYING"

The most widely-used Native American hallucinogens today are those based on the liana, or vine, *Banisteriopsis*. Such usage stems from remote antiquity. The use of the vine is a South American phenomenon. Schultes informs us that thousands of Indians use it in western Amazonia, the Orinoco region, and on the slopes of the Pacific Coast of Colombia and Ecuador.[39] It is known by a variety of names in different places: *caapi, ayahuasca, yagé* (or *yajé*), *natema, pinde,* and *nape,* among others. *Banisteriopsis* infusions—which we will refer to here as *ayahuasca,* the most commonly selected term among Western commentators today— typically promote a sensation of the soul separating from the body. Although this sensation is a common effect of many native hallucinogens,* the very basis of ecstasy, in fact, *Banisteriopsis* concoctions seem particu-

---

*The Shuar (Jívaro) Indians use the term "trip" when referring to the ecstatic state. Such is also the case with the Cashinahua Indians of Peru. They apply the word *bai,* meaning "trip," in the sense of a sight-seeing excursion,[41] to the *ayahuasca* effect, just as Western youth in the sixties invoked the word "trip" when referring to a psychedelic experience.

larly effective at providing this sensation. It is used in initiation ceremonies, for returning to the beginning of the universe to see the gods,
and for prophetic and divinatory purposes, including traveling in spirit
(usually in the form of a bird or animal, such as a jaguar) to distant places
and seeing the things happening there. It is the agent par excellence for
inducing the out-of-body experience—German scholar Hans Peter
Duerr has written that it "seems to be specifically a 'drug for flying.' "[40]
Physical effects of *ayahuasca* intoxication often include nausea and diar-
rhea, but motor coordination is not greatly affected.

In some regions the bark of the *Banisteriopsis* liana is prepared in a
cold-water infusion, but more commonly bark and stem, perhaps
leaves too, are boiled in water for long periods. Sometimes the fresh
bark is chewed. Visions that are caused by *Banisteriopsis* alone tend to be
dull blue or gray unless certain additives are used. These additives
cause one to experience more vivid colors, making the hallucinogenic
effect altogether more potent.[42] Most *ayahuasca* drinks do contain additives, but their full range and chemistry is by no means known to
Western science. Those that have been studied, however, reveal the
sophisticated neurophysiological knowledge possessed by numerous
generations of rain forest Indians. The active elements in *Banisteriopsis*
are principally the alkaloids harmine and tetrahydroharmine, plus the
less important harmaline. (It was first thought these were new alkaloids, and one was named telepathine for its alleged divinatory and
clairvoyant properties, but it was later realized that all the alkaloids
had already long been identified in Syrian rue.) These are beta-
carbolines that act as monoamine oxidase (MAO) inhibitors, which
means that they prevent the degradation of certain neurotransmitters
or amines administered from outside the body. It has been found that
several of the traditional *ayahuasca* additives contain tryptamine alkaloids, specifically DMT (N, N-dimethyltryptamine). This substance is
not effective when ingested orally, as it is broken down by the enzyme
MAO before it can pass the blood-brain barrier. When it is combined
with carbolines, which inhibit the MAO, however, as in *ayahuasca*, it
becomes orally effective. In short, the *Banisteriopsis* base of *ayahuasca*

acts as an enabler of the DMT hallucinogenic effects provided by the additives. Not only do the Indians display sophistication with this practical knowledge, but they also distinguish between different types of *ayahuasca*, all of which have their own names. The Tukano, for example, have six types, while the Harakmbet Indians have no less than twenty-two kinds, each noted for specific visionary effects and symbolism. At least one of these types of *ayahuasca* is said to confer permanent visionary effects.[43]

The strong "flight" effects of *ayahuasca* were noted by outsiders from the beginning. In 1858, only seven years after *ayahuasca* was first identified by Richard Spruce, the Ecuadoran geographer Manuel Villavicencio made the first written report on the *ayahuasca* experience. "Its action appears to excite the nervous system; all the senses liven up and all faculties awaken . . . vertigo and spinning in the head, then a sensation of being lifted into the air," the geographer wrote. "I can say for a fact that when I've taken *ayahuasca* I've experienced dizziness, then an aerial journey in which I recall perceiving the most gorgeous views, great cities, lofty towers, beautiful parks, and other extremely attractive objects; then I imagined myself to be alone in the forest and assaulted by a number of terrible beings from which I defended myself; thereafter I had the strong sensation of sleep."[44] Precisely similar kinds of effects are reported today. An American informant told me that after she had taken *ayahuasca* in a rain forest setting, she suddenly found herself high up in the air above the tree canopy, with the stars overhead. The experience was completely "real" in both appearance and feeling. She spent most of the session in this suspended state.

Some claim the ability to see things at a distance while under the influence of *ayahuasca*. This is usually combined with the out-of-body or soul-flight experience. Peter Gorman, executive editor of *High Times* magazine, has described *ayahuasca* sessions he experienced in 1984 in Peru. During one session, he had a vision of a huge brown bird with long white-tipped wings soaring over snowy mountain peaks. "I was looking at the bird from a great distance when I suddenly felt myself merging with it," Gorman recalled. "I saw from the bird's perspective, my sharp eyes picking out the most minute details of the landscape. I flew over a range of mountains, searching for something. While travelling at great speed, I looked down into a stream and saw fish moving slowly in shallow water. Although I was thousands of feet in the air, I could see sunlight glinting off individual scales on the blue and green fish. The colors were unimaginably rich."[45] After diving down and catching and eating a fish, all in the richest and most realistic detail, Gorman returned to his body. But soon he drifted off again into more flying visions; he would sometimes fly with the bird, sometimes just below it. On two occasions he asked the bird to take him somewhere. First, he "went" to see his wife in California. He glimpsed her making love with someone, but as soon as he experienced a pang of jealousy, the image was snatched from him. The second was a visit to his apartment in New York, which he had sublet to two friends. There was nothing special about the scene, just two people sitting reading, talking occasionally. But they were wearing clothes he'd never seen on them before. Later, when Gorman returned to New York, he saw that these same friends had bought new shirts exactly like those he had seen in his vision.

A more dramatic instance of *ayahuasca*'s powers in promoting apparent remote viewing was brought home to anthropologist Kenneth Kensinger when he was with the Peruvian Cashinahua. He notes that the Cashinahua drink *ayahuasca* in order to learn about things, persons, and events at a distance—geographically, in time, or both. He continues:

> Hallucinations generally involve scenes which are a part of the Cashinahua's daily experience. However, informants have described hallucinations about places far removed both geographically and from their own experience. Several informants who have never been to or seen pictures of Pucallpa, the large town at the Ucayali River terminus of the Central Highway, have described their visits under the influence of *ayahuasca* to the town with sufficient detail for me to be able to recognize specific shops and sights. On the day

A clone of peyote, the gray-green crowns just visible above the surface of the ground. *(Peter T. Furst)*

following one *ayahuasca* party six of nine men informed me of seeing the death of my *chai*, "my mother's father." This occurred two days before I was informed by radio of his death.[46]

AND THE HUNTING OF THE DEER: "THE DARKNESS EXPLODES INTO DANCING COLORS"

Peyote (*Lophophora Williamsii*) is one of the best known of Native American hallucinogens, and the visionary experience and strong metaphysical and intellectual insights the cactus can inspire are relatively well documented. Its magic may have accompanied human beings in the New World virtually from the beginning, for fossilized peyote buttons have been found that are five thousand years old. The cactus has been recorded in stone as art in Mesoamerican tombs dating to 100 B.C., and is represented on a ceramic snuffing pipe from Monte Albán, Oaxaca, dating to 500 B.C. As a symbol employed in the Tarahumara Indian peyote ceremony, it is even depicted in prehistoric rock carvings.

The peyote cactus is small, somewhat turniplike in shape and size, and has no spines, branches, or leaves. The rounded crown of the cactus peeps up above the ground. When cut off and dried, this crown becomes a "peyote button." The surface of the cactus is divided by a radial arrangement of ribs and segments that bear small tufts of gray-white hair. The botanical name *Lophophora* ("I bear crests") refers to this feature. These tufts inspired the Aztec name *peyotl*, which is a reference to cocoon silk. The cactus is rich in phenylethylamine and tetrahydroisoquinoline types of alkaloids. The most active "visionary" alkaloid is trimethoxypheny-lethylamine, called mescaline. However, due to complex and little-understood interactions between the various active constituents, traditional users of peyote feel that taken as an organic whole the substance provides a different experience to that of chemical mescaline taken on its own.

The cactus can be eaten raw or in dried form or drunk as a tea or mash. A "dose" would normally range between four to thirty buttons. The peyote experience is characterized by vividly colored hallucinations, which often follow a sequence starting with geometric patterns and progressing to more complex representational scenes, both familiar and novel. Visual effects can be accompanied by tactile and auditory hallucinations, and by synesthesia, the mixing of sensory modalities, so one "hears" colors, and so forth. La Barre points out that auditory peyote hallucinations are known to have been the source of Indian songs and chants developed in fairly recent times—"Heyowiniho," for instance, came to the 1890s Ghost Dance leader John Wilson (Nishkúntu) from a peyote experience in which he heard the sound of the sun's rising.[47] This inevitably raises an interesting question: How much Indian traditional ceremonial song, dance, and costume had its source in hallucinatory states?

The first historical documentation of peyote use was, as might be expected, by the Spanish chroniclers of Aztec cultures. Francisco Hernández wrote in 1651, "Ground up and applied to painful joints, it is said to give relief. . . . This root . . . causes those devouring it to foresee and predict things . . . and other things of like nature. . . . On which account, this root scarcely issues forth, as if it did not wish to harm those who discover it and eat it."

With their typical severity and assumed righteousness, the Span-

ish attempted to outlaw peyote use. Hence its medicinal and ceremonial use was kept secret by the Indians in the remote Mexican countryside, where it has survived among some Indian tribes up to
the present day. Knowledge of peyote crossed what is now the
Mexican–United States border a number of times in the unchronicled
past, but the first documented reference to its use among North American Indians seems to have been in 1760 in Texas.[48] Around 1880, the
Kiowa and Comanche tribes developed a new kind of peyote ceremony, which ultimately led to the establishment of the Native American Church. Today peyote usage is legal within the highly principled
religious organization, which considers the cactus a sacrament. It
claims around a quarter of a million Indian adherents among many
tribes throughout North America, its influence stretching as far north
as Saskatchewan, Canada. The difficulty nowadays is the shortage of
peyote, caused not only by the demands of the Native American
Church, but by others seeking the cactus.[49]

The best-preserved ancient peyote tradition is that of the Huichol
Indians of the Sierra Madre Occidental of northern Mexico. They an-
nually enact a three-hundred-mile-long pilgrimage to Wirikúta, a high
desert area of mythic ancestral significance situated in San Luis Potosí,
to the northeast of their present homeland. This area is traditionally
rich in the peyote cactus, and the pilgrimage is a ritual "hunt" for peyote that lasts several weeks. The sanctity of peyote is deeply rooted in
Huichol culture, and La Barre has stated that "the unacculturated
myths of the Huichol contain embedded in them elements of manifestly very great antiquity, some harking back to the mesolithic horizons of the paleo-Siberian migrants who became the American
Indians".[50] Anthropologists were allowed to accompany and observe
the Wirikúta pilgrimage for the first time in 1966, and Western outsiders have taken part in subsequent pilgrimages.

Until recent decades the trek was undertaken on foot. Now much
of it is done by car, but holy places on the traditionally defined route
to Wirikúta are still visited as much as possible. Many Huichol aspire
to take this pilgrimage at least once in their lives, but it is not obliga-
tory. It is led by a shaman or *mara'akame*. For the duration of the pil-

grimage, he represents the Great Shaman, Tatewari ("Grandfather Fire"), who led the ancestral gods and goddesses on the first peyote hunt. Those going on the peyote hunt and those who remain behind to maintain the sacred hearth fire in the temple must first undergo a period of purification, abstaining from sex and naming in public every sexual partner they have had since puberty. This is done without recrimination or shame. For the period of the peyote hunt fasting is observed, with only minimal food consumption during the journey and the stay at Wirikúta. Each pilgrim is "newborn," and for the purposes of the hunt represents one of the deities who took part in the original mythic, ancestral peyote quest.

Deer holding peyote cactus in its mouth. A snuffing pipe about 2,500 years old, from Monte Alban, Mexico. *(Peter T. Furst)*

The Huichol call the sacred cactus *bikuri*, and it is thought of as a deer, or, more accurately, a manifestation of the supernatural Master of the Deer Species. To eat the fresh cactus is to eat the flesh of the sacred, primal deer itself. At Wirikúta, *bikuri* manifests as Elder Brother Deer, who bestows the gift of transcendence upon the pilgrims. The Deer-Peyote concept is also associated with maize. Barbara Myerhoff, who took part in the 1966 pilgrimage, has written:

Together, deer, maize, and peyote account for the totality of Huichol life and history. The deer is associated with the Huichols' idealized historical past as nomadic hunters; the maize stands for the life of the present—mundane, sedentary, good and beautiful, utilitarian, difficult, and demanding; and peyote evokes the timeless, private, purposeless, aesthetic dimension of the spiritual life, mediating between former and present realities and providing a sense of being one people.[51]

The *mara'akame* carries a hunting bow and arrows contained in a deerskin quiver. When the region of Wirikúta is finally approached, the pilgrims are led by the *mara'akame* along a mythic route, retracing the ancestral steps, encountering, with much emotion, places that have mythic significance but which, in physical appearance, are unremarkable.[52] A deer deity and culture hero called Elder Brother Kauyumarie is invoked as the *mara'akame's* spirit helper. Those making the trip for the first time are blindfolded on arriving at the boundary of Wirikúta "so as not to be blinded by the glory and brilliant light of the sacred land."[53] When the feature known as "the water holes of Our Mothers" are reached, the blindfolds are ceremonially removed. At the appropriate place, the first campfire is speedily "brought out" of a piece of wood, and all participants feed the sacred fire, the manifestation of Tatewari. A coal is taken from this and all fires lit during the hunt; each coal contains the *kupuri*, the essence or life force, of Tatewari.

Then the hunt for Deer-Peyote begins. Bows and arrows and offerings are readied. Beating the string of his bow, the *mara'akame* creeps forward until he sees the "tracks" of Deer-Peyote, and a cluster of *Lophophora Williamsii* are found. The cactus is "killed" by the *mara'akame* shooting or placing ceremonial arrows into it and in the Four Directions around it. The pilgrims ask Deer-Peyote to not punish them for killing him, for he will rise again. Offerings are made. The *mara'akame* sees the life essence coming out of the cactus like a rainbow of colored rays of light, which are coaxed back into the cactus with a feathered prayer arrow. The cacti are then collected, but with enough root left in the ground so Elder Brother can regrow from his "bones." A piece of "Elder Brother's flesh" is ceremonially given to each participant with the admonition to "chew it well" so as to be able to "see your life." After some singing and dancing, and the consumption of more pieces of peyote, the harvest proper begins, with participants going off into the

Huichol Indians at Wirikúta, their "game bags" full with the sacred deer, peyote. *(Peter T. Furst)*

desert with baskets—"game bags"—looking carefully for the cacti. Ritual exchanges of peyote are made among participants as part of the traditional ethic of the hunt. That night is spent singing and dancing around the ceremonial fire while consuming large quantities of the hallucinogenic cacti. The pilgrims go into trance, experiencing out-of-body flight or falling into visionary reverie. It is thought by the Huichol that the visions of the *mara'akame*, as he stares into the fire, are different from those of the other participants.

Huichol Indians do not talk about their visions, but Prem Das, a yoga student and a writer who has researched altered states of consciousness, attended a Huichol pilgrimage at Wirikúta in the early 1970s and reported on his visionary experience. After receiving his peyote, he sat down to watch a spectacular sunset as the psychoactive plant took effect. When he next looked around, he could see the sacred cacti, or "flowers" as the Huichol called them, glowing with self-luminescence in many places in the desert. He was easily able to collect at least a hundred of the cacti in the bags he had with him. He ate some more. He felt peaceful and felt blessed in this holy land of the Huichol, but this ultimately caused him to weep as he thought of the harshness and lack of harmony of so many aspects of his own, Western society. He wondered why it was that we have become so estranged from the earth.

> I heard an answer that seemed to come from all around me, and it rose in my mind's eye like a great time-lapse vision. I saw a human being rise from the earth, stand for a moment, and then dissolve back into it. It was only a brief moment, and in that moment our whole lives passed. Then I saw a huge city rise out of the desert floor before me, exist for a second, and then vanish back into the vastness of the desert. The plants, rock, and earth under me were saying, Yes, this is how it really is, your life, the city you live in. It was as if in my peyotized state I was able to perceive and communicate with a resonance or vibration that surrounded me. . . . An overwhelming realization poured through me—that the human race and all technology formed by it are nothing other than flowers of the earth. The painful problem which had confronted me disappeared entirely, to be replaced with a vision of people and their technology as temporary forms through which Mother Earth was expressing herself.[54]

The pilgrims leave Wirikúta promptly when their activities are finished (it is considered spiritually dangerous to linger too long), departing as they had entered, in single file, blowing horns. They implore the ancestral beings who inhabit Wirikúta not to leave, not to abandon their places, for they, the Huichol, will come again another year.

"Peyote may be viewed as the Huichol provision for that dimension of religious experience which can never be routinized and made altogether public—that sense of awe and wonder, the *mysterium tremendum et fascinans*, without which religion is mere ritual and form," Myerhoff has commented.

> It provides the ecstatic and enormous moment when the soul departs, flies upward, and loses itself in the other reality. The darkness

explodes into dancing colors. . . . Returning to ordinary reality, the pilgrims are left grief-stricken, exhausted, and exhilarated by the experience. An enormous undertaking has been accomplished. They have traveled to paradise, dwelled there as deities for a moment, and returned to mortal life.[55]

THE PSYCHEDELIC TEMPLE

One of the hallucinogens to have had the longest use in the Americas is undoubtedly *Trichocereus pachanoi,* known in northern coastal Peru as San Pedro. As with peyote, the active principle of this cactus is mescaline. It is found in the general Andes region of South America and is used today in coastal and Andean Peru and Bolivia for curing sickness, and for divination and sorcery. Its use involves a moon-oriented ritual that has a Christian veneer, but which no doubt has a long history. This is indicated on an engraved stone panel in the wall of the circular sunken plaza of the Old Temple at Chavín de Huantar, which was built in the first millennium B.C. In this panel, a piece of the long, ribbed cactus is held by a human-animal figure that has jaguar fangs—the jaguar is a motif strongly associated with South American shamanism. Rebecca Stone-Miller has suggested that this image actually depicts a costumed shaman holding the cactus as a staff of authority.[56]

Chavín de Huantar is a large, profoundly mysterious ruined temple complex, located midway between coast and jungle in northern Peru. It stands at the confluence of two rivers, at an altitude of over ten thousand feet, and appears to have been the New World's greatest temple of psychedelic worship. The entirely windowless building opens only to the east, and has processional routes that would carefully control the movement of people through the complex. Some of its architectural details subtly relate the whole structure to cosmological principles, such as the Four Directions. It has such deeply enigmatic features as a labyrinth of internal, unlit passageways, rooms where the roaring sound of the rivers' rushing water is emphasized by architectural techniques, and other rooms that are completely soundproof.[57]

A drawing of the bas-relief at Chavín de Huantar depicting a supernatural being or priest in ritual garb holding a San Pedro cactus.

The focal point of the complex is a fifteen-foot-high carved stone monument known as the Lanzón, which is situated within a cruciform gallery set deep in the center of the temple structure.

Chavín de Huantar was an active center from about 900 to 200 B.C., the heart of a shamanic cult that projected its influence for many hundreds of miles around, and expressed it through an art style to which the complex gives its name. "Chavín is a very complex, 'baroque' and esoteric style, intentionally difficult to decipher, intended to disorient, and ultimately to transport the viewer into alternate realities," Stone-Miller informs. "Much of the cult's enormous success may be ascribed to the intense visual messages sent by the buildings, their decoration, and the portable ritual objects. Their strong perceptual effect, certainly calculated by Chavín artists, inspires confusion, surprise, fear, and awe through the use of dynamic, shifting images that contain varying readings depending on the direction in which they are approached. The terms 'hallucinatory' and 'transformational' aptly describe much Chavín subject matter and artistic effect."[58]

A number of techniques were employed to produce the powerful psychedelic effects of Chavín art. One of these was to use lines that served double and triple duty, allowing diverse images to form and dissolve in different parts of a visual display—much as the Necker-cube optical illusion allows the viewer to switch mentally from looking inside a transparent cube one moment, to staring at its exterior from another angle the next. Another trick was to make deeply incised lines that used the high-contrast, inky dark shadows cast by the crisp Andean sunlight to produce shifting outlines. The size, scale, and positioning of the art displays relative to the viewer were also used. Dozens of large sculpted heads studded the outside walls of the temple complex. "As if time-lapse photography, they document the dramatic process of shamanic transformation through hallucinogenics," Stone-Miller observes, for there are sequences of heads which show, stage by stage, human features transforming into exotic, hallucinatory creatures.[59] Here, wrought in stone, is the hallucinogenic experience of the body-image changing into a magical animal.

Widespread use of the San Pedro cactus is found throughout the record of Andean cultures. Well-preserved textiles found at Karwa, a burial site three hundred miles from Chavín de Huantar, depict images of San Pedro cacti, as do Chavín-style ceramic vessels. The much later Moche culture (of around A.D. 500) used a stirrup-spout vessel that depicts a female, owl-headed shaman (another image of trance-transformation), strings of mind-altering espingo seeds, and the characteristic star shape that is vividly revealed in a cross section of the San Pedro cactus. Moche pottery designs often depict the tree *Anadenanthera colubrina*, the seeds of which were used to produce the potently hallucinogenic *wilka* snuff, and also contain scenes that anthropologist Marlene Dobkin de Rios interprets as showing actual San Pedro sessions.[60] Pottery of the Nasca culture (approximately 200 B.C. to A.D. 600) often shows "flower" or "star" motifs that can readily be interpreted as San Pedro cross sections. There are also depictions showing or motifs alluding to ecstatic magical flight in various examples of ancient Andean art.

A TREASURE CHEST OF VISIONS

While sacred mushrooms, *Banisteriopsis,* red bean or *Sophora secundiflora,* *ololiuhqui* or morning glory seeds, datura, peyote, and San Pedro cactus represent the most important of native American hallucinogens, there are so many known in the New World (not to mention those that have not yet been identified) that there simply isn't space here to describe all of them; but I will briefly mention a few of the other, lesser-known ones in order to give a sense of the sheer scale of the pharmacopoeia of visionary substances that the ancient Native Americans possessed.

Native American usage of hallucinogens involved not only drinking, chewing, and smoking, but also snuffing: psychoactive snuffs have been employed from remotest antiquity (as have enemas, as well). There is ample evidence that the ancient use of psychedelic snuffs occurred over much of South America, in the Caribbean islands, and, at one time, in Mexico. Snuff samples twelve hundred years old have been found in mummy bundles from northern Chile, while a bone snuffing tray with tubes (nose pipes) dating to 1600 B.C. has been excavated in Peru. "Archaeological remains in Argentina, Brazil, Chile, Colombia, Costa Rica, the Dominican Republic, Haiti, Peru and Puerto Rico testify to the broad range and antiquity of entheogenic [psychedelic] snuff use in the Caribbean and South America," notes Jonathan Ott.[61] In Mexico, evidence of ancient snuffing goes back to "at least the second millennium B.C."[62] People holding pipes to their nostrils are shown in trancelike states in Colima tomb artifacts from western Mexico dating to between 100 B.C. and A.D. 200; a double-stemmed bird-effigy nose pipe from a shaft-and-chamber tomb in Nyarit is of a similar age; nose pipes from Oaxaca date to 500 B.C., while at Xochipala, Guerrero, ceramic nose pipes from between 1300 and 1500 B.C. have been found. There are also Olmec jade "spoons," which were probably used for snuffing, that date to 1200 to 900 B.C. For reasons unknown, snuffing seems to have ceased in Mexico at some point prior to A.D. 1000.

Psychoactive snuff was the first Native American hallucinogen to have been noted by Europeans. In a letter of 1496, Columbus himself

A snuffing pipe in use. This figure of an entranced man is from a shaft-and-chamber tomb in Colima, western Mexico, and dates to between 100 B.C. and A.D. 200. *(Peter T. Furst)*

commented on a strange Antillean "powder" that the Taino Indians would "snuff up," rendering them "like drunken men." This snuff was *cohoba*, which, centuries later, was identified as being prepared from the beans of a tree of the pea family, *Anadenanthera peregrina*. *Cohoba* has been found to be the same as the hallucinogenic snuff *yopo*, used by the Indians of the Orinoco Basin, and it was probably from that region that the use of the snuff spread to the West Indies. Indeed, the use of the drug seems to have diffused outward quite widely from the Orinoco.[63] Another *Anadenanthera*-based snuff has traditionally been used in Peru, Bolivia, and northern Argentina; it is known as *wilka* (also *huilca* or *vilka*, and called *cébil* in Argentina) and derives from *Anadenanthera colubrina*.

The psychoactive elements in *Anadenanthera*-based snuffs are tryptamine derivatives, including DMT and bufotenine (5-hydroxy-dimethyltryptamine). Interestingly, trace amounts of monoamine oxidase–inhibiting beta-carbolines have also been found in the bark of *Anadenanthera peregrina*.[64]

Another important range of hallucinogenic snuffs derives from the bloodred sap of *Virola* trees, which are of the nutmeg family. Four or five different species have been used. Tryptamine alkaloids are present in high concentrations in the scrapings of the inner bark of these trees. *Virola* snuffs are used by Indians of the Colombian Amazon, in the Orinoco Basin in Venezuela, and in the Rio Negro Basin of Brazil. There are many names for *Virola* snuffs among the various Indians groups involved, including *yakee, yato, epena, parica*, and *nyakwana*. DMT and 5-MeO-DMT has been found in all *Virola* snuffs analyzed.[65]

Peter Furst has drawn attention to the iconography used on snuffing paraphernalia found in the Americas. There is "an unmistakable symbol complex that ties shamanism and the ecstatic experience to the already familiar bird-feline-reptilian configuration we find so prominently in Mesoamerican and Andean cosmology and iconography."[66] Birds, serpents, and, particularly, the jaguar, the dominant shamanic symbol of tropical American shamanism, are prominent representations in the imagery to be found on ancient snuffing equipment. Similar but more subtle associations are made by fashioning snuffing pipes out of bird bones. "Where the bird motif is unspecific," Furst further comments, "it seems to stand for the power of flight that is the shaman's special gift and that is activated by the hallucinogen."[67]

The most widespread substance snuffed by tribal Native Americans is tobacco, and no review of New World hallucinogens would be complete without mention of the genus *Nicotiana*, which is a branch of the nightshade family. It is thought that about twelve species of *Nicotiana*, including *N. rustica* and *N. tabacum*, were originally cultivated in South America for religious and healing purposes perhaps as long ago as six or eight thousand years. The theory is that tobacco became a sacred plant because it, like other members of the nightshade family, such as datura, has the ability to grow spontaneously in disturbed soil. Its sprouting from graves, for example, might make it seem to be a gift from the ancestors.[68]

Tobacco use was unknown in the Old World prior to the colonization of the Americas, and it was rapidly taken up widely in Europe as a hedonistic drug. In the Americas, its use had been restricted to shamanic practices, but after about 1700 a gradual shift toward more general and profane use occurred. Westerners do not think of tobacco as being hallucinogenic, but the Native American shaman took extremely large doses, and in sufficiently large amounts tobacco can cause altered states of consciousness. It was and is used in vision quests to induce trance states, and as an aid in curing procedures. Tobacco is taken in all manner of ways: by chewing or sucking quids, by snuffing, by administering suppositories and enemas, by smoking, by drinking tobacco juice and syrup, by licking tobacco paste, by eating it as a cake, and by applying tobacco preparations to the skin and eyes. When smoked, it is usually fashioned into large cigar-type rolls, combined with additives from other plants, or used in pipes.

When used for trance-induction purposes, in whatever manner, vast dosages are taken. In Guiana, for instance, shamans' apprentices are obliged to consume liters of tobacco juice, force-fed through a funnel, bringing them "to the brink of death," as anthropologist Johannes Wilbert puts it.[69] Among the Tupinamba of Brazil, shamanic initiates are fed tobacco juice until they pass out and vomit blood. "South American shamans are known to ingest up to five three-foot-long cigars (while simultaneously chewing tobacco) in the course of a single seance," Wilbert informs.[70] These kinds of massive doses cause convulsions, seizures, and transitory respiratory failure, causing the "temporary death" of the shaman. In this state he can have his out-of-body experience and visit the otherworlds of the spirits and ancestors. These doses can also cause "actual" death—it is as dangerous a shamanic technique as it is an incredibly ancient one.

Noteworthy body changes occur in the shamans who chew, smoke, or drink tobacco. Their voices take on a guttural, deeply hoarse quality. Their eyesight becomes keenly effective in dim, twilight conditions due to neural changes in the retina, so they have "night vision" like the jaguar. Because of increased perspiration and the liberation of norepinephrine, which causes a drop in skin temperature, shamans can demonstrate their elemental mastery by performing heat-defying feats with fire.

Some of the other mind-altering substances that have been, or are believed to have been, used by Native Americans include other species of cacti and mushrooms. But there are also plants that are known in the Old World which possess surprising properties. For example, the white water lily (*Nymphaea ampla*) is pictured in ancient Mayan art, often in conjunction with animal transformations and other visionary subjects.[71] It has been found to contain apomorphine, which is psychoactive. Mayan art also depicts frogs or toads, and Marlene Dobkin de Rios has argued that the Mayans may have used the psychoactive giant toad, *Bufo marinus*, which secretes bufotenine and buftalin.[72] Other native hallucinogens are simply bizarre: *Heimia salicifolia*, for instance, a shrub the Mexicans call *sinicuichi*, is specifically an auditory hallucinogen—it does not produce visions. A person drinking an infusion made from its leaves will feel giddy and drowsy, and will experience a darkening of the surroundings, accompanied by alterations of time and space, and auditory hallucinations. Actual sounds will appear distorted and seem to come from far away. Indians consider the plant to be sacred and to have supernatural powers. They claim that it helps them to recall long-ago events with great clarity, and even to remember prenatal events.[73] Its ancient use is confirmed by the fact that a *sinicuichi* bud appears on the Aztec statue depicting Xochipilli, the "Prince of Flowers."

Plants used include some that are virtually unknown to us, and have very localized use. One such is *Calea zacatechichi* ("bitter grass"), which seems to be used only by the Chontal Indians of Oaxaca, who call it *thle-pelakano*, "leaf of god." This inconspicuous low, branching shrub is put to various uses by the Indians, but its main use is in inducing dreams. A person taking an infusion of *Calea zacatechichi* falls into a drowsy sleep punctuated by very intense periods of dreaming. These dream states, during which the person makes contact with the spirit worlds, are used for divination. Controlled scientific tests and anecdotal evidence from researchers have shown that *Calea zacatechichi* does indeed produce brief catnaps with intense sequences of vivid and meaningful dreams, including precognitive ones. And yet, no hallucinogenic constituent has so far been isolated in the plant. (My own experience included a rush of strongly colored dreams. In one brief but "realistic" dream I saw a group of colorfully dressed Indians looking down at me with a mix of amusement and gravity in their expressions.)

When contemplating the richness, depth, and subtlety of the Native American knowledge of naturally occurring visionary substances, our own naïvité is apparent. Some of the New World's ancient treasure chest of hallucinogens has already been lost to us, and much more will be unless the dominant culture respects, nurtures, and values those tenuously surviving Native American tribal groups who have experience with these traditions.

four
Drawing Conclusions on the Wall

Patterns of the Past,
Signs of All the Times

Entering any prehistoric chambered monument is an exciting and eerie experience: the stone surfaces of the roof and wall slabs press in on all sides, and there is literally a smell of antiquity, of a strange, lost world. Nowhere is this more the case than at Gavrinis. One cautiously moves down the passage in the dim lighting, observing the deep, beautifully engraved swirling lines on the walls, like gigantic fingerprints set in stone. Emerging into the rectangular chamber, the full impact of the designs is felt: the walls seem as alive as the tortured skies of a later Van Gogh painting. The lines curve and flow about the chamber, clustering and radiating around bumps and hollows on the slab surfaces like water rippling against a rock. If one looks carefully, a few representational symbols can be made out, such as the triangular glyphs thought to represent the ceremonial axes associated with the region; but most of the lines appear to be simply abstract curvilinear patterns. Some consider the designs to be highly abstracted goddess figures, but more recent interpretations reveal much about the nature of this place. According to later theories, markings such as those at Gavrinis are *psychedelic signatures*; they tell us that people used the place while in trance, during altered states of consciousness. If this is so, then these patterns offer us a glimpse into the ancient mind, and in so doing prompt us to look more closely at the workings of our own.

Some of the carved stones in the passage at Gavrinis. *(Paul Devereux)*

THE PATTERNED WINDMILLS
OF THE MIND

Discovering the significance of such ancient patterns resulted from investigations into the effects of psychedelic drugs. It is fair to say that the main catalyst in this process was the work of Heinrich Klüver, which spanned three decades, beginning in the 1920s with his study of mescaline. Drawing on his own experimentation with the hallucinogen, and on the work of previous German, French, English, and American researchers, Klüver became fascinated not so much with the *content* of hallucinations provoked by the substance, as with their *structural form.*[1] He surveyed his own observations, and the accounts deriving from the work of the others, finding certain recurring motifs embedded within the descrip-

Triangular glyphs thought to depict ritual axes surrounded by psychedelic curvilinear designs on a stone inside Gavrinis. *(Author's drawing)*

tions of hallucinatory material. Consider, for instance, the account of one of the subjects of experimenters A. Knauer and W. Maloney in 1913: "Immediately before my eyes are a vast number of rings, apparently made of extremely fine steel wire, all constantly rotating. . . . These circles are concentrically arranged. . . . Now a beautiful light violet tint has developed in them. As I watch, the center seems to recede into the depth of the room, leaving the periphery stationary, till the whole assumes the form of a deep funnel of wire rings." After glorious color changes, the wire rings transformed into bands or ribbons that moved "rhythmically, in a wavy upward direction suggesting a slow endless procession of small mosaics." The subject next seemed to be standing beneath a huge domed ceiling covered in harmoniously colored mosaic pieces. "The dome has absolutely no discernible pattern," the account continues. "But circles are now developing on it. . . . now they are rhomboids; now oblongs; and now all sorts of curious angles are forming. . . . The colors are changing rapidly." Hours later, the subject was seeing "a beautiful palace, filled with rare tapestries, pictures, and Louis Quinze furniture."

Klüver cited the mescaline experiences of the Philadelphia physician and novelist Weir Mitchell, who wrote the first modern published accounts of mescaline experimentation in 1898. Sitting in a dark room, Mitchell saw "delicate floating films of color . . . then an abrupt rush of countless points of white light swept across the field of view, as if the unseen millions of the Milky Way were to flow a sparkling river before the eye." Later, "definite objects associated with the colors" appeared for the first time. He saw a tall, elaborate Gothic tower. "As I gazed every projecting angle, cornice, and even the face of the stones at their joinings were by degrees covered or hung with clusters of what seemed to be huge precious stones, but uncut, some being more like masses of transparent fruit. . . . These were green, purple, red, and orange, never clear yellow, and never blue. All seemed to possess an interior light." He saw a giant stone bird claw projecting over the edge of a deep abyss, with "clusters of stones hanging in masses" from it. His last vision was of a beach, where "huge and threatening" waves of rich green, red, and purple "broke on the beach with myriads of lights" of the same colors.

Mitchell sent peyote buttons to the great American psychologist William James, whose only reaction to them was to be "violently sick for 24 hours." Mitchell had better luck with British psychologist Havelock Ellis, who had similar experiences to Mitchell's. "The visions never resembled familiar objects; they were extremely definite, but yet always novel," Ellis observed. "I would see thick, glorious fields of jewels, solitary or clustered, sometimes brilliant and sparkling, sometimes with a dull rich glow. Then they would spring up into flowerlike shapes beneath my gaze, and then seem to turn into gorgeous butterfly forms or endless folds of glistening, iridescent, fibrous wings of wonderful insects." The imagery that paraded before Ellis was a mixture of "kaleidoscopic, symmetrical groupings" and "living arabesques." He was impressed not only by the brilliancy of the colors, but also by "their lovely and various textures—fibrous, woven, polished, glowing, dull, veined, semi-transparent."

Decades later, the German researcher Dr. Kurt Beringer, a friend of the great esoteric novelist Hermann Hesse and psychologist Carl Jung, conducted some sixty mescaline trials with subjects at the Psychiatric Clinic in Heidelberg (mescaline had been synthesized from the peyote cactus in 1919). One of his subjects reported seeing "transparent oriental rugs, but infinitely small" with eyes closed; then, with his eyes open, at lunchtime, he saw them projected onto the surface of a bowl of soup. Other descriptions included phrases such as "wallpaper designs," "the chessboard motive repeated," "cobweb-like figures or concentric circles and squares," "architectural forms, buttresses, rosettes, leafwork, fretwork, and circular patterns," "modern cubist patterns," "lightnings," "comets," "explosions," and "a kaleidoscopic play of ornaments, patterns, crystals, and prisms which creates the impression of a never-ending uniformity."

Klüver's own experience with mescaline included similar perceptions. With his eyes closed he saw the tail of a pheasant transforming into a bright yellow star, which then turned into sparks. A moving "scintillating screw" became " 'hundreds' of screws." He saw a "rotating wheel . . . in the center of a silvery ground." "Sparks" looked like "exploding shells" that turned into "strange flowers which remind me of poppies in California." He saw moving wheels and stars in various colors crossing a "[s]oft, deep, darkness." Then images appeared: nuns in silver dresses who quickly disappeared; bluish ink bottles with labels; autumn leaves turning into peyote buttons; "gold rain falling vertically"; "rotating jewels revolving around a center." He saw a strange animal that turned rapidly into arabesques. With eyes open, Klüver saw streaks of green and violet projected onto the wall of his room. Shadows took on the appearance of a head that turned into a mushroom.

Klüver figured that there was a basic set of structural forms behind this phantasmagoria, but he was not the first to think so. Knauer and Maloney had already identified a sequence "characteristic of all the poisonings": ". . . wavy lines; mosaics; carpets, floral designs, ornaments, wood-carving; windmills; monuments; mausoleums; panoramic landscapes; statuesque men and animals; finally scenes picturing episodes in a connected manner."[2]

The French researcher A. Rouhier had also attempted to establish various stages of the mescaline experience. The first stage characteristically included the perception of geometric and kaleidoscopically changing forms. The second stage typically involved more familiar objects and scenes—landscapes, faces. The third stage was marked by novel mixes of imagery—monstrous forms and fabulous landscapes. Rouhier admitted that such stages were "intimately mixed" rather than distinctly sequential.

Klüver felt that such a scheme was "extremely arbitrary." He accepted a more general stage progression in which "very elementary visions are followed by visions of a more complex character," and identified four essential types of the elementary hallucinations, which he called "form constants." One of these he refers to using terms like "grating . . . lattice . . . fretwork . . . filigree . . . honeycomb, or chessboard-design." Closely associated with this was the "cobweb" form constant. A third form constant that Klüver felt deserved special mention was the "tunnel, funnel, alley, cone or vessel." Today, we particularly recognize the "tunnel" image from the accounts of those who undergo near-death and "out-of-body" experiences. A very important

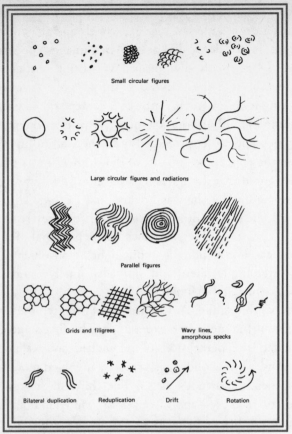

Basic forms and motion in entoptic imagery as deduced by Mardi J. Horowitz. *(From* Hallucinations, *Siegel and West, eds. Reproduced by permission from John Wiley & Sons.)*

property of this form constant is that it often heralds the moment when the subject stops merely *observing* the geometric and patterned motifs, and begins to *enter into* the hallucinatory or visionary world. The subject is engulfed by the imagery and begins to *participate* in it. The person's consciousness slips down the tunnel into the otherworldly realm. Klüver saw the "spiral" image as the fourth basic type of form constant, but this is essentially the same as the tunnel or funnel effect.

A. Serko experienced in 1913: "The luminous spiral and the haptic spiral blend psychologically, that is to say, the same spiral which is optically hallucinated is also haptically experienced."

Klüver categorized other recurring aspects of the hallucinogenic experience. In particular, he noted that these form constants provided fields of images that were arranged symmetrically and multiplied themselves into infinity—what we now recognize as fractal proliferation. He was also aware that the hallucinatory effects of mescaline could take the form of sensations other than visual. He especially singled out the feelings in which the mental image of the body becomes distorted. One characteristic element of this is a type of somatic hallucination in which the body feels elongated, and Klüver reported instances in which the subject felt that an arm became suddenly long or a leg seemed to be several meters long.[3] Serko also reported seeing his own leg assume a spiral form.[4]

Various studies concerning brain-stimulated geometric imagery were conducted in the 1950s and 1960s, including the research of Mardi J. Horowitz. He was initially unaware of Klüver's findings when he studied the varieties of hallucinatory experience, hoping to abstract redundant elements in the perceived imagery.[5] Nevertheless, he came up with very similar results to those of Klüver. Horowitz reasoned that the universality of these form constants seen in trance states was due to the fact that they were visualizations arising from elements within the human optical system itself, from the anatomical structure of the eyeball, the optical blood vessels, the retina, and the visual cortex. Indeed, the term *entoptics*, deriving from Greek words meaning "within vision," was now one of the labels used for these types of mentally generated patterns.* Horowitz agreed with Klüver that the basic geometric pat-

---

*Debate over which elements of the human visual system cause the form constants continues. Suggestions have been numerous, and include specific firing patterns of neurons within the visual cortex, phosphenes, fibrous and folding structure of the eyeball, structure of the retina, "floaters" in the liquid of the eye, and red blood cells passing through retinal capillaries. It is probable that most or all parts of the system are involved in various ways.

terns could become embellished, forming the basis of more complex and representational hallucinatory imagery as the trance state deepened: the entoptic imagery "may be elaborated by adding internal information to these basic forms."

In 1975, Ronald Siegel and Murray Jarvik published an overview of the whole field of entoptics and provided results from their own clinical trials.[6] These two researchers noted that in 1845, the French psychiatrist Jacques Moreau had observed that the structural nature of hallucinations was basically the same for a wide range of mind-altering conditions: certain kinds of mental illness, the influence of hashish, nitrous oxide (laughing gas), opium, alcohol, thorn apple, belladonna, henbane, dreaming sleep and hypnagogia, fever, and hallucinatory states arising from hunger and thirst. Ahead of his time, he also suspected that processes within the brain provided the sensory impressions underlying visions and auditory hallucinations.

In 1888, P. Max Simon studied the imagery of schizophrenic hallucinations in his patients. He observed the repeated occurrence of spiderwebs, ropes, meshes, and balls. These images were always in flux, and displayed specific movement patterns. In 1924, Louis Lewin, author of the seminal work *Phantastica: Narcotic and Stimulating Drugs, Their Use and Abuse,* noted the similarity of imagery elicited by several drugs. He observed that marijuana frequently produced hallucinations such as "fireworks, rockets, and many-colored stars" while mescaline produced forms such as "colored arabesques," "carpets," "filigree lacework," "stars," "crystals," and "geometrical forms of all kinds." Following this observational trend, Siegel and Jarvik noted that "surprisingly similar imagery" had been experienced with a variety of other trance-inducing agents, including alcohol (in delirium tremens), fly agaric mushroom (*Amanita muscaria*), antihistamines, numerous anesthetics, the South American "soul vine" (*Banisteriopsis*), *Datura stramonium,* harmela alkaloids, ketamine, psilocybin ("magic") mushrooms, and tobacco in heavy doses. They remarked that entoptic-style imagery can also be provoked by some chemicals used in chemotherapy, and can occur during high fevers caused by illnesses such as measles and malaria, and during epileptic seizures, half-sleep (hypnagogic or hypnopompic) states, and psychotic states.

Siegel and Jarvik also drew attention to the fact that entoptic imagery can be seen projected like an overlay on the physical environment. An account of delirium-driven hallucinations given by V. Kandinsky in 1881 gives a particularly good idea of this:

> These vivid visual pictures completely covered real objects. During a week I saw on one and the same wall, covered with uniformly colored wallpaper, a series of large pictures set in wonderfully gilded frames, landscapes, views of the seashore, sometimes portraits. . . . Hallucinations . . . were projected on the surfaces of the floor, the ceiling, or the wall, or they appear in space, covering the objects that lie behind them. . . . With closed eyes the complicated hallucinations appeared in the form of corporeal objects surrounding me; the less complicated ones, like, e.g., pictures, microscopic preparations, or ornamental figures, were drawn on the dark ground of the visual field.[7]

"Form-constants and allied phenomena have also been observed by subjects in sensory deprivation situations," Siegel and Jarvik further note, "following photostimulation . . . electrical current . . . crystal gazing . . . while gazing at a light bulb . . . during migraine scintillating scotoma . . . and even during 'swinging' or 'pendulumlike' motion." But the investigators add an important observation: "In general, drug-induced patterns appear to be more vivid, more colorful, more regular, and more ornate than those elicited by other methods."

Siegel and Jarvik conducted scientifically controlled tests to better study the production of hallucinatory imagery. Their first experiment involved fourteen untrained subjects who self-administered cannabis in eight weekly sessions. After administration, the subjects were seated in a dark and lightproof room and asked to give a running commentary on whatever imagery they saw with their eyes closed. On the basis of the material produced it was possible for the experimenters to construct a list of eight basic forms underlying the imagery (random, line, curve, web, lattice, tunnel, spiral, kaleidoscope), eight colors (black, violet, blue, green, yellow, orange, red, white), and eight movement patterns exhibited by the imagery (aimless, vertical, horizontal, oblique, explosive, concentric, rotational, pulsating). The tunnel was a recurring form, and many subjects reported a blue lattice-tunnel in particular during the first stages of intoxication. One described the tunnel form as an experience in which "I was traveling through the inside of a tube and the background faded towards the center of the tube and so that all of it seems to be going from behind, below, over, above me. . . . I am traveling into a tunnel and out into space." Numerous subjects experienced distinctive memories of objects and scenes, "and these were projected onto the visual field, often overlaid by form constants."[8] Combinations of images were also noted, such as a horse and a man combining to form a centaur, as was repetition and the overlaying of images. Many subjects likened the display of visionary imagery to a movie or slide show being projected in front of their eyes.

In another controlled experiment, subjects were trained in describing various forms and over several weeks were randomly administered substances ranging from hallucinogens to placebos. Form constants were cited by sixty-seven percent of all subjects using the hallucinogens, the rest being complex imagery. Combinations of forms were often reported, such as "nested" sets of curves that turned into "curved lines in a tunnel-like arrangement." This shift to tunnel-like forms occurred about thirty minutes after the administration of the drug and tended to coincide with the "peak high" of the experience. While placebos and nonhallucinatory drugs did not significantly alter the normal base line distribution of form imagery, it was found that "the hallucinogens THC, psilocybin, LSD, and mescaline induced a significant and dramatic shift to the lattice-tunnel forms, as seen in the earlier marihuana data."[9] Complex imagery "usually did not appear until well after the lattice-tunnel shift was reported." This is significant further evidence that the tunnel form constant heralds a shift from observation to participation in the visionary experience. While form imagery initially appeared like a slide show located about two feet in front of the eyes, subjects felt themselves becoming part of the imagery itself as each session progressed. The complex imagery included "recognizable landscapes, scenes, people, and objects subjects could identify as memory images, but often presented in unique combinations and arrangements."[10] When the blindfolded subjects were taken outdoors, memory content decreased and associative imagery from sounds and touch increased. The experimenters also acknowledged the findings of other researchers that personal psychology and cultural conditions profoundly affected the content of hallucinations.

Siegel and Jarvik initially thought that some elements of entoptic phenomena, particularly those connected with the eyeball and retina, only occurred when there was a light source. But this was not supported by their work with subjects sequestered in totally blacked-out rooms. They felt that only some aspects of entoptic imagery "provide the basic structural templates" for form constants, and they gravitated toward the idea that phosphenes (bright images sometimes seen with eyes closed under various conditions) are produced by electrical output from cells in higher centers of the visual system than the retina. Gerald Oster, who also felt that there are mechanical ordering processes affecting hallucinations, used LSD in the 1960s to investigate the neurological "languages" that may geometrically order hallucinations. Noting the work of Max Knoll,[11] he reported that phosphenes "can be produced also by applying electrical current to the temples, especially if the voltage is in the form of a square-wave pulse at about 20 cycles per second."[12] The actual geometrical figures produced could be modified by changing the frequency of the electrical stimulation. In 1990, Thomas Lyttle and Elvin D. Smith described how

> hallucinogens are particularly valuable as mind-mapping instruments because neurostructure and associated processes become visible. . . . The particular characteristics that each type of hallucinatory constant has are reflective of what is going on in the perception processing circuitry—the neurostructuralism—of the brain. . . . The constants can be understood as "neurological landmarks" that serve to orient oneself within the progression of the trip, as well as being primary symbols which reveal structural organization of the brain.[13]

They warn against simplistic reductionism, however, pointing out that there is a "difference between *information processing* and *information*, between the *structure* (brain) and the *content* (symbol)."[14]

Whatever mechanics are involved, it seems certain that the basis of hallucinatory imagery lies in the actual structure of or processes within the human visual system, whether at the optical or the cellular, electrical levels (or most probably, at all levels). These can underlie more complex imagery, in the same manner that the dots of a newspaper photograph can "carry" a photographic image.

While these mechanics specifically focus on visual effects, we must bear in mind that the haptic sense of travel down (or up) the tunnel form constant (that is, the experience of the soul flying out from the body) is a very *real* sensation. However, mind-altering substances operate across all the senses. An example is the phenomenon of synesthesia, when sense modalities switch from one to another, examples of which we have already described earlier in this work. This experience is well expressed by a mescaline subject who was pricked with a sharp instrument: "I've got concentric circles like round the top of a radio mast. If you touch me, jagged things shoot up, little-sort-of-jagged things, from the center." Then there are the changes in the perception of body image. We have already noted that shamanic literature is replete with accounts of the shaman turning into an eagle, a jaguar, and so on. Here is a graphic, instructive account reported by a friend of William James who took a large dose of hashish. We see the progression from cognitively enhanced entoptic imagery to a full-blown sensation of being transformed into another creature caused by associative thinking:

> Directly I lay down upon a sofa there appeared before my eyes several rows of human hands, which oscillated for a moment, revolved and then changed into spoons. The same motions were repeated, the objects changing to wheels, tin soldiers, lamp-posts, brooms, and countless other absurdities. . . . I saw at least a thousand different objects. These whirling images did not appear like the realities of life, but had the character of the secondary images seen in the eye after looking at some brightly-illuminated object. . . . A strange

fear came over me, a certainty that I should never recover from the effects. . . . I thought of a fox, and instantly I was transformed into that animal. I could distinctly feel myself a fox, could see my long ears and bushy tail, and by a sort of introversion felt that my complete anatomy was that of a fox. Suddenly, the point of vision changed. My eyes seemed to be located at the back of my mouth, I looked out between the parted lips, saw the two rows of pointed teeth, and, closing my mouth with a snap, saw—nothing. . . . The whirling images appeared again.[15]

But how does all this fascinating neuropsychological and neurophysiological information help us understand the archaeology of ecstasy, the physical remains of past human activity in altered states of consciousness?

OUT OF AFRICA

The association of neurological findings and ethnological research currently revolves around the work of David Lewis-Williams and Thomas Dowson, two South African archaeologists from the Rock Art Research Unit at Witwatersrand University in Johannesburg.* For their model, these two archaeologists have identified three stages in the progress of trance-induced hallucinatory imagery. In Stage One subjects experience entoptic-style hallucinatory form constants alone. While these forms are "human universals," the symbolism attached to them varies from culture to culture. In Stage Two the subject's mind applies cognitive processes to the imagery, trying to "recognize" or "decode" it as representational forms. Lewis-Williams and Dowson refer to such hallucinatory material as "construal" imagery. Associations leading to the development of these construal images would be culturally determined

---

*In 1974, J. Eichmeir and D. Höfer had argued that the abstract motifs in megalithic art derived from entoptic phenomena, but their work was more generalized than that of the South African researchers.

to a large extent, mixing with a smaller body of idiosyncratic images arising from the individual's own psychological disposition. The onset of Stage Three is frequently marked by the experience of the "tunnel" form constant, in one version or another, in which the subject participates in complex, fully representational ("real-looking") hallucinatory imagery. Though presented in novel and creative forms, this complex imagery seems to be memory-based and emotion-associated. The South African researchers use the term "iconic" to describe this type of visual product. "This shift to iconic imagery is also accompanied by an increase in vividness," Lewis-Williams and Dowson note. "Subjects stop using similes to describe their experiences and assert that the images are indeed what they appear to be. . . . Nevertheless, even in this essentially iconic stage, entoptic phenomena may persist: iconic imagery is 'often projected against a background of geometric forms.' "[16]

Lewis-Williams and Dowson adopted a basic range of six entoptic pattern-types for their model, recognizing that images can be subject to fragmentation, to replication, to reduplication, to rotation, and to merging with one another: "In such an experience, a grid, for example, may be integrated with an animal; in other instances an animal may be blended with characteristics of another species."[17] They also accept that the three stages of trance do not necessarily always occur in a neat sequence, but that there can be jumps from one to another, and even mixed versions of each process occurring more or less simultaneously. The brain mind is mercurial.

The principal focus of study for these two researchers and their colleagues is the rock art left by the Bushman (or San) peoples who once roamed the vast expanse of southern Africa and whose culture became extinct about a century ago as a result of colonization. Only some groups of !Kung in the Kalahari Desert still follow the traditional life. The Bushmen were the original inhabitants of southern Africa, and along with the Khoikhoi belonged to the Khoisan group of people. Their phonetically complex language was distinguished by a variety of "click" sounds, which have become represented in writing by such punctuation devices as ! or / or //. The main Bushman groups were not

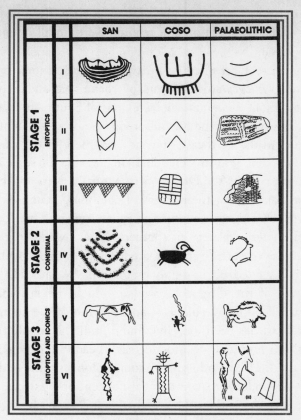

Entoptic and visual phenomena from the three stages of trance consciousness as depicted in examples of San (Bushman), Coso (Native American), and Paleolithic rock art. *(David Lewis-Williams and Thomas Dowson, 1988)*

tribal but linguistic. They were a hunter-gatherer people, just as the !Kung still are. The nomadic movement of the Bushman peoples followed yearly cycles along planned annual routes; the men hunted, the women gathered. "Egalitarianism and changing membership of groups, even across linguistic boundaries, led to widespread uniformity of Bushman life and belief," Lewis-Williams and Dowson note. "This is not to say that all Bushman groups were identical, certainly there were regional differences, but research has shown that the fundamentals of Bushman social organisation and religion were, to all intents and purposes, universal."[18]

Bushman rock art offers of a rich legacy of paintings and engravings. Paintings occur in rock shelters, overhang sites, and on boulder surfaces, primarily in the mountainous regions of South Africa, such as the Natal Drakensberg and the Malutis around Lesotho, the Waterberg and other ranges in the northeast, and the Cedarberg to the west. Another range rich in paintings is the Brandberg in Namibia. "In some areas of the subcontinent, such as the Drakensberg, virtually every inhabitable rock shelter has paintings or the remains of paintings," state Lewis-Williams and Dowson.[19] The rock engravings, or petroglyphs, are found principally in the interior plateau of southern Africa. Many engravers chose rocky outcrops of dolerite and diabase forming low rises. Other sites are found in rocky riverbeds or simply on rocks in the flat veld.[20]

Because of the disgraceful way in which the Bushman peoples were regarded by many colonists, appreciation of the complex nature of Bushman art has been long in coming. Initially, people thought the Bushmen "too primitive" to produce such beautiful, sophisticated, and mysterious art. On the other hand, some colonists dismissed this sensitive work as "childlike." A further misconception was that the art depicted "foreigners"—the Abbé Henri Breuil was one of the great promulgators of this misconception. He is famous for calling a marvelous painting of a figure in the Brandberg "the White Lady." In fact, it is neither white nor a lady.[21] Breuil thought the White Lady figures represented "a mixed group of foreigners . . . and that they brought with them beliefs such as are found in Egypt and Crete. . . . The Lady's costume is obviously Cretan. . . . My supposition is that a population of Nilotic-Mediterranean origin came south through Kenya in a rapid migration."[22] This was sheer fiction created by the eyes of the old French paleontologist, celebrated for his work in the European Paleolithic (Old Stone Age) painted caves, such as Lascaux in France. That the White Lady was partly white had to do with the color symbolism used by the Bushmen and did not relate to skin color at all—elephants, for instance, could be painted red, black, or white.

Another dismissive view of rock art held that the images and scenes simply depicted episodes of daily life: people dancing, hunting, and battling. This approach ignored the possibility that the art was actually more than it appeared, that it could be symbolic of deep spiritual experiences, because it was assumed that the Bushman peoples were incapable of abstract thinking. This attitude toward the art is akin to assuming that the statues of lions in Trafalgar Square are simply zoological references, or that the depiction of a lamb in the stained glass of a Christian church window is merely a farming scene. Strange images in the rock art, such as antelopes with human hind legs, or men with antelope heads, or half-human, half-buck creatures flying through the air trailing lines or streamers, were understood to be some expression of "sympathetic hunting magic," a practice for which there is no evidence among the Bushman groups.

Despite these red herrings, however, it became generally accepted that the Bushman peoples were responsible for the paintings. Lewis-Williams and Dowson recount a moving episode:

Those few Bushmen who were interviewed on the subject or to whom copies were shown accepted that the art had been made by their own people. For instance, in the 1870s, George William Stow showed some copies he had made of rock paintings to an old Bushman couple. On seeing a depiction of a dance, the old woman began to sing and dance. Her husband was so moved by the memories she awakened that he begged her to stop. "Don't," he said, "don't sing those old songs, I can't bear it! It makes my heart too sad!" She persisted, however; finally, the old man joined her. They looked at each other, Stow wrote, and were happy, the glance of the wife seeming to say, "Ah! I thought you could not withstand that!"[23]

The real nature of the Bushman rock art, which has caused us to revolutionize the way we now look at much prehistoric rock art throughout the world, came to be understood by collecting together a variety of sources of information. The documentation left by those colonists in the nineteenth and early twentieth centuries who recorded the language and beliefs of the Bushman groups gave us valuable information about Bushman rock art, which has radically altered the way in which we now interpret prehistoric art around the world. Ethnological studies of the Kalahari !Kung have also been helpful. While the !Kung do not belong to the particular Bushman groups who produced the art, they nevertheless share the same lifestyles and religious beliefs as those extinct groups. Finally, there has been the dedicated and detailed archaeological study of the rock art over recent decades. As a consequence of all this, it is now possible to understand the essential nature, meanings, and contexts of the rock art.

Predominant pigments used in the paintings include red (ocher or ferric oxide), white (silica, clay, gypsum), and black (charcoal, soot, manganese, etc.). The last known painter used *qhang qhang*, a glistening hematite, for his red pigment. *Qhang qhang* was traditionally prepared by a woman, out-of-doors, during a full moon. Researchers are unsure about what methods were used for binding the pigments, but they likely included blood, egg white, urine, sap, and other ingredients. Paint was applied with the finger. Thin bones and quills were used where fine lines were needed. It is difficult to date the paintings themselves, and many are damaged because the rock shelters in which they exist are often shallow and exposed to the elements.* Nevertheless, various techniques have provided important information concerning their antiquity. Examining extracted particles of carbon from the black paints of rock art in the western Cape, an atomic accelerator has dated the site to five hundred years ago. Strata of rocks containing paintings that were found in the Apollo 11 shelter in southern Namibia have yielded a date of over twenty-six thousand years ago, much earlier than the Paleolithic paintings of Lascaux. Other samples have been dated to between 6000 and 2000 B.C. But researchers are satisfied that the rock art tradition was practiced up until the arrival of colonists, so

---

*These rock shelters may have been seen as more than mundane refuges—they "may well have been considered particularly powerful places," as Lewis-Williams and Dowson observe.

some examples of rock painting may be no older than a century or so. Southern African rock art therefore represents "the longest artistic tradition human beings have produced."[24]

The content of the rock paintings relates directly to Bushman shamanism. Although Bushman shamans can operate independently, the primary expression still practiced by the Kalahari !Kung is the healing or trance dance. There are various versions of this dance, some of which take a linear form, others that are horseshoe-shaped arrangements of dancing women. But the most dominant form is the *dwa* or Giraffe Dance, where women sitting around a central fire clap the rhythm of special songs while men stomp in a circle around them. Rattles are tied to their legs to enhance the rhythmic effect; sometimes sticks or staves add to the pounding beat (and, at later stages, help support them). This form of dancing can go on for many hours and can cause a supernatural potency called *n/um* to "boil" and "awaken" from its resting place in the pit of the stomach or at the base of the spine and rise up the spinal column. When the potency reaches the base of the skull, the dancer enters a profound state of altered consciousness or *kia*. One old !Kung healer, Kinachau, described the process to anthropologist Richard Katz:

> You dance, dance, dance, dance. Then num lifts you up in your belly and lifts you in your back, and you start to shiver. Num makes you tremble; it's hot. . . . When you get into kia, you're looking around because you see everything. . . . Rapid shallow breathing draws num up. What I do in my upper body with my breathing, I also do in my legs with the dancing. You don't stomp harder, you just keep steady. Then num enters every part of your body, right to the tip of your feet and even your hair. . . .
>
> When we enter kia, we are different from when our num is not boiling and small. We can do different things.[25]

One of several supernormal abilities the trance dancer acquires during *kia* is the ability to perceive disease. The dancer becomes a healer and can see with X-ray vision into the bodies of ill people, curing their disease by sucking it out or by the laying on of hands. (This ability of X-ray vision in trance is often portrayed in "X-ray style" shamanic art around the world.) Experienced healers can control their stages of trance so that they can still perform healing activities, but the less experienced are apt to collapse on the ground unconscious or to throw themselves uncontrollably into the embers of the fire. When young men seek the ability to acquire *n/um* and enter *kia*, a trance dance will include the respected healers accompanied by youngsters, at various stages of initiation. Some seekers never achieve the ability to perceive disease, even after many years of trying. And they suffer no discrimination within !Kung society, because it is recognized that achieving *n/um* is a task not easily mastered. The sensation of *n/um*, of supernatural potency, is viewed with some fear, even by experienced trance dance healers themselves. The state of *kia* is regarded as a kind of "death," and is accompanied by great risks. "As we enter kia, we fear death," one trancer stated. "We fear we may die and not come back!" Other metaphors for the deep trance state include "being under water" and "flying" (flight is a universal shamanic metaphor for the dissociative feeling of soul flight encountered in trance states). A person in deep trance was said to be "spoiled."

The dancers often carry fly whisks while trance dancing. These whisks help maintain balance and serve to symbolically flick away the "arrows" of disease—it is these that cause illness, and sometimes people are affected without knowing it. The arrows come from ill-wishing spirits or malevolent shamans. The entranced healer can see these arrows and the *n/um* itself.

Shamans enter trance for other purposes besides healing. A major one is rainmaking, which has its own set of protocols and imagery. Some trancers are famous for their healing, others for their rainmaking skill, and so on.

In the course of a dance, only a few men will enter *kia* at various times. A dancer's arms and legs will shake and tremble; he may collapse or rush toward the fire. But the whole affair is well managed, with people on hand to support and look after the person entering *kia*. Those with strong *n/um*, and who are able to control their altered state, will begin healing observers. Those in *kia* adopt characteristic postures. They may hold their arms out sideways, bending their elbows upward. They may lean forward or drop to their knees, their arms stretched back behind them. They may raise a knee or extend an arm in a pointing gesture. (This posture is an act of directing supernatural potency, and it is said to freeze or slow down running animals or even knock over human beings.) Nosebleeds often occur during the trance state, blood streaking across dancers' faces. While in the trance state, a dancer might see glowing spirits standing in the dark beyond the illuminated fringes of the dancing ground. He may be able to see a relative at some distant physical location. His soul can leave his body, usually through the top of the head, and he can travel cross-country as an animal—he may have the sensation of hairs growing on his skin as he transforms into the creature. Or, quite often, he will see a hole open in the ground before him in which his spirit will enter to travel a subterranean route. On the other hand, his soul may "climb threads" and go up to heaven to see God and the ancestral spirits, battling with supernatural forces. There is always the risk that things could go wrong; the healer's spirit may not get back to his body, and the "death" of *kia* would become a permanent state.

Certain animals are associated with extra potency. While a healer could "own" giraffe power or elephant power, the greatest animal source of potency is the eland, the largest African antelope. The animal power of the eland is thought by the Bushmen to reside in the creature's fat, particularly in the male's large dewlap. This fat is used widely in Bushman society, both as a food and as a ritual substance.[26] When an eland has been shot with a poisoned arrow, its death throes exhibit many of the characteristics of a dancer in trance—staggering, sweating, trembling, nose bleeding, drooping head. As the arrow's poison takes effect, its leg muscles go into spasm, so that it staggers along dragging an extended rear leg. This posture is also sometimes adopted by a dancer experiencing the rush of *n/um*. The eland, therefore, presents a complex and powerful symbolic image to the Bushmen.

Once the details of Bushman shamanic practice were properly understood by modern researchers, it became possible to interpret much

The tracing of a Bushman rock painting showing a shamanic curing ritual. The patient lies at the center of the scene with knees drawn up, while an entranced healer lays on hands and a trance dance goes on around them. The arrows are probably not material arrows, but "arrows of sickness" sent by malevolent shamans or spirits. *(David Lewis-Williams and Thomas Dowson, 1989)*

of the imagery found in Bushman rock paintings. While some scenes are of a practical nature, the vast majority of images without doubt relate to hallucinatory scenes, including stages of trance, trance dancing and healing, the adventures of out-of-body shamans, and the physical sensations of trance and *n/um*. One scene depicts a trance dance, with a healing taking place in the center. Arrows are either lying or flying about. No longer simply understanding the picture as a "battle scene," we now see these as "arrows of disease." Other "battle scenes" probably relate to shamans' struggles in the supernatural world. "Fight" was a Bushman metaphor for a particularly strong charge of *n/um*. Some scenes may indeed show what would have been visible to anyone present. But others depict those things visible only to the eyes of the entranced shaman.

In 1985, David Lewis-Williams interviewed an old woman who was probably the last survivor of the southern Drakensberg Bushmen. She was the daughter of a shaman whose sister had been the last of the rainmakers. She could recognize paintings that had been done by her father, and confirmed that eland blood had been used in the manufacture of certain paints. She could recall various rituals and insisted that "all paintings had been done by shamans."[27] Lewis-Williams comments that during trance itself the shamans would not have had sufficient control over their motor functions to paint. It seems likely that they depicted their trance experiences later, while in a normal state of consciousness. By using eland blood in their rock art, the shamans ensured that the paintings themselves became repositories of power. Also, by glancing at the paintings as they danced, it was believed that trancers could receive an extra charge of supernatural potency.

Rock paintings show figures exhibiting the telltale signs of trance. They may hold fly whisks, for instance, which are used only at trance dances. Many figures show the characteristic postures of *kia*, while others have lines running from their noses or across their faces, depicting the trance-induced nosebleeds. Some painted figures are shown with raised hair on their outlines. A number of figures are distorted in various ways, expressing the somatic impressions of changes in body image prevalent during trance consciousness. Elongated figures are frequently depicted. This parallels observations made by Klüver during his mescaline research. (One !Kung dancer pointed to a tree and said that he became its height during trance.)

Another recurring and fascinating type of distortion shows an extended protuberance emanating from the top of a figure's head. While a few of these depictions may be interpreted as headdresses, others are simply too long to be explained this way. "The explanation for this feature again lies in a combination of neuropsychological evidence and Bushman beliefs," suggest Lewis-Williams and Dowson. "Laboratory research has shown that people in certain altered states of consciousness experience a tingling sensation in the top of the head. Schizophrenia, which has much in common with trance experience, sometimes produces a similar feeling. One patient described it as a fish hook in his scalp being drawn upwards."[28] Dowson notes that the lines are believed to depict the spirit leaving on out-of-body travel.[29] Birds or fish (or bird-headed or fish-tailed human figures) appear in some paintings and engravings, referring to the underwater and flight metaphors for trance. "Some shamans say they 'took feathers and flew,' " Dowson observes.[30]

A particularly clear Bushman rock painting depiction of the nasal bleeding that can be produced in trance dancing. Most of the paintings simply show lines dropping away from the face of a figure. *(David Lewis-Williams and Thomas Dowson, 1989)*

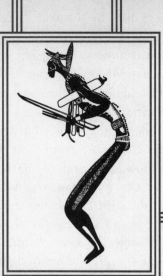

Elongated figures are common in Bushman rock art. Rather than it being a stylistic feature, Lewis-Williams and Dowson argue that it is in fact an expression of the sensation of body-image changing frequent in mind-change experiments. In this particular case, dots can be seen running along the figure's spine: this is probably an entoptic effect that was interpreted as the supernatural potency, or *n/um*, which rises up the spine during trance dancing. *(David Lewis-Williams and Thomas Dowson, 1989)*

This wonderful rock-painted figure has a long line extending from its head expressing the sensation of ecstasy, of the spirit leaving the body via the top of the head. It is an ancient Bushman depiction of what we call today the "out-of-body" experience. *(David Lewis-Williams and Thomas Dowson, 1989)*

The Bushman rock-art picture stresses the ecstatic element by showing a shaman transformed into a bird, a symbol of spirit flight, from the head of which runs a line. Some paintings show a trancing figure with a bird on its head from which in turn emerges a line. *(David Lewis-Williams and Thomas Dowson, 1989)*

A series of tracings of Bushman trance-buck paintings from various sites, showing a sequence of transformations from human to visionary animal. This is the very image of an out-of-body experience. *(Harald Pager)*

This drawing was done for anthropologist Richard Katz by !Kung trance healer Kinachau, showing the Kalahari Bushman in trance. Kinachau said the shorter zigzag lines were his body, and the longer one was his spinal cord. Katz comments that the lines are reminiscent of descriptions of *n/um*, and that the trancer's self-image is determined more by his inner states than by anatomical details. *(From* Boiling Energy *by Richard Katz. Copyright 1982 by the President and Fellows of Harvard College, reproduced with permission of Harvard University Press.)*

A detail of a southern African rock painting showing the mysterious connecting line that appears in some rock art. *(After David Lewis-Williams and Thomas Dowson, 1989)*

Above all, there exists classic Bushman shamanic imagery showing antelopes and other power animals, especially men with hoofed feet or antelope heads. These half-man, half-animal depictions, which are classic expressions of merging hallucinatory imagery, are called "therianthropes." There is an extreme version of this image that occurs only in the paintings found in the southeastern mountains of South Africa. It is currently called the "trance-buck" and is an especially well melded image of human and antelope. It is often shown in the arms-back trance posture and seems to be flying, or, in some cases, kneeling. Joseph Campbell remarked that this figure-type in Bushman rock art represented "the released soul of the trance dancers as well as of the dead. . . . The 'half-dead' visionaries in trance fly forth and about in the forms of antelope men."[31] The following illustrations show depictions from various rock art sites, with the fully fledged flying trance-buck shown in the image on the next page. Researchers think that the lines emanating from (or rushing into) the figure's shoulders depict

Part of a large panel of entoptic images engraved on the bedrock of a spring. *(Thomas Dowson, 1992)*

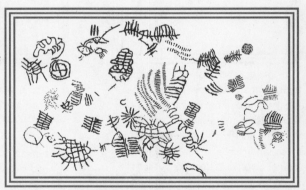

The body markings of the giraffe in this Bushman petroglyph echo the patterns in the connected entoptic grids on either side. *(Thomas Dowson, 1992)*

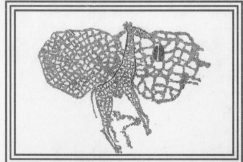

n/um. This particular illustration comes from a boulder overlooking the Mlambonja River in the Drakensberg. The deep and complex experiences of trance were emblazoned by the ancient Bushman on the very landscape.

The engravings show more evidence of specifically entoptically based form constants than do the paintings, but they nevertheless appear in the paintings in various forms. Strange dots appear on or around figures in trance. In some cases, small dots are seen along a figure's spine. This suggests that the busy entoptic flickers were probably interpreted as *n/um* itself. Some dots represent bees, which were symbolic to the Bushman. The beehives are drawn in the form of entoptic nested curves and the buzzing of bees represent the tinnitus that occurs in altered states. Zigzags flicker around other figures and groups. In one picture, a zigzag entoptic has become a construal, buck-headed serpent. One !Kung healer gave Richard Katz an illustration of himself in trance that showed his body made up of curves, dots, and zigzag lines—reminiscent of Serko's 1913 vision of his leg as a spiral. The hole in the ground that frequently appears to !Kung trance dancers is, of course, a version of the tunnel form constant. There is also a most mysterious element that creeps into some of the rock paintings: a serpentine line that is studded with entopticlike dots and often interlinks individual figures and groups. Lewis-Williams and Dowson speculate that this dot-encrusted line could represent *n/um* or even "the trajectory of a shaman on out-of-body travel."[32] They further note that this ser-

In this rubbing of a southern African petroglyph, we see a figure placing one hand to its face (a gesture thought to be associated with trance-induced nasal bleeding) while holding a fly whisk with the other, a sure symbol of the trance dancers. It faces the Bushman's ultimate power animal, the eland. An entoptic pattern hovers above the animal's fatty hump, thought to be the greatest concentration of *n/um*. *(Thomas Dowson, 1992)*

pentine image, like other features of both the paintings and engravings, seems often to relate to the nature of the actual physical surface of the rock on which it is executed, reacting to undulations and perhaps disappearing into a crack. What was supposed to happen to the image on the *other* side of the rock surface? Perhaps the spirit world was thought to lie behind the rock face. Perhaps the rock shelter was the entrance to the spirit world. Archaeologists are unsure.

The engravings on the interior plateau tend to be more geometric, with more animal figures depicted than human. The geometric elements are clearly entoptic, ranging from complex abstract imagery to grids of pecked dots on rock surfaces. This is so prevalent that in his 1992 book on the subject, Thomas Dowson was able to allocate specific groups of engravings to the three specific stages of trance. Dowson also stressed that the actual sites where engravings occur were probably considered significant, and the act of producing the rock art actually enhanced the power of such places.

The origins of rock art are located in the altered states produced by techniques of hyperventilation and extended periods of rhythmic motion, combined with a cultural framework for *kia*. It is not known if Bushmen used hallucinogens in the past or not. Today, certain Bush tribes do occasionally use marijuana. There is an old Bushman legend that associates *cannabis* with the snake, which figures in rock art and is a Bushman symbol of out-of-body travel. (It sheds its skin, it slithers underground.) Anthropologist Richard Katz informs us that the drug is used "if a fellow fails to find kia,"[33] and is sometimes smoked in conjunction with the trance dance. Certain herbs "strong in num" are often taken during the dances, and, as noted in Chapter 2, Katz learned of a root that the !Kung call *gaise noru noru*. Knowledge of its preparation existed in antiquity, it seems, but Katz's source was ambiguous as to whether its proper usage was presently known.[34] It is reported that some African Bushmen used kwashi bulbs (*Pancratium trianthum*) as a hallucinogen.[35,36]

But this matter is of relatively minor importance. The Bushman rock art of southern Africa is the archaeology of ecstasy par excellence. Not only is it the longest record of human artistic activity, it is also the most heroic expression of consciousness distinct from our mono-phasic (i.e., single mind-state) culture. It reminds us, from mountainside to riverbed, from sea to shining sea across a whole subcontinent, that there are other, additional ways of perceiving the world. As our Western culture eclipses other peoples and lifestyles, so we increasingly risk losing sight of a broader, wiser, and older understanding of the mind. Fortunately, the ghosts of Bushmen now extinct can have a last word: out of Africa, from time out of mind, comes the visionary imperative for us not to become too narrowly and exclusively entrenched in just one mode of consciousness we call "normal."

MIND-SIGNS OF THE AMERICAN INDIANS

Evidence for a shamanic source exists in varying degrees in Native American rock art, and for decorative artistic traditions involving imagery derived from hallucinogenic experience.

David S. Whitley, a member of the Witwatersrand Rock Art Research Unit, came to focus his studies on rock art in the eastern Californian Coso Range. Located at the western edge of the Great Basin, a vast tract of largely desert country lying between the Rockies and the Sierra Nevada, punctuated by short chains of rugged mountains, this range has one of the greatest concentrations of rock art anywhere, with approximately twenty thousand petroglyphs scattered through it. The Great Basin area had been occupied by Native American people for thousands of years, most recently Numic-speaking people like the Shoshone. Archaeological evidence indicates that a mixed subsistence of hunting and gathering involving small- and big-game hunting gave way after about A.D. 1200 to a subsistence based primarily on plant foods. Various forms of dating techniques, ranging from analyzing the desert varnish covering some petroglyphs to evidence contained in the themes and imagery of the art, indicate that most of the engravings date from this later period—and some seem to have been produced in recent centuries. The most common image in this rock art is that of mountain sheep, some of them shown being hunted or killed. In addition, there are male figures (often with patterns covering their bodies), animals, weapons and fight scenes, snakes, objects identified as medi-

A petroglyph image from the Coso Range showing a shaman, his body filled with entoptic imagery. *(David S. Whitley, 1994)*

cine bags, and a large element of geometric patterns "representing 'entoptic designs,' the patterns experienced cross-culturally during altered states of consciousness."[37] Indeed, the telltale form constants have been identified in the Coso images.

Whitley notes that although "not widely recognized as such, there are numerous ethnographic references to rock art production in the western Great Basin." This provides "a clear and coherent indication of the creators of the art. . . . However, rock-art researchers (and some ethnographers) have overlooked these references or have undertaken only a superficial examination."[38] There have been simplistic and erroneous interpretations that the art has to do with "hunting magic," but Whitley has conclusively demonstrated that it derives from shamanic experiences, and that the artists were shamans and shaman-initiates.

The engravings were produced following visionary episodes experienced during vision quests. It seems that altered states in the shamanism of the western Great Basin were also aided by the ingestion of psychoactive plants, such as jimson weed (*Datura stramonium*), and the use of tobacco.[39] These vision quests, undertaken at locations thought to be especially strong in *poha*, or supernatural power, were considered perilous. "The distribution of engraving sites, then," Whitley observes, "corresponds to the perceived distribution of *poha* across the landscape, which was correlated with high peaks, rocks and caves, and permanent water sources."[40] The Coso mountain range was considered to be the place where humans were created in mythic times, and was therefore a potent region of power itself. Such a place was known as *pohakanhi*, "house of power," and shamans and shamanic initiates entered the supernatural world at these locales to acquire *poha*. *Poha* could manifest itself as objects of power for shamans' medicine bags or bundles, as special songs, and as the appearance of spirit helpers. Certain places yielded special-ized kinds of *poha*, including a generalized curing power. The shaman was a *pohagunt*, meaning a "man of power" (also translated as "a man who writes," meaning a man who writes on rocks). Spirit helpers in the west-ern Great Basin were traditionally known as "water babies" or "rock ba-bies," reported as elements in jimson weed trances, and "ethnographic informants consistently and unanimously referred to rock art as made by shamans' spirit helpers."[41] Dreaming, shaman and spirit helper were so linked as to become effectively a single dynamic entity.

Whitley's impressive study has revealed much about the meaning of the rock art. "Rattlesnake shamans" who could cure snakebites saw rat-tlesnakes in their visions or dreams, and engraved images of snakes on the rocks. "Bulletproof shamans," previously "arrowproof shamans," saw battle scenes, weapons, and fighting. There were also "horse-cure shamans" whose spirit helpers were horses. Ultimately the Coso Range was the center for rainmaking shamanism, and the last living Numic rain shaman traveled specifically to those mountains to make rain.[42] The mountain sheep, so prevalent an image in Coso rock art, was the spirit animal of the rain shaman. While wooden bull-roarers were considered to be little more than toys, serious rainmaking bull-roarers were fashioned from mountain-sheep horns. A "mountain sheep singer" or rain shaman would dream of "rain, a bull-roarer and a quail tufted cap of mountain-sheep hide." Figures displaying such ritual objects, obtained during vision quests, feature in the rock engravings. To increase his power, a rain shaman would hang a thong of mountain-sheep hide wrapped in eagle down from his belt or staff. The shaman's dream of a mountain sheep had to have special char-acteristics. It was believed that rain fell when a mountain sheep was killed, so a dream of killing a mountain sheep gave power—it was a metaphor for the acquisition and application of a particular type of power, namely, weather control.

The Chumash Indians who once occupied the Santa Barbara coastal region of Southern California also produced rock art of an un-doubtedly shamanic nature. It contains animal and human images, unidentifiable anthropomorphs and zoomorphs, therianthropes, fish, insects, and handprints, together with entoptic-style form-constant im-

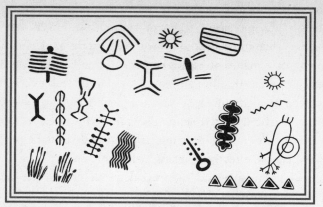

Some examples of the abstract motifs in Chumash rock paintings. *(From* The Rock Paintings of the Chumash, *by Campbell Grant. Published by the University of California Press, 1965.)*

agery—a bewildering array of lozenges, grids, cobwebs, zigzags, dots and circles, wheels, chevrons, ladders, parallel lines, checkerboards, comets, stars, diamonds, pinwheels, sunbursts, triangles, and so forth. Chumash paintings occupy hundreds of sandstone caves and rock shelters, ranging in size from a few feet to over forty feet in length. Techniques varied from simple line drawings in red to complex six-color designs. In some cases, a single rock has hundreds of designs on it. Sites were always near permanent water sources, in the mountains. Pigments came from a variety of sources, as did the Bushman pigments, mixed with animal and vegetable oils, juice of milkweed, egg white, and other binders. Paints were applied by brush (probably frayed yucca fiber among other material), by finger, or by sharpened stick. Sometimes a lump of hematite was used to draw on the stone. There are only a limited number of engravings or petroglyphs showing animal (particularly bear) tracks, or entopticlike grids formed by grooves and pecked holes. There are a few zoomorphic engravings. What ethnography has been gleaned about the rock art indicates that, as with the Numic peoples of the Cosos, the act of producing art at a location enhanced the power of that place. Such places were supernatural power points known as *Trip'-ne*. It is thought that many of the paintings were done within the last one thousand years, and that the practice was continued into historical times.

"It seems likely that most of the abstract paintings in the Chumash country are visualizations of supernatural beings or forces to be used ceremonially in much the same manner as the Navajo sand figures," Campbell Grant wrote in 1965. "Many of their pictures certainly represented things that existed only in the mind of the painter. Others were regional and stylistic formulas to represent objects, creatures, and phenomena known to the shamans of the area. In the western states, there are doubtless some rock pictures that record events, but this does not seem to be true of the southern California abstract pictographs."[43] Grant was writing before the neuropsychological understanding of such imagery was available, but he clearly had the measure of the matter even then. "It seems certain that most of them [the paintings] were painted by the shamans," Grant asserted.[44] As with the Coso Indians, the Chumash had different kinds of shamans. Their main function, of course, was the curing of disease, but there were rattlesnake shamans, bear shamans, and the rain shamans. Bull-roarers were found in caves in the Santa Barbara area. In Bowers Cave, four were found with feathered bands, stone-tipped ceremonial wands, and Chumash-style baskets. Chumash shamanism was associated with the ritual drinking of the powerfully hallucinogenic datura. The link between the rock art and this hallucinogen was originally made in 1925 by A. L. Kroeber. The Indians ground up the dried roots of the plant and mixed it with hot water. Ceremonial bowls and pestles used by the Chumash for datura have survived to this day.

One type of Chumash shaman was an astronomer-priest known as an 'alchuklash, who was responsible for maintaining the ceremonial calendar. He also acted like an astrologer and issued names for newborn children that related to the celestial configurations presiding at the times of their births. The 'alchuklash also administered jimson weed to boys at their puberty rites. At the midwinter solstice, the 'alchuklash would himself take jimsonweed in order to foresee the outcome of the gambling game between Sun and Sky Coyote (Polaris, the polestar), as the solstice was a critical time in the Chumash calendar. The astronomer-shaman would perform a (probably) solitary vigil, often in the caves and locales where rock art is now to be found. We can picture him, then, sitting in the darkness of the mountain recesses, experiencing his visions and perhaps singing or chanting, awaiting the first rays of the midwinter rising sun. Astronomer E. C. Krupp witnessed this astronomical event at a Chumash painted rock panel at Burro Flats in the Simi Hills just beyond the northeast corner of the San Fernando Valley, where a slot in an overhanging ledge was thought to provide an opening for the rays of the rising winter solstice sun. He reported:

> As our vigil began, the dawn grew brighter. The upper ledges caught the sun, and a golden sheet of light gradually edged down the ridge. At about 7:35 A.M., Pacific Standard Time, the first direct sunlight fell upon the "window" and produced a momentary image of a bright white triangle of light. It cut across a set of five concentric rings, painted in white, and pointed towards their shared center. This brief impression of a triangle was followed by the full silhouette of the opening. It looked like a spike, its sharp tip cocked to the left and towards the center of the rings. . . . Later observation confirmed that the same effect can be seen each morning for about a week before and a week after the winter solstice. During the rest of the year, however, the sun rises too far north and passes too high to illuminate any of the pictographs.[45]

A finger of winter solstice sunlight reaching in to touch the Chumash paintings on the wall of the Burro Flats rock shelter, California. (E. C. Krupp)

We can only imagine the impact of the rays of sunlight penetrating the shaman's dark and powerful place of vigil, its brilliant light searing and dazzling his hallucinogenically sensitized eyes. Interestingly, the image of the sunbeam is one of the widespread traditional metaphorical means for a shaman's soul to leave the body and ascend heavenward. We cannot know what visions were generated by such an event, but we can be sure that the rock art imagery we find at places like Burro Flats depicts the psychedelic mental patterns that were part of them.

There can be little doubt that the zigzags, dots, grids, lattices, chevrons, and other elements in North Native American rock art in general, principally in western and southwestern locations in the United States, relate to entoptic experience in trance states, and that most of such rock art belongs to shamanic traditions. In his guide to the rock art of the greater Southwest, Alex Patterson identifies imagery at a wide variety of sites in Mexico, New Mexico, Arizona, and California as entoptic, singling out those specifically resulting from jimson weed intoxication.[46] They can be seen by any visitor to rock art sites in such regions. For instance, Boca Negro Canyon, better known now as Petroglyph National Monument, is a volcanic escarpment on Albuquerque's West Mesa. This site is within the domain of Pueblo peoples, such as the Zuni, who are known to have used jimson weed, and is home to at least fifteen thousand

A pre-Columbian Indian rock marking at Boca Negro Canyon, Albuquerque, New Mexico. This is a classic "construal-iconic" zigzag entoptic pattern perceived as a snake or serpent. *(Paul Devereux)*

prehistoric petroglyphs. It is certainly one of the main rock art sites in the country. Humans, animals, birds, plants, and weird therianthropes are depicted there, as are shamanic and ceremonial images of masked figures. The visitor will glimpse spirals, zigzags, or construal images such as wriggling snakes flickering along the edge of a rock face or boulder. On the top of the escarpment is a curious cleared area surrounded by a low wall made of small rocks laid out in a horseshoe configuration opening toward the sacred Sandia Mountains, dramatically visible to the east. The authorities are puzzled by the nature and purpose of this site. Some believe it was used for vision questing—such "dreaming beds" have been found within view of numerous Indian sacred peaks in North America. Some are very ancient, and others still seem to be in use.

Rock paintings are found in over forty rock shelters in the Pecos River region of Texas and the adjacent portion of the Mexican state of Coahuila. The dominant image is of large, stylized human figures, some headless, that have elongated bodies that taper off to short straight legs. Some of the figures wear horned, antlered, or feathered headdresses. They are sometimes accompanied by what appear to be cultic regalia, smaller humanoid figures and animals, especially deer. In 1958, T. Campbell suggested that these images show shamans "engaged in mescal bean cult activities," a theory supported by Klaus Wellman in 1978.[47] We saw in the previous chapter that extremely ancient deposits of mescal bean (*Sophora secundiflora*), as well as peyote, had been found in a number of caves or shelters in this region. One site near Comstock, Texas, also contained red pigment, the main color used in the paintings.

The legacy of ancient hallucinogen-usage is not confined to rock art: it can be found in Native American decorative art as well. The best of many examples is the art of the Mexican Huichol Indians, whose religion centers on the use of the hallucinogenic peyote cactus. Susan Eger has observed that the colorful, symmetrical imagery in Huichol embroidery and yarn paintings "reflects the omnipresence of peyote."[48] Ronald Siegel accompanied the Huichol on their 1972 peyote pilgrimage and learned that the imagery the Indians saw in their peyote visions "was virtually identical to the symmetrical and repeating patterns used in Huichol embroidery and weaving."[49]

In South America, the San Pedro cactus (*Trichocereus pachanoi*), containing mescaline, is found depicted on ancient vases and tapestries in conjunction with shamanic power animals such as jaguars.[50] It is in South America too where the most detailed anthropological study conclusively linking hallucinogens, entoptic patterns, and decorative art in living tribal societies was conducted, by Gerardo Reichel-Dolmatoff. In the 1970s he reported on his studies with the Tukano Indians of the Colombian Amazon. These people take a number of hallucinogens related to their ritual life, which is closely tied to their everyday existence. In particular, they use the "soul vine," of the genus *Banisteriopsis*. Mixed with other plant substances, the drug is prepared from the bark of the vine and is usually infused to form a beverage or a finely powdered snuff, and is known by numerous names throughout Amazonia. This hallucinogenic infusion plays an important part in the Tukano collective rituals, in which they see spirits, visions, and mythical beings important to the history and spiritual life of the tribe—indeed, to its entire cosmology—and is also used for divination and healing practices.

Describing the experience of *Banisteriopsis* intoxication, Reichel-Dolmatoff refers to an often reported initial period of vertigo, accompanied by nausea and vomiting. After a while, vividly colored visions will appear, frequently containing images of felines and reptiles. There can be threatening monsters, aggressive people, and other disturbing scenes, accompanied by feelings of considerable anxiety. But Reichel-Dolmatoff notes that the individual can also find himself or herself "flying on the winds, visiting far-off places, or communicating with divine beings, dead relatives, or shamans of neighboring groups."[51] He goes on to summarize what the Indians themselves told him about their perceptions of the *Banisteriopsis* trip:

> According to the Indians, there exist essentially three stages of *Banisteriopsis* intoxication. Shortly after the ingestion of the drug, after an initial tremor and the sensation of rushing winds, harmaline produces a state of drowsiness during which the person concentrates with half-closed eyes upon the luminous flashes and streaks which appear before him. This first stage is characterized by the appearance

of small, star-shaped or flower-shaped elements which flicker and
float brilliantly against a dark background, in repetitive kaleidoscopic
patterns. There is a marked bilateral symmetry to these luminous perceptions which sometimes appear as clusters of fruits or feathery
leaves. Grid patterns, zigzag lines and undulating lines alternate with
eye-shaped motifs, many-colored concentric circles or endless chains
of brilliant dots. . . . The person watches passively these innumerable
scintillating patterns. . . . After a while the symmetry and the overall
geometrical aspect of these perceptions disappears and the second
stage sets in. Now figurative, pictorial images take shape; large blots
of color will be seen moving like thunderclouds and from them will
emerge diffuse shapes looking like people or animals, or unknown
creatures. The Indians interpret these images as mythological . . .
which to them bear witness to the essential truth of their religious
beliefs. In a third stage, all these images disappear. There will be soft
music and wandering clouds, a state of blissful serenity.

While the second stage obviously marks the onset of hallucinations, the first stage is a trance-like state during which the person, while not divorced from reality, visualizes elements that appear
in external objective space as geometrical patterns . . . which cannot be designated as true hallucinations. The Indians themselves
recognize quite clearly that this is . . . quite different from the
emotion-charged images of the second stage.

. . . It should be kept in mind here that the sphere of hallucinations is one of subjective interpretations in which the person projects a set of pre-established, stored material upon the wavering
screen of shapes and colors.[52]

We can see that this hallucinatory progression closely resembles the
three-stage model of David Lewis-Williams and Thomas Dowson, a fact
the South African researchers themselves draw attention to, remarking
that their stages one to three conform to Turkano's stages one and two.

Reichel-Dolmatoff underscored the fact that the entoptic images
are form constants common to all human beings, irrespective of culture, as they are a neurophysiological product. He asked a group of

nonacculturated Tukano men, all experienced *Banisteriopsis* takers, to draw the visual images they perceived under the hallucinogen's influence, and gave them sheets of paper and a choice of twelve colored pencils. The Indians enjoyed the task, but because of their highly sophisticated sense of color, they complained that the choice of colored pencils was inadequate. Some of these drawings represented entoptic images, which the Tukano clearly distinguished from the figurative hallucinations. Reichel-Dolmatoff isolated and numbered each of the basic entoptic images the Indians had drawn, and found that there were "twenty well-defined design motifs." These he checked against the fifteen universal phosphene motifs obtained by Max Knoll in his electrically induced phosphene experiments and found a good match—"too close to be mere coincidence." Reichel-Dolmatoff discovered that each of the images had a meaning for the Tukano, revolving around sexual themes—patterns represented the uterus, the male organ, the female organ, drops of semen, and so forth. Some of the other designs were associated with concepts surrounding incest and social groupings. In essence, the entoptic imagery provided a codification that brought the threat of incest and the necessary laws of exogamy to the regular attention of members of Tukano groups.

Crucially, he further found that this code was "extended beyond the narrow confines of individual trance and is applied to the wider physical environment of everyday life." This was because the Tukano used the entoptic patterns seen under *Banisteriopsis* influence as the basis for their decorative art. "Practically all decorative elements that adorn the objects manufactured by the Tukano are said by them to be derived from the photic sensations perceived under the influence of the drug; that is, are based on phosphenes."[53]

So the entire art style of the Tukano is based on hallucinogenic imagery, and the message it carries is to urge the Indians to practice exogamy.

The most outstanding examples of Tukano psychedelic art are the paintings found on the flattened bark walls at the front of their longhouses. When the Colombian anthropologist asked about the longhouse imagery, the Indians merely replied that it represented what they saw when they drank *yagé*. The same geometric motifs also find a place in the decorative work on ritual bark-cloth aprons and masks, and on the large stamping tubes, gourd rattles, and large drums used in ceremonial dances. Older Tukano assured Reichel-Dolmatoff that the imagery also adorned many ceramic vessels in the past, though now the Tukano rarely produce pottery. "The ritual vessel in which the narcotic beverage is prepared is always adorned with painted designs," the anthropologist noticed, "generally in red, yellow and white, showing wavy lines, rows of dots, or a series of rainbow-shaped patterns."

During his ethnographic fieldwork with the Tukano, Reichel-Dolmatoff realized that they frequently experienced "flashbacks" or afterimages of the entoptic/phosphene imagery after they returned to normal consciousness, a phenomenon noted by Western researchers from the time of Klüver onward. The patterns could repeat themselves in this manner for up to six months, within which period the individual would have taken part in further *Banisteriopsis* sessions so the "afterimages are likely to persist in a latent, chronic state." It seems that the Indians are able to engineer environmental cues and make use of bodily and emotional states to encourage and enhance the occurrence of entoptic phenomena. During these flashback periods, they see the physical world overlaid with entoptic geometry, and it has been experimentally confirmed that when seen in this combination such patterns can take on a more definite form. Reichel-Dolmatoff was able to photograph Indians tracing out entoptic geometry on the sand.

Musing generally about the origins of native art in drug-induced experience, Reichel-Dolmatoff noted that the Chocó Indians, separated from the Tukano by over a thousand kilometers, have developed a similar "entoptic" art style, and that they too take *Banisteriopsis*. "It would not be difficult to find parallels to phosphene-derived design motifs in prehistoric artifacts, such as the decoration of ceramics, or petroglyphs and pictographs," the anthropologist concluded. "The pottery of a prehistoric burial cave in northern Colombia, associated with snuff tablets and bone containers suggesting the use of narcotic snuff, is decorated with designs clearly comparable to the Knoll-Tukano series."[54]

Ethnobotanists Richard Evans Schultes and Robert F. Raffauf note ancient rocks in the general Amazonian region of the Tukano group that contain images of winged beings. These "may be the result of the experiences of ancient Indians who made the engravings—experiences of flying though the air, a very frequent initial symptom of intoxication with hallucinogens."[55]

STONE AGE PSYCHEDELIC ART

Returning to where we started out at the beginning of this chapter, we can now see why the crazy carvings adorning the walls of Gavrinis have come to be seen by some archaeologists as the psychedelic signatures of Neolithic people in altered states.[56] Mark Patton notes a range of forms in the wall art at Gavrinis—which include specific images such as wheels, or sun images, as well as "grid patterns, zig-zags, concentric right angles and semi-circles and chevrons"—that are "very close to patterns recorded by Lewis-Williams and Dowson in neurophysiological experiments, and in ethnographically documented rock art in Africa and North America."[57] He further observes that this geometrical artwork is a profound switch from the earlier, clearly representational rock art that survives on the opposite side of the Gavrinis capstone and elsewhere in Armorica, indicating that some strong socioreligious change rippled through the people of the region during which these passage grave monuments were built.

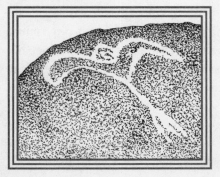

One example of a petroglyph of a winged being on rocks in Tukano country. *(Author's drawing after a photograph in Schultes and Rauffauf, 1992)*

In 1989, British archaeologist Richard Bradley pointed out that motifs that may well be entoptically based form constants are to be found in rock carvings at numerous Neolithic sites in Europe in addition to Gavrinis.[58] After discussing the Breton sites, he turns his attention to the great chambered mounds of Newgrange, Knowth, and Dowth in the Boyne Valley in Ireland, and the chambered monuments and artifacts of

Orkney, off Scotland's northern coast. The Irish motifs are even more geometric than the ones in Brittany, with greater emphasis on circles and spirals. While there is a definite relationship between some of the rock carvings and the movement of sunlight and shadow at astrologically significant times of the year,[59,60] this does not rule out their origination in trance imagery effects (any more than it did for the patterns on the walls of the Chumash shaman's midwinter sunbeam rock shelter). Bradley goes on to mention the Orkney sites, where two distinct traditions probably existed side by side, each with its own art and architectural styles and portable objects. Of these, Bradley singles out Grooved Ware pottery, which is characterized by entoptic-style decorative markings. (Indeed, a researcher named Pokorny has compared the geometric decoration from several Neolithic artifacts with mescaline-induced form constants and entoptic phenomena and found clear similarities.) Between 3000 and 2400 B.C., this distinctive style of pottery spread through Scotland and southward as far as southern England, many hundreds of miles away. Because it is found primarily in ceremonial contexts, it could be that it was associated with "ritual specialists," as Bradley puts it. We can envisage a hallucinogen-based shamanic cult focused around monuments such as the Boyne Valley group and certain ones of the Orkney sites, spreading through the British Isles.

Lewis-Williams and Dowson support the theory that the Neolithic tomb art of western Europe contains entoptic imagery. In the megalithic markings they note the use of reduplicated motifs, which recall the endless, moving repetition of geometric elements and images seen under trance (a phenomenon called *polyopia*), and other elements that can be seen as representations of the visual mechanics experienced under trance. They observe that "naturalistic" images, such as the axhead engravings at Gavrinis, are embedded in thick clusters of "contour lines," suggesting entoptic phenomena surrounding real images perceived in altered states. In a similar manner, human figures are seen covered or surrounded by zigzag and wavy lines, dots, and flecks in Bushman art. Developing the arguments of Bradley and Patton, they argue that access to altered states of consciousness became a more political, controlled activity in Neolithic Europe than it had been earlier, in the Mesolithic (Middle Stone Age) and Paleolithic eras. They speculate that there was a shift from the general shamanic experiences in the deep

A nineteenth-century engraving of rock-art carvings inside Cairn T, Loughcrew, Ireland, showing motifs typical of Neolithic Irish rock art.

caves of the older eras to the use of altered states specifically to access the spirits of the ancestors. Perhaps this access was used as a way to control lineages—to legitimate dynasties. Limited numbers of people would be allowed into the chambered tombs. These were built by humans (unlike the caves used for rituals in earlier ages), and were closer to everyday human life than the deep cave sanctuaries of the Paleolithic had been. Rock art displaying entoptic imagery from the different stages of trance appears in different parts of some of the more complex monuments, suggesting that there may have been a "geography" of trance levels within such monuments. This might reflect hierarchical control over access to the ultimate mysteries—contact with the ancestral sources of supernatural power. Only the elite could enter the inner sanctum and "converse" with the ancestral spirits in the spirit realms.

Lewis-Williams and Dowson also liken the structure of the chambered mounds, entered along a passageway, to the key entoptic phenomenon of the "tunnel," the experience of which marks entry to deep trance and the out-of-body experience:

> The act of placing a body in a chambered tomb recalls laboratory subjects' reports on mental imagery's being related to a tunnel-like perspective. . . . One subject puts it like this: "Images tend to pulsate, moving toward the center of the tunnel or away from the bright light and sometimes moving in both directions." . . . As subjects move deeper into trance, the rotating tunnel seems to surround them. . . . The sides of this vortex may be marked by a lattice of squares like television screens; the images on these "screens" are the

Some researchers suggest that the entrance passage of Neolithic passage tombs may have been designed to imitate the tunnel entoptic pattern reported in modern themes as part of the "near-death" and "out-of-body" experience. Here, we are looking into the entrance passage of Gavrinis. *(Paul Devereux)*

first spontaneously produced stage 3 hallucinations. . . . The parallels between this experience and looking along a chambered tomb when there is a light in the distance are close. When new human remains were placed in a tomb, they and those who bore them were entering a human-made replica of the spiritual, or hallucinatory, world, with its darkness, engulfing vortex, and mental imagery. The geometric motifs and the tombs themselves may well have been designed, in part, to recreate the tunnel experience, and physical entry into the dark passages may have been seen as parallel, perhaps even equivalent, to psychic entry into the spirit world via the mediating vortex.[61]

The trance states could have been produced by nondrug techniques, but in the light of the Er Lannic braziers described in Chapter 1, the use of hallucinogens is probable. This matter has begun to be understood through the innovative work of Jeremy Dronfield, an archaeological researcher at Cambridge University. He notes that cannabis may possibly have been available to Neolithic Britons. Ergot is also a distinct possibility, while psilocybe-containing hallucinogenic mushrooms would almost certainly have been available in the British Isles five and six thousand years ago—as they are now. Dronfield also reports that seeds and pollen of psychoactive henbane (*Hyoscyamus niger*) were found in an encrusted deposit on shards of Grooved Ware at a megalithic ceremonial complex at Balfarg, in Fife, Scotland. As henbane is not found at this latitude, it must have been deliberately imported. This, of course, supports Bradley's suspicions about Grooved Ware and also Sherratt's observations.

Dronfield conducted highly detailed and sophisticated diagnostic analyses of pattern shapes in the rock art of twelve Irish passage tombs, including Newgrange, Knowth, Dowth, and the several Neolithic cairns at Loughcrew, comparing them with those drawn by both modern Westerners and traditional people experiencing entoptic imagery while under the influence of hallucinogens. Dronfield was careful to select results from hallucinogens that could have been available to the megalith builders, or which, like psilocybin, produce similar neurophysiological effects. He was able to distinguish the results from different hallucinogens. Dronfield went further and included entoptic patterns drawn by modern Western subjects as a result of controlled electrical stimulation of the eyes. This method creates a consistent and prolonged flickering effect closely mimicking the effect obtained by facing a powerful light source such as the sun with eyes closed, and clapping hands or waving fingers between the eyelids and the light source. This "strobing" effect can induce trance and produce entoptic pattern characteristics different from those caused by drugs.

Dronfield also considered types of entoptic imagery produced in pathological conditions such as migraine and forms of epilepsy. All these were compared with a randomly generated control sample of patterns. As expected, this scientific analysis showed no significant matching between Neolithic tomb art and the random control set, and cannabis imagery did not match either. Interestingly, there *was* matching in some sites with entoptic imagery produced by migraine and epilepsy. As these conditions tend to occur in genetically related groups, especially in the maternal line, Dronfield argues that such conditions, seen as disabilities by our culture, might have been an element—perhaps a prized ability—in a shamanistic society. The hallucinogens such as psilocybin, and those that act like it, showed correlations with the megalithic art in about half of the sites in the test sample. But the most prevailing correlation was between the rock art and light flicker (electrical stimulation) entoptics. This of course has great significance, as all the chambered mounds were astronomically oriented and had searchlightlike beams of sunlight directed down their passages at key calendrical moments in the year. Overall, Dronfield concluded that hallucinogenic mushrooms, light flicker, and pathologically based methods of mind change were all employed at these Neolithic sites. Some sites, such as Knowth, Newgrange, and Cairn L at Loughcrew include rock art exhibiting all three types of imagery, but the other sites show matching with only one or two entoptic sources.[62]

"This clinches the debate," Andrew Sherratt states.[63]

Dronfield intends to extend his research to the study of decorated monuments all across Europe, that evidence might be found of drug use across the whole continent. We are at the dawn of an extremely sophisticated approach to decoding megalithic rock art, turning it into a written record of trance states across the ages.

LET THE SUN SHINE IN

It is worth considering that studying the Chumash astronomer-shaman could help us understand activity at some of Europe's Neolithic ceremonial chambered mounds. As a classic example, Newgrange is known to have had astronomical functions, though probably within a ceremonial, rather than scientific, context. Above the entrance to the sixty-two-foot-long passage into the great mound is a rectangular opening known as the "roof-box," the top lintel of which is carved with lozenge patterns. As the winter solstice sun rises, a pencil-beam of direct sunlight is directed through this roof-box and down the passage, the floor of which rises as it meets the twenty-foot-high corbeled chamber near the heart of the mound. The solstitial sunbeam moves as a circle of light along the passage, then opens into a "fan" of light as it cuts across the chamber floor and hits the end wall. For several minutes it makes the whole interior glow with a remarkable golden light. A wide range of lozenges, spirals, triple spirals, and other form constants are engraved on stones in the passages and within the chamber. Outside, there is an entrance stone in front of the passage entrance that is richly carved with similar patterns, as are three of the mound's exterior kerbstones to the mound. Are these markings the equiva-

Entrance to Newgrange. Note rock art on entrance stone. There are also rock art motifs on the upper edge of the "lightbox" above passage entrance. This aperture lets a laser-like beam of the midwinter rising sun into the inner chamber of the great mound. *(Paul Devereux)*

lent of those in the Chumash shaman's cave? Did an astronomically connected, ritualized vigil of mythic significance take place here, where the ancient Lords of Light are said to have dwelled? Did some Neolithic shaman-or shamanic elite take a mind-altering infusion and sit within the inky blackness of the awesome chamber, perhaps among the ancestral bones, intoning deep chants until the very walls reverberated, waiting to receive the ecstatic golden blast of soul-searing solar light at the dark turning of the year?

We may never know for certain, but the evidence leads to interesting speculation. The structure was clearly related to midwinter solar astronomy, and the entoptic-style rock art there does speak of altered mind states. In 1994, Robert G. Jahn and I conducted acoustical tests within the chamber. These tests showed that the resonant frequency of the Newgrange chamber was 110 Hz (cycles per second), well within the male vocal range.[64,65,66] Chanting at the resonant frequency of the chamber might itself "drive" the brain and help induce trance states. Inside the chamber great shallow bowls were found. If these had contained water in which hot stones were placed, as some have suggested, clouds of steam would be produced, creating a "sweat lodge." (There is evidence of this kind of practice in prehistoric Ireland and the British Isles.) Not only is such an intense environment traditionally a part of ritualized mind change, but the droplets of moisture would probably vibrate with the resonant chanting or singing within the chamber. The solstitial sunbeam would also cut a vivid shaft of light through the steam, revealing shifting light and dark patterns affected by relating to the vibrations of the sound. These visual sound patterns would be similar to the sort of rock art motifs we find at Newgrange. The acoustically driven steam patterns would probably also enhance eyes-open entoptic visions, and—a particularly intriguing possibility—they could have assisted the "flicker" mechanism in the sunlight which Dronfield has found. In this admittedly hypothetical scenario we witness the combination of at least five mind-altering techniques: the use of a hallucinogen (be it psilocybin mushrooms, an ergot derivative, or henbane) taken at the start of a long initial period of sensory deprivation in the silent blackness of the chamber, followed by prolonged resonant chanting prior to the creation of a steam atmosphere, culminating in powerful flickering light, all within the strong, mythic set and setting of a solstice.

CAVES OF INITIATION

That the trance element, or perhaps basis, of Neolithic religion, and its expression in sacred art, is becoming increasingly certain shouldn't surprise us, for, as remote in time as the Neolithic period is from us today, we can glimpse evidence of trance states in the art of the Paleolithic era, which is many thousands of years older still. Having studied Bushman rock art, David Lewis-Williams and Thomas Dowson looked at the painted Paleolithic caves of France and Spain, such as Les Trois Frères, Niaux, La Mouthe, Lascaux, and Altamira, among others. Most of us are familiar with the remarkable animal depictions in these caves, but Lewis-Williams and Dowson point out that "dots, zigzags, and grids, for instance, are ubiquitous throughout the Upper Palaeolithic. The accurately delineated animals of Bushman art show that realism is not incompatible with the imagery of altered states," they add.[67] Earlier ideas of "sympathetic hunting magic" and other simplistic notions and modern projections are now on the wane. "The neuropsychological model orders and fits Upper Palaeolithic art as well as it does San art," David Lewis-Williams explains.[68] It is certainly the case that when one studies the recurrent "signs" in Upper Paleolithic art as assembled by André Leroi-Gourhan,[69] one of the great scholars of cave art archaeology, it is not difficult to pick out numerous entoptic form constants, excluding "the very numerous zigzags, flecks, filigrees, and festoons," as the South African researchers indicate.[70] There is a scatter of form constant imagery on the cave walls, and sometimes the representational imagery also displays entoptic nuances, such as the exaggeratedly curved ibex horns with a zigzag outer margin at Niaux, or the tusks of mammoths depicted in Rouffignac, which form nested curves. In addition to the imagery emblazoned on the cave walls themselves, mobile Paleolithic art such as engraved stones, tusks, and bones displays a bewildering array of zizags, lozenges, cross-hatched grids, chevrons, and other repeated forms. Alexander Marshack has argued convincingly that some of these were notations for lunar calendrical purposes,[71] but this use does not contest the origins of the forms, nor can all the engraved items be lunar calendars. Lewis-Williams and Dowson have pointed to examples of entoptic imagery engraved on bones that are even older than the Upper Paleolithic. The earlier art seems to be primarily geometric, with more construal and iconic imagery appearing gradually on later artifacts.[72]

We can be certain of the shamanic origins of Bushman and Coso rock art, less so with Paleolithic art. But both the content and the context of the rock art suggest such origins. First, the rock art contains clear examples of both shamanic imagery and shamans themselves. A famous example of the former is the so-called sorcerer in the cave of Les Trois Frères, who dominates a cramped cavern deep beneath the earth, staring out of the rock wall. It is a classic therianthrope. The body is of some unknown large animal, possibly a deer; the lower part of the back legs are human, the tail is that of a wolf or fox, the front legs have hands, the face seems birdlike with a mix of vaguely human characteristics, and there are deer's antlers on the head. Elements of the image could refer to some kind of supernatural power of

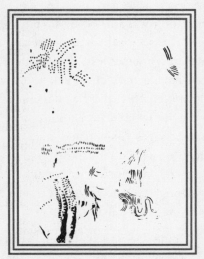

Details from the Paleolithic rock art panels in the Llonin Cave, Panamellera Alta, northern Spain, showing entopticlike abstract motifs. *(After Magin Berenguer, Prehistoric Cave Art in Northern Spain Asturias, published by Frente De Afirmacion Hispanista A.C. Mexico)*

The "sorcerer" from the cave of Les Trois Frères. *(Henri Breuil)*

sight. Another therianthrope is on a panel nearby. Indeed, animals with human hind legs, or hooves on human figures, are not uncommon elsewhere in cave art. Lascaux contains the picture of an entranced shaman wearing a bird mask in a supine position. His penis is erect, perhaps suggesting that he is dreaming (erections and increased vaginal blood flow occur in REM or dreaming sleep) or in trance. Nearby is the depiction of a bird-headed stick. This type of artifact was symbolic of shamanism in Eurasia even up to recent centuries.[73]

The location of rock art—often in pitch-black caves—is also ideal for experiencing altered states of consciousness. Deep within subterranean natural rock chambers (which the much later Neolithic chambered mounds may well have been mimicking) at the end of labyrinthine passages, illuminated only by flickering torches, or in utter darkness and silence—these are unsurpassed as conditions for sensory deprivation and profound experiences by well-prepared initiates.

Entranced shaman with bird mask and bird-headed stick in painted panel at Lascaux.

It is almost as if the whirl of altered states of consciousness became somehow affixed to the rock walls of the painted caves of western Europe.

A PATTERN OF POSSIBILITIES

It is clear that the pervasiveness of ecstatic trance and hallucinogenic consciousness in antiquity is recorded on the walls of monuments, caves, rock surfaces, and tribal buildings in many locations around the world. This rock art describes and represents an overlooked legacy.

Rock art of places other than western Europe, southern Africa, and the Americas awaits study. For instance, the rock art of the Kimberley (a remote region of Western Australia), thought to date back tens of thousands of years, has yet to be analyzed from an entoptic point of view. Finding myself in this simmering, brickred wilderness on other business in 1995, I inspected one of the painted rock shelters we happened to pass. At first glance, there was nothing particularly suggestive of trance imagery, other than the strange otherworldly painted figures, which included the famous round-headed Aboriginal spirit beings called *Wondjina*. I could see no sign of entoptic markings, at first. Then I noticed a boulder at the entrance to the rock shelter that was covered in a regular grid of pecked dots. It was easily overlooked because the whole petroglyphic panel was a dark chocolate brown due to thick deposits of desert varnish, indicating the profound antiquity of the markings.

Extremely ancient pecked rocks at the entrance to an Aborigine rock shelter containing rock paintings. The Kimberley, Australia. *(Paul Devereux)*

In 1996, archaeologists found carved circular markings on rocks in the same area, and tentative dating suggests a possible age of 70,000 years. If this turns out to be correct, then not only will Aboriginal rock art in the Kimberley become the earliest known human art, but whole migration patterns of early human beings will have to be reappraised. It is possible that the pecked markings shown here are of a similar exceptional age. Were the very first markings of humanity entoptic patterns?

Other hallucination-derived imagery is much closer at hand. We noted earlier this chapter that the vessels used for hallucinogenic infusion by the Tukano were decorated with entoptic patterns. This seems to be the case for the braziers and other Neolithic ceramic artifacts discussed in Chapter 1 as well. And we have heard the ideas concerning the markings on the mysterious Grooved Ware pottery. Gordon Wasson also drew attention to *grecas* or "frets," abstract, meandertype designs that can be angular, curvilinear, or serpentine, usually repeated in bands or strips as decorative borders. This type of pattern got its name because it is characteristic of the painted pottery of ancient Greece, dating to the Archaic period, which ended around 620 B.C. Wasson particularly noted the marvelous fret designs that grace a superb amphora found at Eleusis, the temple of the Mysteries in ancient Greece where hallucinogenic drinks were almost certainly drunk. Wasson considered these type of designs to be formalized versions of entoptic images encountered in hallucinogenic trance. "I can hardly believe that, of all people, it falls to me to draw attention to the inspiration for these frets, these *grecas*," he wrote with a hint of exasperation.[74]

We have also noted the psychedelic content of woven art such as that of the Huichol Indians. Andrew Sherratt has theorized that hallucinogenic entoptic imagery is reflected "in the geometric designs of traditional Persian and central Asian carpets" and that the sensations of flying produced by many hallucinogens may have been the source of the idea of the "flying carpet."[75] It is a fascinating chicken-and-egg question: Did the marvelous "tapestries" so often reported in entoptic and construal stages of trance visions come from memories of carpets and textiles seen, or did hallucinogenic "tapestries" provide the original inspiration for such artwork? R. Fischer has similarly speculated that "both the rose windows of Gothic cathedrals and the mandalas of Tantric religions are ritualized hallucinatory form constants."[76] Stained-glass windows and mandalas are, again, images frequently used when people describe geometrically based visions in hallucinogenic sessions. It is possible that these most august forms of decorative, architectural, and religious imagery come from the depths of all our cultures, and speak to us of altered consciousness. Psychedelia probably underpins our most treasured religious iconography.

five

The Long and Not-So-Winding Road

Did Archaic Ecstacy Leave Its Mark on the Land?

There is one more place to look for imagery that resulted from or was useful in the altered state. This imagery is drawn in bold strokes on the land itself. In numerous locations there are dramatic remains of mysterious old straight tracks, roads, and ground markings. As we shall see, these are trance-inspired trails, and are principally found in the Americas.

THE LINEAR ENIGMA

I began to explore this subject in the 1980s. At that time I had been editor of a small journal called *The Ley Hunter* for about ten years. My focus in this publication was (and still is) "leys" or "leylines," supposed alignments and linkages of ancient, sacred sites across the landscape. Antiquarians from Britain, Germany, France, and the United States had made claims of finding the remnants of such ancient alignments in their respective countrysides since at least the nineteenth century. The greatest champion of the idea of these earth lines was Alfred Watkins, a resourceful businessman, inventor, and amateur archaeologist who lived in England near the Welsh border. In 1921 he had a flash of insight in which he suddenly saw that prehistoric burial mounds, standing stones, and earthworks all over the country were positioned along and linked by straight lines. He felt these alignments must be the remnants of old trade roads laid down in prehistory by surveyors using line-of-sight ranging techniques to plot straight courses across what was then wild country. He felt that the old sighting points along these straight ways had evolved into sanctified spots, marked by stones or mounds. (It's true that as far back as Celtic times, certain roads and crossroads were viewed as special, magical, or sanctified places.) Watkins's theory was that in a second stage of evolution some of the marker sites had been Christianized. This explained why there were so many old churches located on the leys. In fact, there are numerous instances throughout western Europe where churches stand on pagan and prehistoric holy sites. Though Watkins assumed there would, for the most part, be no trace of the old tracks today, he nonetheless found segments of stray track that still followed the course of his map-drawn alignments. Watkins lectured and wrote various books on his ley findings until shortly before his death in 1935.[1] Though orthodox archaeology dismissed Watkins's ideas, a straggling band of fringe researchers kept his research alive until the 1960s, which saw a new wave of interest in the subject of "leylines," as they began to be called. During the psychedelic sixties they were considered as being linked to UFOs and as some kind of energy circuitry in the landscape, detectable by the dowsing rod. The actual origin of the idea became lost to all but a few enthusiasts.

I worked as an editor on *The Ley Hunter* during this period. The readership ranged from analytical groups who trekked out into the field with maps and compasses, to New Agers more interested in the "vibes" of "earth energies" than the history of ancient landscapes and their inhabitants. In the mid-1980s, a beautifully produced booklet crossed my editorial desk. I went through it with increasing weariness and in the end I tossed it aside. It was one of many such texts I had received for publication from men confident that they had discovered *the* "energy line system." By then prominent New Age writers were already publishing their various claims about energy lines, past and future energy leylines, and even interplanetary and intergalactic ones.

But what exactly *were* leys, and did they exist at all? Archaeologists said they were a mirage, and there had been a period of fairly inconclusive statistical wrangling over whether lines between sites on maps were chance effects or not. Aerial archaeology, which used air pho-

Alfred Watkins, discoverer of "leys" and pioneer photographer, shown taking a picture of one of his alignments. *(Major Tyler/Northern Earth Mysteries)*

tographs to reveal the existence of roads and earthworks thousands of years old, was clearly showing that Watkins's theory was incorrect. From my own experience I knew that many published ley-type alignment studies were either carelessly mapped or included marker sites that were invalid for one reason or another. It was apparent that if progress on properly evaluating the linear enigma was ever to be made, then we had to start with undeniably real, observable, ancient, straight landscape lines and work from there. At that point, the only examples I knew of that fit this description were the mysterious "Nazca lines" in Peru. I was soon to learn that the Americas contain many more such enigmatic linear features.[2]

ROADS TO NOWHERE: THE MYSTERY LINES OF THE AMERICAS

We can start as far north as Ohio, which was the central domain of the Hopewell Indians. The Hopewell culture flowered roughly between 150 B.C. and A.D. 500, and evidence of its presence can still be found far afield from its Ohio Valley heartland. It is thought that rather than being a distinct tribe, the Hopewell culture was a religious phenomenon, a sphere of influence. We know that the Hopewell religion was shamanically based, as evidenced by finds such as the copper-sheathed wooden effigy of a hallucinogenic mushroom in the Mound City necropolis at Chillicothe. The Hopewell built burial mounds and huge, geometrical earthworks, including circular and hexagonal enclosed areas covering many acres, and giant earthen mounds and truncated pyramids, along with linear features that seem to have been ceremonial

Sacra Via, in Marietta, Ohio, marking the course of a two-thousand-year-old Hopewell Indian ceremonial way. *(Paul Devereux)*

roadways. Many Hopewell earthworks were destroyed during the early centuries of settlement, but fortunately, some survived. The good people of Marietta, Ohio, took great care of the earthworks they discovered (their library can be found even to this day perched on a Hopewell mound). Fortunately, they also preserved the course of one Hopewell graded, ceremonial way leading up from the Muskingum River to a fifty-acre enclosure containing truncated earthen pyramids. This was almost seven hundred feet long, with its one-hundred-foot width bounded by high banks. Its straight course can today be traced by the now pink-surfaced road the settlers called "Sacra Via."

In 1995, Bradley T. Lepper, curator of archaeology at the Ohio Historical Society, announced the finding of even more extensive Hopewell linear sacred geography.[3] He has evidence that a sixty-mile-long Hopewell ceremonial road connected modern Newark and Chillicothe in a straight line across the Ohio countryside. Newark's Octagon State Memorial Park contains a circular earthwork over a thousand feet in diameter, which is connected to an octagonal earthwork covering some fifty acres. Parallel earthen walls, presumably the remains of a sacred way, extend two and a half miles southward from the octagon. Lepper recently discovered documents dating to 1862 left by James and Charles Salisbury, which describe how the brothers walked farther southward along the line of these earthen walls, and found traces of the same walls six miles farther south—"through tangled swamps and across streams, still keeping their undeviating course." They didn't investigate further, but some years later another investigator noted that the line of an ancient road could be "easily traced" through the forest even farther. In 1930, a Newark businessman traced the course of this apparent road from the air, following remnants of earthen walls "southwards in a straight line" about twelve miles from Newark. Using this evidence, Lepper placed a ruler on his Ohio map, angled it parallel with the walls of the reported road segments, and found that the resulting line went right to another circle-and-octagon earthwork complex, similar in size to that at Newark, on the banks of the Scioto River opposite Mound City in Chillicothe. Since then Lepper has driven, walked, and conducted aerial surveys of "the Great Hopewell Road," as he has called it, and had aerial infrared photographs taken of it by the Ohio Department of Natural Resources. Further sections have consequently been revealed at widely separated locations along the route, and there can be little doubt that an entire straight sixty-mile-long "road" did once exist and was probably used as a pilgrimage route. Although there are no surviving records or traditions concerning the ancient Hopewell culture, it's possible that there may be other now lost "roads" elsewhere. We can hope that further archaeological discoveries may some day shed more light on this vanished culture.

In the California Sierras, the prehistoric Miwok Indians left behind the remains of dead-straight tracks. In 1950, Laetitia Sample wrote, "The trails of the sierra regions followed natural passes. Many trails were wide and worn a couple of feet deep from long use. They

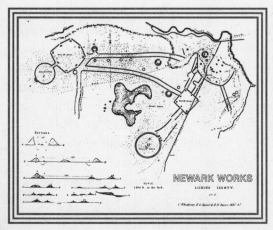

Plan of the Hopewell earthworks at Newark, Ohio. The twin lines running south from the hexagonal earthwork at upper left form the beginning of the sixty-mile ceremonial road discovered by Bradley T. Lepper. *(As surveyed by Whittlesey, Squier, and Davis, 1837–47)*

could be traced long after the Indians had gone and the paths were abandoned. They seem to have gone in straight lines . . . without detouring for mountains in the way."[4] This last point was also noted by S. Barrett and E. W. Gifford, who both observed in the 1930s that the Miwok trails were "usually almost airline in their directness, running up hill and down dale without zigzags or detours."[5] The Miwok were a shamanic culture, like their Chumash neighbors, and we recall that they did use datura ritually.

Narrow parallel trails edged in places with small stones have been noted in California's Colorado Desert. Stone mounds or cairns thought to be "shrines" punctuate these tracks. Based on pottery fragments found nearby, the tracks date from before A.D. 900 to around A.D. 1300. Similar trails also appear in Arizona, and, though little is known about them, they seem to be related to California's old straight tracks. There is very limited knowledge of prehistoric paths found in Nevada, and similarly those in Colorado, where vestiges of two old tracks at altitudes of over eleven thousand feet were reported in 1878. But the most dramatic examples of prehistoric straight roads discovered so far in the American Southwest, and in United States as a whole, are those that converge on (or diverge from) Chaco Canyon. This ragged, rocky gash in the high, arid desert country in northwestern New Mexico was a cult center of the lost Anasazi people. The vast domain of the Anasazi (the Navajo word for "the Ancient Ones") spanned what is now known as the Four Corners region, where Utah, Colorado, Arizona, and New Mexico meet. Their culture reached its height between the eleventh and thirteenth centuries A.D., when the Anasazi mysteriously disappeared—possibly because of severe drought. They may have dispersed into other existing Pueblo Indian groups of the American Southwest, so Anasazi elements may have survived in cultures such as today's Hopi and Zuni. (The pre-Columbian Zuni, we recall, left a kiva wall-painting of a medicine man holding a species of datura.) The Navajo now occupy the area vacated by the Anasazi.

The Chacoan roads are thought to have been built between approximately A.D. 900 and 1150. They stretch for fifty or sixty miles be-

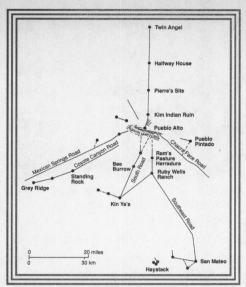

A simplified map of the major "roads" around the Chaco Canyon, showing some of the shrine sites and Great Houses occurring along them.

yond the canyon, and possibly much farther. They link Anasazi "Great Houses," of which there are many dozens scattered throughout the desert area surrounding Chaco Canyon. A number of roads converge at a narrow gap in a wall leading from the ruins of Pueblo Alto, a Great House on the northern rim of Chaco Canyon. These pueblo complexes seem to have been designed to specifically accommodate the passage of the strange roads, with doors opening out only onto the roads and not into the interior of the building. It is thought that a Great House had a small "caretaker" staff occupying it for most of the time, with seasonal influxes of visitors probably gathering for ceremonial purposes; they were not normal domestic dwellings. Where the roads meet the rimrock of the canyon, stairways were carved out of the rock walls reaching down to the canyon floor, and Great Houses within the canyon were also linked by the roads.[6,7]

These mysterious roads are not mere tracks, but engineered features. Primary roads are between twenty-three and thirty-six feet in width, while secondary roads are about half that. They were constructed in various ways, usually being cut down to the bedrock or clay hardpan. Some were ramped to cope with slopes and were edged with earthen "berms," rows of stones, or even drystone walling. The roads are, for the most part, strikingly straight ("arrow straight" was one description), changing direction in a sudden dogleg, not a curve. They

North Wall of the Chaco Canyon, containing eroded rock-cut stairway (upper center). Ruins of the Great Houses left and right foreground. *(Paul Devereux)*

were first documented in modern times in an army report of 1879, which referred to "remarkable trails" in New Mexico "extending as they do in a straight line from one pueblo to another." In 1901 a government agent's report mentions them, as does Neil Judd, a pioneer Chaco archaeologist active in the 1920s. A woman told another Chaco archaeologist, Gordon Vivien, that "in the old days" a wide roadway running north from the canyon "was clearly defined in the spring or early summer because the vegetation on it was different from any other." Early photographs show this road—called "the Great North Road" by archaeologists—quite clearly, but now it and all the roads are very difficult to see at ground level with the untrained eye. (This deterioration in visibility seems to have been due to a change in human usage of the area, such as altered grazing patterns resulting in changed vegetation cover, and also in shifting climatic conditions.)

Study of the road system as a whole has been mainly from the air. In 1929 the famed flier Charles Lindbergh took the first aerial photographs, and more were taken and analyzed in the 1970s. In the 1980s, NASA conducted a probing survey using a Learjet and state-of-the-art thermal infrared multispectral scanning (TIMS) techniques. It was delicate work, with the surface temperature of the features being suitable for imaging for only a few minutes in every twenty-four hours.[8] Not only did this work extend the mapping of the road system, it also revealed multiple parallel sections to some lengths of the roads.[9] These parallel sections,

Old photograph showing a Chacoan road made visible by change in vegetation coloring. Horse and carriage show scale of the road. *(F. A. Wadleigh, 1916)*

invisible to the naked eye or even the normal airborne camera, only deepened the mystery of the roads, whose very existence puzzled researchers, as the Anasazi did not have wheeled vehicles (the wheel was unknown in the Americas prior to European contact).

"Why were the Chaco roads designed with exacting linearity, which surmounted any topographic obstruction . . . and constructed by people who did not even employ beasts of burden in their lives?" ask NASA investigators Thomas Sever and David Wagner.[10] Judd spoke with Navajo informants, and though we do not know what he learned, he subsequently took to referring to the roads as "ceremonial highways." We also know that one Navajo elder, Hosteen Beyal, told Judd that they were "not really roads," although they looked like them. A Hopi elder suggested to writer Kendrick Frazier that the roads might be symbolic: the Hopi had myths that said their ancestors came from specific directions. Perhaps the directions of the Chacoan roads related to migratory myths of the Anasazi.[11] Frazier also notes that Zuni oral traditions relate to a migratory quest for the mythical "center of the Earth." Modern Zunis told Frazier that Chaco Canyon appeared in these legends, and that the Anasazi were Zuni ancestors.[12] The Zuni male-female Sun Father/Moon Mother figure, Awonawilona, is "the One Who Holds the Roads," relating to the Four Directions and "Center Place," the mythic center of the world.

The major road at Chaco is the Great North Road. Kathryn Gabriel has suggested that it may be related to these kind of Pueblo cosmological principles.[13] She notes that the people of Zia (Sia Pueblo) have a rain song that includes the lines

> "We, the ancient ones, ascended from the middle of the world below, through the door of the entrance to the lower world. . . . We entreat you to send your thoughts to us that we may sing your songs straight, so that they will pass over the straight road to the cloud priests."

In Zuni cosmology, north can also stand for the zenith-nadir axis, the shamanic cosmic axis, which is also an image of the world center, where the First People emerged from the underworld. In addition, Gabriel points out that the road metaphor is very powerful in Pueblo imagery, and in Tewa, one of the Pueblo languages, the word *road* translates as "channel for the life's breath." Life itself is a road, and there are important spirit keepers along it. (This concept of a straight landscape feature being a spirit line of one kind or another is a universal concept we will encounter a number of times.) However, Gabriel also warns that the Pueblo peoples have been through many changes; it may be unwise to put too much store in the assumption that what is now believed and taught is an infallible guide to what their ancestors believed a thousand years ago.

Broken pottery found along the Chacoan roads suggests damage in transport or the ritual breaking of vessels, a worldwide practice in ancient cultures. Chipped stone debris found at places on the roads could also have resulted from ritual actions.[14] The Great North Road passes through some unusual terrain, the most distinctive being a group of dune pinnacles. One dune on the path is known as El Faro (the Lighthouse) because on its summit archaeologists found a hearth on which many fires had been lit. A kiva (a circular, semisubterranean ceremonial and ritual enclosure) may also have existed there. Segments of the road were found on either side of the pinnacle. A find like this further strengthens the idea of the roads being ritual or ceremonial routes. Archaeologist Thomas Windes reports finding a carved stone figure on a mesa top near Chaco Canyon. He feels that some of the roads "may once have been marked at high points by stone animal figures set alongside the roads, perhaps as road markers or shrines."[15] This in itself hints at possible shamanic associations with the roads. An authority on prehistoric Native American roads, Charles Trombold, suggests that each road may be "represented by a spirit" and it might therefore have had ritual behavior associated directly with it.[16] Windes has suggested that the roads were probably essentially trade routes, but this view now finds less favor with investigators, for although archaeologists now tend to agree that a prehistoric road of this kind could have been used for both mundane and religious purposes, it is the ceremonial aspect that has to be seen as most important. "The early road systems with their careful planning and construction would not have served primarily as a means of transport of goods or people. Simple paths would have served as well," another researcher, Timothy Earle, makes clear.[17] John Hyslop, a veteran of Inca roads research, puts it simply: "Roads constructed in extraordinary ways may reflect ritual or symbolic concerns." He goes on to caution Western interpreters not to project their own cultural prejudices. He insists that prehistoric Native American roads "often had meanings and conceptual uses not found in our society. . . . Attempts to interpret all aspects of prehistoric roads in purely materialist terms are bound to fail."[18]

With these thoughts in mind, we can look farther southward in our quest for the enigmatic old straight roads of prehistoric America. We note in passing that a roadway system has been observed at the Casas Grandes ruins in northern Chihuahua, Mexico, but little information is available on this yet. Farther south in Mexico, the land where the greatest variety of ancient hallucinogen usage has been recorded, we come to the archaeological site of La Quemada, in Zacatecas. This place is possibly a fortified ceremonial center, a citadel, built on the slopes and summit of a twin-peaked mountain. About one hundred miles of ancient roads have been discovered in this area, dating to between A.D. 700 and 800. They were first mapped by Charles de Berghes in 1833, and Trombold began research on them in 1974. The La Quemada roads are masonry structures built on the surface of the ground like causeways: two parallel rows of stone were laid out in a straight line, and the area between filled with rubble and capped with flag-

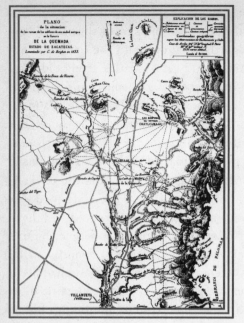

Charles de Berghes' 1833 map of the straight causeways (shown as dashed lines) around La Quemada, Mexico.

stones. Wider roads connected areas of higher population density while narrower ones ran to a variety of dispersed sites. The first detailed written descriptions of the roads were made by an English mining engineer, G. F. Lyon, in 1828. He described numerous "perfectly straight" roads. One well-engineered road, about twenty-five feet wide, descended across a valley in the direction of the rising sun, crossed a stream, and rose two miles up a mountain, ending at "an immense stone edifice, which probably may also have been a pyramid."[19] He noted other paved causeways up to forty-six feet wide and raised over a yard above the surrounding terrain. One ended at the foot of a cliff beneath a cave, and its other end was at an artificial mound. Another seemed to run up into the mountains. Trombold has found that square altars were occasionally placed in the center of causeway routes, and that most roads seemed to terminate at the site of some kind of ceremonial architecture.

Similar straight causeways have been reported in other areas of north central Mexico—at least five sites in the Bajio, Río Lajas, and middle Lerma districts. They have also been noted at an archaeological site in Durango.[20] Trombold notes that the roads around La Quemada are structurally similar to the later Chacoan roads in their straightness. He speculates that possibly a cultural influence moved northward from Mexico into New Mexico over the period of a few centuries.

Further south is the Yucatán Peninsula and the domain of the ancient Maya. They emerged during the first century B.C., but the flowering of their culture, known as the Classic Period, occurred between the late third century A.D., when they began working in stone, and A.D. 900. (There are still Mayan-speaking Indians in southern Mexico.) They had advanced masonry skills, had ceremonial life based on astronomy, developed a complex and sophisticated calendrical system, and kept records by means of hieroglyphic writing on stone stelae and in plaster-coated bark paper or animal-skin "books" now called codices. And they built long, straight roads called *sacbeob* ("white ways"), which interconnected with plazas and temples in some Mayan ceremonial cities, and also linked cities themselves. These roads now exist only in fragmentary sections.

The longest-known surviving *sacbe* is the sixty-two-mile-long section that runs between Coba and Yaxuna in the northern part of the Yucatán Peninsula. This was discovered by explorer Thomas Gann in the 1920s. He described it as "a great elevated road, or causeway thirty-two-feet wide. . . . This was one of the most remarkable roads ever constructed, as the sides were built of great blocks of cut stone, many weighing hundreds of pounds. . . . It was convex, being higher in the centre than either side, and ran, as far as we followed it, straight as an arrow, and almost flat as a rule."[21] Altars, arches, and curious ramps are associated with the *sacbeob*, and, according to local Mayan tradition, the physical network of the *sacbeob* is augmented at various places by spiritual routes: mythical *sacbeob* that are supposed to pass underground, and others, called *Kusam Sum*,[22] that run through the air. One of these "air lines" is said to link the Mayan cities of Izamal and Dzibilchaltun.

The vast Mayan territory extended south through modern-day Belize, Guatemala, El Salvador, and Honduras, the same territory in which ritual hallucinogenic mushrooms and ancient mushroom stones were found. *Sacbe* segments are known throughout much of this region—at El Mirador in Guatemala, for instance[23]—and many more, long since covered by the jungles, await discovery.

NASA has employed light detection and ranging (LIDAR), infrared aerial photography, and L-band radar techniques to detect paths running through the mountainous rain forest of the Arenal area of Costa Rica.[24] These paths "follow relatively straight lines" despite the difficult terrain. They have been examined at ground level and have been dated to Costa Rica's "Silencio Phase," A.D. 500–1200. Researchers Payson Sheets and Thomas Sever discovered that the paths are "death roads": one goes straight over the top of a hill, rather than going around it, linking a village with a Silencio Phase cemetery. The paths had been used for carrying corpses to burial, and also for transporting *laja*, volcanic stone, used in the construction of tombs and cemetery walls.[25] (We will find this "death road" aspect to have surprising echoes in the Old World.)

The Sierra Nevada de Santa Marta on the northern coast of Colombia, South America, is the territory of the Kogi Indians. Scattered among the forests of the sierra are the remains of the stone-built cities of the Taironas culture.[26] The cities were linked by paved roads or paths, some of which were straight. Archaeologists know of about two hundred miles of these roads, but do not know their full extent. The Kogi, whose immediate ancestors made gold objects embellished with mushroom shapes, consider the roads to have been built by the ancestors, and therefore sacred. Their traditions place them under a spiritual obligation to maintain and to walk the roads. We will return to these points.

South and west, along the Andes region of South America, we encounter a number of different "roads," desert lines, and alignments. Peru, the home of the hallucinogen-based shamanic cult centered on the psychedelic temple of Chavín de Huantar, has many. Very ancient straight roads have been found and studied in the Moche Valley of northern Peru.[27] Further south along the western coast of Peru we come to the most famous of the linear markings in the Americas, the "Nazca lines." These date to between fifteen hundred and two thousand years ago. Unfortunately, Erich Von Daniken incorrectly identified these lines as landing strips for ancient astronauts in the 1970s. The lines are to be found on the desert tablelands or pampas at Cuzco and farther afield. They were made by the removal of

One of the broad rectangular markings on the Nazca pampa. *(Courtesy of the Peruvian Tourist Board)*

the relatively dark, oxidized desert pavement, leaving lighter soil beneath. There is virtually no rainfall on the pampas, and the wind has long ago removed what it can, so marks made in this fashion remain visible for very long periods of time. The linear markings vary from broad rectangular and trapezoid areas to narrow, very straight lines, some of which run parallel to one another. They can run for up to several miles in length, passing over hills and ridges as if they did not exist. Toribio Mejia Xesspe was the first archaeologist to notice them. He thought they were ceremonial roads and that their distribution suggested an association with prehistoric aqueducts and cemeteries on the pampa. In 1941, American historical geographer Paul Kosok looked at them and was sure they were astronomical markings of some kind. He introduced the German mathematician Maria Reiche to the features, and she has remained at the lines all her long life, helping to keep them preserved in the face of increasing public interest—which was particularly strong after the publication of Von Daniken's best-selling books.[28] Smithsonian astronomer Gerald Hawkins studied the lines in the late 1960s, and found no basis for thinking that the lines were oriented in relation to astronomical phenomena.[29]

The best study of these fascinating and enigmatic desert markings came two decades later. An interdisciplinary expedition led by Colgate University astronomer Anthony F. Aveni brought a new rigor and wide-ranging approach to the mystery.[30] One of the fundamental findings of this study was that there was a network pattern embedded in the apparently haphazard mesh of straight lines: the expeditionary team identified over sixty "nodes" or "ray centers" consisting of mounds or natural

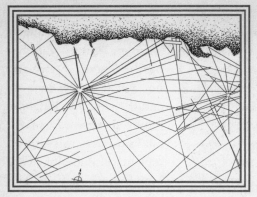

Part of the northern edge of the Nazca pampa showing the layout of straight lines, trapezoid areas, and a "ray center" (upper center left).

hillocks, often topped with boulders, from which several lines would radiate like spokes form the hub of a wheel. Moreover, at least one line from each ray center would connect with another node somewhere else. The team also confirmed Hawkins's findings that the lines had nothing to do with astronomy,[31] and Xesspe's observation that the lines were associated with the locations of the old aqueducts, and, indeed, with other water features, such as numerous dried-out riverbeds on the pampa. The lines present an almost ethereal sense of mathematical precision, of exact straightness, yet a good number of them also contained *paths*: they had been *walked*. And walked and walked—perhaps like the Kogi's paved ancestral paths. Archaeologist Persis B. Clarkson, one of Aveni's team, studied the Nazca lines on foot. She noted that some had "been preferred for an undefinable amount of time as footpaths, as evidenced by twisting trails that weave within the confines of the straight lines."[32] The Nazca lines are the classic example of roads to nowhere. But nobody thinks the Nazca lines were ordinary footpaths; rather, they were for "ritual walking along straight predetermined routes."[33]

Helaine Silverman, another member of the research group, feels that some of the pampa lines were oriented to Cahuachi, a ruined ceremonial complex immediately south of the Nazca pampa, and were used as pilgrimage routes. Cahuachi contains some natural mounds that had been artificially faced with adobe to turn them into pyramids, and the remnants of a temple structure. Lines on another pampa, the Pampa de Artarco, also point toward Cahuachi, whose name, Silverman discovered, may relate to the Quechua Indian word *qhawachi*, which means "prediction." Silverman feels that "the Nasca priest-scientists observed the natural and supernatural world from Cahuachi and from the pampa. . . . [This] observation [was] for the purpose of prediction."[34] She also found evidence indicating that the lines had been kept *ritually clean*, by sweeping and other means. She and Gary Urton had seen ritual cleaning behavior still taking place in a Christianized context in contemporary Andean Indian communities: a village square in front of a church would be swept across in strips by various kinship groups on a saint's day, before bringing the saint's effigy out of the church and parading it.[35]

Deep in the Peruvian Andes, some two hundred miles northeast of Nazca, is Cuzco, the old Inca capital. The Incas rose to supremacy over other Andean tribal groups around A.D. 1200 and met their demise at the hands of the Spanish during the sixteenth century. The Great Plaza in Cuzco was the focal point of a huge road system estimated to contain twenty-five thousand miles of roads through the Andes. Some sections were paved while others, especially those in desert areas, were simply marked by stone edgings. The roads were punctuated with cairns or shrines, and wayside stations (*tampu*) were placed at frequent intervals along them. These were used by the *chasquis* or runners carrying messages or special goods. The roads ran straight between any two points, though they sometimes detoured to avoid obstacles. Archaeological examination has shown that considerable lengths of Inca roadways were based on much older straight tracks.

The Coricancha in Cuzco, the so-called Temple of the Sun, a place of ancestor worship and a ceremonial seat of the divine king of the Incas, was the center of another system of straight lines. This was the *ceque* system, forty-one alignments of sacred places or *huacas*, such as temples, shrines, holy hills, caves, standing stones, natural boulders or outcrops, sacred trees, bends in rivers, springs, and waterfalls that had been imbued with special significance. These alignments fanned out over the landscape surrounding Cuzco and different kinship groups or *ayllus* were responsible for keeping up and managing specific *ceques*. The system had complex associations with the ancestors, and with water (thought to be a gift from the ancestors in the underworld).

It helped social organization among the Incas as well as performing a ceremonial calendrical function. The alignments themselves had multiple purposes. Ten of them seem to have been used for ceremonial solar observation, others marked the routes along which sacrificial victims were escorted back to their respective parts of the empire for ritual execution, and yet others were for straight-line pilgrimages.

Five hundred or so miles south of Cuzco, lines crisscross the altiplano of western Bolivia. Some of these lines are twenty miles long, considerably longer than any found at Nazca. French anthropologist Alfred Métraux came across them in the 1930s when he investigated earthen shrines set out in a straight row from a small village. He found them to be standing on a pathway that was "absolutely straight, regardless of the irregularities of the ground." In more recent years, explorer Tony Morrison conducted an expedition to study the lines, and confirmed that they are indeed as straight as laser beams (as his laser surveying equipment demonstrated) and traverse ridges and valleys without deviation.[36] The lines are simply paths cut through the tola bushes and cleared of debris. Consequently they can easily be overgrown, and Morrison found that some of the younger Aymara Indians were not bothering to maintain them.

A straight and ancient Indian path crosses the arid plains of Carangas, Bolivia. *(Tony Morrison/South American Pictures)*

The shrines along them were of various kinds—Christianized adobe structures, piles of rocks, places where lightning had struck, and other sanctified spots. There were also churches standing on some of the lines (much in the manner that Alfred Watkins had imagined with his leys), as at the community of Sajama, for instance. The Quechua word the Indians used to describe the lines or paths was *siq'i*, meaning "a row of things," and relates to the Quechua word *ziqui*, which the Spanish transliterated as *ceque* when referring to the alignments around Cuzco. Either the Indians did not remember what the lines had originally been for, or they were not telling Morrison, but in 1985 anthropologist Johan Reinhard witnessed a ceremony near a remote Bolivian village in which the Indians walked in single file along a two-mile straight path to a mountaintop, playing pipes and drums. At the summit they made offerings and said prayers, appealing for water.

Lines—single or in groups, desert markings or long rows of small stone heaps—have been seen at other places in the Andean region, at least as far south as the Atacama Desert in Chile.

Prehistoric roads and rumors of lines occur as well in lowland, rain forest parts of South America, east of the Andes, where we have seen that the use of hallucinogens such as *ayahuasca* is still widespread. "Somewhere deep in Amazonia, early Spanish explorers encountered Indian roads and were greatly impressed: 'betwixt Peru and Bresill . . . the waies [are] as much beaten as those betwixt Salamanca and Valladolid,'" writes William Denevan, quoting a Spanish account from 1590.[37] When he landed on the west coast of Puerto Rico in 1493, Christopher Columbus himself reported seeing "a wide road leading to the sea and bordered by towers of cane on both sides." Today, researchers are uncovering a number of examples of prehistoric roads across the tropical lowlands, despite initially considering the vast region an unlikely place for such discoveries. Over nine hundred miles of causeways have been reported and studied to some extent in the Llanos de Mojos, a savanna in the upper Amazon region of northeastern Bolivia. Denevan remarks that "the straightness of most of the causeways is impressive" and that they are "unusually straight."[38] At least some of them seem to connect burial and ceremonial sites. He makes the important point that while engineering a straight road in flat terrain is not all that difficult, "building a long straight road to a destination that cannot be seen is not easy."[39] Further, he notes that the causeways occur in dry, drained ground and not just in wetlands, and thus they take on "other significance" than can be explained merely by providing dry transport across swamp country. Elsewhere, knowledge of prehistoric roads is still extremely sketchy. Some have been seen leading out of the eastern Andes to the edge of the tropical lowlands, but little is known about them and they have not even been properly mapped.[40] In 1942, Alfred Métraux reported "broad, straight, and perfectly clean highways" between the upper Rio Guapore and the Serra dos Parecis in the Mato Grosso of western Brazil; causeways have been reported in the Rio San Jorge region of northern Colombia, and causeways connected with artificial mounds have been given cursory study at Hato la Calzada de Paez, Barinas, in the Orinoco Llanos of Venezuela.[41] There also appears to be emerging ethnological evidence in the Amazon of features somewhat similar to Australian Aboriginal "songlines."[42]

SHAMANIC LANDSCAPES

I was staggered at the quantity, forms, and geographical range of Native American "roads" and linear ground markings. The famed Nazca lines were obviously but one example among many. Clearly, the most remarkable feature shared by all of them is their *straightness*. "If there is one attribute that characterizes New World road systems, it is straightness," archaeologist Charles Trombold similarly observes.[43] In some instances the "roads" occur on open deserts, so it is easy to speculate that in such a situation a straight road would be the obvious choice. But the roads are straight even in difficult terrain—straightness was clearly a fundamental design factor. And the roads, paths, and "lines" all seem to have had religious and ritual significance, even where they may have been multifunctional. It seemed to me that perhaps all these features were expressing one general, fundamental idea, using various structural methods and with varying cultural emphases. But what could the unifying factor have been? Perhaps the key is that these linear displays occurred in the territories of people who were known to be shamanic and who in most cases used hallucinogens. Deep down in time and consciousness, there must have been an underlying shamanic impulse that led to these forms of expression. Could the lines on the land be signatures of trance, as are the paintings and symbols of prehistoric rock art? Perhaps they

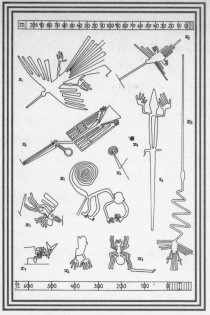

A selection of Nazca ground drawings or geoglyphs. *(Maria Reiche, 1968)*

were ceremonial and/or politically symbolic expressions—such as impressive processional paths for social elites. In any case, the straightness seems to be the key to discovering the origins of the form.

I became convinced that the lines or roads are elements of shamanic geography—*shamanic landscapes*. It became clear that the straight line or path was just one element in such landscapes. Another characteristic component was the *terrestrial effigy*. Effigies are of two basic types: ground drawings (properly called *geoglyphs*) and earthen effigy mounds.

Geoglyphs tend to occur in desert areas. As a prime example, an amazing variety of images are scattered among the lines at Nazca, engraved into the desert pavement in the same manner. They include bizarre abstract shapes, spiral forms, and animal, plant, human, and supernatural effigies. One of the smaller representational shapes is a spider, about 150 feet long. The larger creatures extend for over 3,000 feet. They are all drawn in a beautiful, symmetrical fashion, and the line is usually unicursal: it is a single unbroken line that does not cross over itself. This feature has led some commentators to suggest that they may be ritual dance patterns.

It is difficult to understand how these huge images were executed so perfectly at ground level without the aid of scaled drawings. They can be seen at their best from the air, and this fact has led people to speculate that they were really signs for ancient astronauts, or that they were created under the direction of observers in hot air balloons.

Ground drawings exist elsewhere in the Andes too, sometimes

taking the form of crude human figures outlined with small rocks, other times engraved, as at Nazca. Figures have been reported in northern Peru, Bolivia, and Chile. In Chile there are giant hillside effigies that are "stylistically and thematically distinct from Nazca figural geoglyphs."[44] Geoglyphs made by rock outlines or ground markings edged in rocks, referred to as *intaglios*, occur in North America too. Probably the best known is the 150-foot-tall human figure on the desert at Blythe, California. This is part of three groups of intaglio figures depicting men and animals thought to be panthers. There is an 80-foot human figure at Winterhaven, near California's boundary with Mexico. In Kansas there are snake intaglios at Lyons, the largest 160 feet in length, and a giant male figure outlined in small stones at Penokee. Human figures are marked by rocks in Montana and South Dakota, and human and turtle effigies occur at various locations in Alberta, most of them associated with medicine wheels.

Although there are some in Canada, most surviving earthen effigy mounds are concentrated in the north-central United States, with Wisconsin having the greatest surviving number. They take the forms of birds, panthers, turtles, bears, snakes and serpents, lizards, and deer, as well as humanoid and a variety of geometrical and abstract forms, some of which we have already noted in discussing the Hopewell earthworks. The most celebrated of the great North American mounds is the quarter-mile-long Serpent Mound in Adams County, Ohio. This is not a burial mound, but some kind of ceremonial earthwork. It appears to have been built by the Adena, with later work completed by the Hopewell peoples. Another example of a large effigy mound is a six-foot-high bird mound with a wingspan of over six hundred feet in the Mendota State Hospital Mound Group near Madison, Wisconsin.

South of the Río Grande, Marlene Dobkin de Rios has drawn attention to a massive effigy earthwork believed to date to the Olmec culture of the first millennium B.C., the forerunner to the Maya and Aztec civilizations. It is located at the archaeological site of San Lorenzo on Mexico's Gulf Coast, and is three-quarters of a mile long, "reaching out like fingers on its north, west and south sides with long narrow ridges divided by ravines." She continues:

Serpent Mound, Adams County, Ohio. *(Squier and Davis,* Ancient Monuments of the Mississippi Valley, *Smithsonian Institution, 1848)*

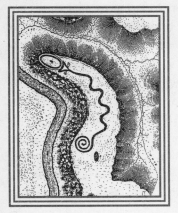

A pair of ridges on the western side exhibit bilateral symmetry, with every feature on one ridge matched in mirror fashion by its counterpart. The ridges are artificial and consist of fill and cultural debris as deep as 25 feet. Coe [Michael Coe, the investigating archaeologist] suggests that this construction is a gigantic bird flying eastward, its extended wing feathers forming ridges on the north and south, with its tail trailing to the west.... Coe comments that such a grandiose plan can only be appreciated from the air and suggests that an ancient Olmec ruler/priest, inspired by cosmological ideas, ordered this construction to impress the gods and men.[45]

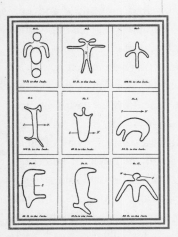

Plans of Wisconsin effigy mounds, showing animal, bird, and human-bird forms. *(S. Taylor, in Squier and Davis,* Ancient Monuments of the Mississippi Valley, *Smithsonian Institution, 1848)*

We understand all these terrestrial effigies as representing totem animals or shamanic familiars, or, at least, ceremonial structures based on such ideas.

In addition to these figurative and abstract shapes, there are also *nonstraight* shamanic lines. At Sears Point on the south bank of the Gila River in southwest Arizona, for instance, there are about fifty ground figures that trace meanders and geometrical designs. They are formed by rocks and intaglio methods.[46] This group is accompanied by about two thousand petroglyphs and a few straight-line ground markings.

FLY SHAMAN AIRWAYS: THE OLD TRANCE TRACK

The straight roads, paths, and lines may be one characteristic component of shamanic landscapes—the variability in their structural form apparently depended on the complexity of the society that produced them. But what, exactly, did they mean? What were they for? In trying to imagine an answer it helps to remember that people have not always seen the world, or interacted with the landscape, in the way we do today. It is only in comparatively recent years that archaeology has really considered this truth, and has attempted to "get inside" other, ancient worldviews at the same time that it tries to expose the unconscious assumptions we make in interpreting ancient monuments and landscapes. We need to heed this "cognitive archaeology" approach if we are to appreciate the significance of the mystery lines of the Americas and their relationship to shamanic trance.

One cognitive archaeologist, Julian Thomas, has expressed unease with the way the landscape concept has been used within mainstream archaeology: "Landscape is not a universal concept, applied in the same way by all people at all times. . . . The modern West has developed a particular and distinctive way of looking."[47] He explains that prehistoric and non-Western art tends to depict place in terms of impression, feeling, significance, or meaning rather than as outward appearance, while, on the contrary, Western art since the Renaissance has been dominated by the "realistic" depiction of appearance using the device of linear perspective. Thomas feels that "perspective art" represents a form of visual control, which freezes time, and distances the viewer from the relationships depicted.[48] This visual innovation has trained us in a particular way of seeing for generations—the *gaze* has become the dominant mode of perception within our civilization. Thomas draws on the work of Susan Ford to suggest that we moderns characteristically look at landscape through the medium of the *male gaze*.[49] He warns that archaeology may be guilty of studying ancient landscapes in just such a manner. It characteristically uses the distribution map, the air photo, the satellite image, and other techniques that all imply a considerable distance between subject and object, and "present a picture of past landscapes which the inhabitant would hardly recognize."[50]

Taking the same approach to the problem, another cognitive archaeologist, Christopher Tilley, attacks the tendency of modern geography and archaeology to falsely assume that there is no difference between our understanding and perception of the environment and that experienced by prehistoric peoples. Tilley stresses that earlier and non-Western peoples experienced the space around them as a *medium* rather than as simply a "container" for things and events. "A centered and meaningful space involves specific sets of linkages between the physical space of the non-humanly created world, somatic states of the body, the mental space of cognition and representation," Tilley writes. "What space is depends on who is experiencing it and how."[51]

Cambridge anthropologist Caroline Humphrey has made a study of shamanic landscapes in Siberia, the home of classical shamanism, the shamanism that informed the essential spiritual sensibility that migrated with the Paleo-peoples across the Beringia land bridge and into the Americas. In a vein similar to that of the cognitive archaeologists, Humphrey argues that landscapes are "ways of thinking and speaking in particular contexts."[52] For us, this is an unfamiliar way of thinking about landscape, which is something we just assume is there in the background, more or less the same all the time. By contrast, the shamanic landscape is filled by spirits of many kinds. In Siberia, one of these involves the shaman directly. When he or she dies, the Siberian shaman is temporarily buried, then is later permanently reburied in another, particular spot. The geography is important because the shaman's soul will become the spiritual guardian of that locality; it has its "seat" in that ultimate burial place.[53] From that locale, the shaman's spirit can move out and about on "journeys." In such a manner, a deceased shaman's soul can be associated with a whole area, but in other cases it may be limited to a particular location; it might "become cliffs" (*xada bolxo*, as the Buryats say). There are also other "spirits" inhabiting the land, and the land can even *be* the spirit. Humphrey cites a Selenga Buryat belief that involves the worship of a female spirit envisaged as wearing dark blue clothing and mounted on a black stallion. The legend is that it is the spirit of a woman who was traveling to a tribal group of the Buryats to the north, and stopped to rest on the southern slope of Bayan-Tugud hill, tethering her horse to a tree. Unfortunately, she died of a disease there, and was buried by the locals, who set her horse free. The horse was captured and eaten by the Selenga Tubsheten clan, which then began to die of a terrible disease. Sacrifices had to be made to the spirit (both the woman and the horse as one) to make the sickness go away. Humphrey continues:

> Although sacrifices are now (1980s) made at the tree, the spirit is considered to be the *ezen* of a lateral section of land which extends between the Bayan-Tugud hill and another called Olzeitie-Ondor and this area is known as *güideltei gazar* (literally, "running-track land," a *güidel* being a track or a run of a spirit or animal). . . . The idea of the "track" is homologous, in many other stories.[54]

Humphrey stresses that the shamanic landscape crucially acknowledges movement. In other words, it is a dynamic medium, not a passive backdrop. If we are to understand the landscape lines of shamanic Native America, we have to accept that idea. The Cambridge anthropologist also points out that in the "purely shamanic" view, the world of the dead is not a discrete "state" of existence located in some separate underworld, but "is just nearby, across the mountains, or round some bends in a river, or inside a cliff, but it is just that ordinary people have lost the knack of finding it." She goes on:

> But ordinary human organs of perception are not enough. This explanation is used to account for why shamans must acquire the abilities of their ancestor-spirit and animal helpers, which can see better, track down better, fly or swim underwater. The exercise of such abilities constructs the "ways" or "paths" of shamans and spirits.
>
> A vision of this kind in effect transforms the landscape. The souls of the dead are no longer trapped underground in a king's dungeon, but are somewhere in this world.[55]

Humphrey reiterates that the way or path is an "extremely important shamanic concept."

So in thinking of shamanic landscapes and trying to interpret markings that have been developed on some of them, we have to be prepared to adjust our "normal," relatively recent, Western perceptions.

With all this in mind, we can direct our attention again to the straight roads and paths of shamanic America.

Taking a cue from the entoptic patternings in some rock art, it is possible to see the landscape lines as another formalized expression of shamanic trance, derived from the tunnel form constant, which is an *experiential straight line*. If the tunnel entoptic form is implicated in the straightness of the shamanic paths, then it follows that we are dealing with the sense of out-of-body spirit travel. In this view, the basis of the straight shamanic landscape lines is an expression of ecstasy: the quintessence of the shamanic experience.

Interpreting the straight lines and images as symbols, however, is more problematic, and would inevitably involve specific cultural factors in the various societies that built the straight roads and paths. Much of the detail may never be known. But in general, it seems reasonable to think that the straightness represented the "other" of the otherworld or spirit realm. Because of the tunnel or "participation" experience, the *sense of movement* into or within that realm was implied, and this was the critical dynamic of the shamanic landscape. The original nature of the straight landscape line appears, therefore, to symbolize spirit travel, journeying into the otherworld of spirits, of the ancestors, which, as Caroline Humphrey has implied, can be seen in shamanic terms as simply another level or dimension of the physical landscape. The line was a sign, or even an actual mapping, of the shaman's ecstatic journey, in the same way trance imagery in rock art was used to express ideas within a given tribal context. We have also noted in previous chapters that the rock art patterns were themselves often considered to be the source of spiritual power. If a similar idea prevailed with regard to the shamanic landscape lines, then that would explain the purpose of *walking* the straight lines or paths by tribal members. In more stratified societies, this activity would not only be an expression of specific beliefs, but would also act as a religious framing exercise to give the shaman, or shamanic priesthood, social power. Silverman has argued, for instance, that the construction and use of the Nazca lines would have helped to augment priestly-shamanic power and to strengthen social organization and cohesion, especially in a hierarchical sense, and would have had other social consequences. The lines were "myriad religio-political phenomena."[56]

There are numerous ways in which travel in the spirit realm was envisaged. However, we have seen repeatedly in foregoing chapters that *spirit flight* is the preeminent form. It is the one most emphasized throughout shamanism worldwide: the allusions to flight, particularly through the medium of bird imagery, can be found in rock art, in geoglyphs, in effigy mounds, on a shaman's robes, in ceremonial dancing and costume, in ritual paraphernalia, in shamanic gestural symbolism (such as the flapping of the arms atop ritual poles), and in the legends concerning shamans (the exploits of flying shamans are particularly prominent in Inuit lore, for example). In addition to bird references, the flight concept is sometimes expressed by the use of the arrow as a symbol: the Siberian Koryak shaman, for instance, says he leaves his body along a path traced by an arrow shot from his ritual bow; the Samoyed shaman holds two arrows pointed upward during his seánce. (There are many other shamanic images of soul flight, including travel along a chain of arrows, along a sunbeam, or along a rainbow.) Another powerful image associated with movement in the spirit realm is that of transformation into an animal.

Flight is the very image of ecstasy, of course, and it is the central experience of shamanic trance. Further, we have seen amply how the plant hallucinogens used by shamans expressly provide the sensation of flight out of the body, some alkaloids seeming to fit perfectly the specifications for "drugs for flying." *Within the context of soul flight, straightness lends itself to an extra dimension of symbolism,* for flight is the straight way over the land—we say "as the crow flies" or "as straight as an arrow," using the very metaphors used by shamanic tradition itself.

THE GEOGRAPHY OF TRANCE

It turns out that in arriving at this theory about the mystery of the old straight tracks I was covering territory that had for the most part already been described in a short, somewhat obscure paper by anthropologist Marlene Dobkin de Rios in 1977. De Rios had argued that "due to shamanistic, out-of-body experiences, the so-called aerial voyage, prehistoric New World, massive earthworks were constructed."[57]

She felt that this work was done to make signs to the supernatural forces, to members of the community, and to "other shamans in conflict with the social group."* After reviewing a selection of three ancient Native American groups, their use of hallucinogens, and the ground markings themselves, she wrote:

> Shamans are famous for their ability to transform themselves into powerful animal figures. . . . In my opinion, the effigies of animals found throughout the New World massive earthworks represent these shamanic familiars. . . .
>
> I would argue that the drug-using shaman, steeped in a religion of hunters, with spirit familiars on call to serve him, has a subjective experience which includes the sensation of flying. My point is quite simple. One need not fly in the air to really fly. Thus, the New World massive earthworks, difficult for the Westerner to conceptualize visually outside of an airplane voyage, are perhaps more simply explicable as the projection by the shaman of the animal or totem familiar from the heights of ecstasy through which he soars.
>
> Geometries in the earthworks, on the other hand, may be linked to . . . the kaleidoscopic visionary patterns reported by drug users.[58]

Since Dobkin de Rios wrote this, further discoveries have indicated that both linear features and traditions of shamanic use of hallucinogens were even more widespread in the New World than was previously recognized. I add to Dobkin de Rios's analysis the suggestion that the lines specifically refer to the participatory tunnel entoptic, and relate both neuropsychologically and symbolically to travel in the spirit realm in general, and with soul flight in particular.

In 1982, R. T. Zuidema, the leading authority on the Cuzco *ceques*, equated ancient Native American lines with the divinatory aspects of shamanic experience. In personal communication with Helaine Silver-

---

*In the "sweetness and light" New Age circles, it is not usually appreciated that there is often a great deal of sorcery and other forms of supernatural warfare among shamanic societies.

man, he suggested that the *ceques* extending over the visible horizon could "tie in to shamans who, on their hallucinogenic journeys to get knowledge of distant places and times, go 'over the horizon' and then return."[59] Earlier, in 1973, Zuidema had emphasized the nature of *ceque* as "line," as nonvisible tracings that were, rather, "straight directions." More recently, Tom Hoskinson has been able to show that it is "ethnographically well supported" that two straight lines in the Sears Point, Arizona, group of ground markings mentioned earlier—which both have astronomical (solstitial) orientation and indicate a common far horizon terminal point, Granary Basket Mountain, sacred peak or power mountain of the Yuman and Pima Indians—were created "in contemporary shamanic contexts." He usefully points to other examples of ground lines that figure in Indian legends and that have been ethnographically recorded.[60] Both straight and circular ground lines in this region could often symbolize mountain ranges thrown up by shamans as protection from enemy shamans. One of the Sears Point lines, however, is called Haak Vaak (Haak Lying), and relates to a creation myth. Indians still use the site, and it is one of the Indian special places where it is said that, if one has the power, one can access the time and space of past, present, and future. The other line, which Hoskinson feels may be up to fifteen hundred years old, indicates the June solstice sunrise in one direction, and the December solstice sunset and Granary Basket Mountain in the other. Granary Basket Mountain was an important point of shamanistic dream power and knowledge, and Hoskinson notes that the Yuman Indians commonly used datura to induce and enhance their dreaming. When the datura (*tolache*) was drunk, "the earth shone with dazzling colors." The shaman would be transported to the summit of his or her tribal mountain during the dream, "always the first stop." And in this case that means along the direction or orientation of the line. This is a specific instance of a line representing the course of spirit flight.

The use of the Costa Rican roads as death roads or corpse ways tells us that the idea of shamanic spirit travel along a straight landscape line included spirits in general. This is to be expected, because the entranced shaman was universally assumed to have temporarily died. It was only in spirit that he or she could meet the ancestors and other spirits. During the period of the shamanic trance, the shaman's spirit was no different than any other spirit.

The old straight ways, be they roads, paths, or lines, were *spirit ways* in one form or another. They were *güidel*, to use the Buryat term. Like so many other aspects of shamanism, this one is, at heart, a universal concept.

JOURNEYING IN ALUNA

As I struggled to put the pieces of this most ancient and unusual jigsaw together, I wanted actual living *proof* that these roads or landscape lines were used as shamanic spirit ways. We had the structures and markings themselves, we had the ethnography, and we had at last started to assemble the pieces, but we were trying to see something that was far back in time. Fortunately, I learned of a remarkable documentary film by Alan Ereira called *From the Heart of the World*.[61] It concerned the Kogi Indians, who live in the mountain fastness of the Sierra Nevada de Santa Marta in northern Colombia. These Chibcha people are the descendants of the pre–Columbian Tairona civilization and are the least acculturated of the three surviving indigenous groups in the sierra. After a bloody encounter with the Spanish in A.D. 1600, they withdrew into the mountains, and their lifeway became fairly fixed at that point. The dense forest and rugged terrain, and the presence in surrounding areas of such dangerous figures as tomb robbers, drug traffickers, and guerrillas, all conspired to keep them relatively undisturbed by the outside world. Anthropologist Gerardo Reichel-Dolmatoff made a study of them many years ago. He showed the Kogi cosmology to be essentially based on the shamanic "three world" model—underworld, middle earth plane, and heavenly upperworld—though elaborated into a complex nine-world scheme. The Kogi think of their domain as the "Heart of the World;" their mountain massif rises from the tropical coast and in twenty-six miles soars to the altitudes of perpetual snows. It contains all the ecological niches to be found on Earth. In *From the Heart of the World*,[62] the BBC filmed their remote society—a rare event—and they told of their concerns that the actions of Younger Brother (the Western world) were affecting the workings of nature. They could see things going wrong in the ecology of their environment, and they, as Elder Brother, wanted to send a warning. This important, primary message is well handled in the film and book, but our concern here is an aspect that emerged tangentially in Ereira's study.

Kogi society is hierarchical, a smaller and modified version of the Tairona culture of which it is a vestige. It is ruled by a shamanic theocracy—Kogi shamans being called *mamas*, "enlightened ones." Ordinary tribal members are best described as vassals, and there are intermediaries who see that the *mamas'* bidding is carried out by the vassal level. Kogi shamans can be male or female, though the men appear to dominate, and are chosen by divination. The selected child or baby is traditionally sequestered for years in a dark environment, often a cave, where it is fed minimal food and massaged to keep its muscles healthy. If brought out from this environment of stark sensory deprivation, it is at night, and the child has its head covered so that it cannot see the moon or stars. Eventually, under this strict regime, the child learns to tune in to Aluna, which we may perhaps think of as the spirit earth, a sort of spectral version of the physical earth. Things happen first in Aluna, their effects manifesting in the physical world. Eventually, under guidance, and if he is to develop into a *mama*, the child begins to sing and dance in an ethereal way. He is attuning to the inner music of the spirit world. He also begins to develop the ability to see in Aluna, and to talk with the "fathers and masters of the world," the ancestors and spirits. After many years, the fledgling *mama* emerges into the full light of blinding day, for the rest of his life able to see and act in the material world while simultaneously able to see and act in the spirit world, in the realm or dimension of Aluna. A Kogi mediator told Ereira that when a *mama* sees a rock he also sees a spirit rock, and when he "sees that river . . . he also sees the spirit river."

The Indians believe that the network of paths running through Kogi territory were built by the ancestors and "are sacred, and must be maintained and must be walked." The film includes a sequence in which the *mamas* supervise the cleaning of a section of one of these

The "Kogi Map Stone." *(Author's drawing after a photograph by Alan Ereira)*

tracks: it is clear that something spiritual is going on within the apparently mundane physical act of path maintenance.

The film also shows a standing stone with incised lines crisscrossing its surface. It stands on a pathway at the edge of one of the lost towns of the Tairona. Ereira nicknamed it the "Map Stone." "The *mama* has to walk in a world visible only to the mind's eye, the world of Aluna. . . . The stone paths of the ancestors are traces of the spirit paths which the *mamas* walked, in a space we do not understand. These are the paths in the Map Stone," Ereira intoned in his commentary. I contacted Ereira and asked if the Kogi *mamas* had explained this in more detail. It seemed to me to be "spirit travel in a spirit version of the physical world," and Ereira agreed that this described the *mamas'* work "in a way which they themselves would recognize."[63] The Indians participating in the path-maintenance ritual had been subjected to ritual drumming and instructions from the *mamas* the night before the activity, to instill in them the importance of the work they were to do. The path they worked on ran in a straight line from a river to the center of a *pre*-Tairona town, where it seemed to disappear under a building. The path was one of the oldest features in the place, and the *mamas* carefully explained to Ereira that it was but the physical trace of a spirit path that continued straight on beyond the building to another river. But the section beyond the building existed only in Aluna, and had no physical trace. The lines on the Map Stone showed the paths of Aluna, both the physical and the invisible portions. Some "mundane" paths that physically exist were not included in this map. This path clearing echoes Silverman's theory about the Nazca lines—that they had been ritually cleared, probably by means of sweeping. It suggests that the practices of the Kogi continue traditions that are at least fifteen hundred years old, with whatever "spin" may be particular to Kogi culture.

The *mamas* appear to attain their altered states by dancing and singing in ways that seem to aid the process of mental dissociation. However, they continually ingest a mixture of coca and lime by sucking on a stick inserted in a gourd container. The use of coca among high-altitude Indians in South America is a common trait; it helps them cope with hunger, fatigue, and the rigors of life in a high-altitude environment. Its consistent use is also likely to engender a mildly dreamy, dissociated state. But in addition, we must also recall that the culture group of which the Kogi are remnants produced the gold artifacts that display mushroom shapes: Ereira cites anthropological views that the Tairona culture experienced a "hallucinogenic explosion" at a particular point in its history. Although not mentioned in Ereira's film, it would be surprising, in the light of their history and the wide range of flora in their habitat, if the Kogi did not use fungal hallucinogens.

Surviving Kogi tradition confirms that some of their pathways represent (or "trace") spirit ways that are linked to shamanic practice involving ecstatic experience which can be found widespread in Native American time and space.

ROADS OF THE DEAD (A PASSAGE OF SPIRITS)

Can signs of the old trance track be found in the Old World? If the Native Americans emerged from the Paleo-peoples who migrated from Siberia, and if they trace their shamanic roots back to the classical shamanism of archaic Eurasia, might there not be lines on the landscape in Siberia? No one yet knows. Siberia is vast, and no one has undertaken the sort of sophisticated aerial survey work that NASA has done in the Americas. It's a delicate operation in any case—the conditions required to successfully get images of the almost lost Indian roads around Chaco, for instance, only occur for a few minutes each day. The shamanic landscapes of Siberia simply haven't been subjected to such scrutiny, but admittedly there is little in the ethnology of the region to suggest that such lines will be found. Nevertheless, Caroline Humphrey has noted that the concept of the path is strong in Siberian shamanism, and that there is at least the concept of *güidel*, "spirit tracks" related to some sense of a moving spirit. Moreover, not all spirit lines are visible (as was the case with the Mayan *Kusam Sum*); many exist in the "folk mind," in the "mythological land," rather than on the physical landscape. Feng Shui, for example, is an ancient Chinese art of landscape divination that has its roots in ancestor worship and Taoism, which in turn derived from shamanism. According to Feng Shui, the straight lines of troublesome spirits upon which houses and tombs should not be built are invisible. And invisible spirit lines occur throughout Europe, as we will see, including such features as fairy passes in Ireland, and ghost paths in Germany.

La Barre has pointed out that because the change from prehistory to history is so recent in the Americas, we can still document a good deal of Native American shamanism, including hallucinogen usage, artifactual ritual material, ritual practice, and, as we have seen, even the fugitive shamanic landscape markings. Eurasian prehistory is a deep, dark, murky well by comparison, with great religions having long ago wiped out the shamanic roots of early societies there. Migrations, invasions, wars, the rise and fall of religions and cultures, have made it virtually impossible to see any direct evidence of shamanic landscape lines. But, we can nonetheless gather some intriguing indirect evidence.

The archaeological record still offers some clues. In Malaysia, in the Middle East, in France, and in the British Isles, there are stone rows that seem to fit the description of spirit lines. On Dartmoor in southern England, for instance, there are rows of stones that date back nearly four thousand years. These stones are usually relatively short, they can be in single or multiple rows, and they usually pass through or incorporate small burial sites. We have no ethnography to help explain such sites, but the association of these rows with burial sites alone would suggest a spirit function of some type. This idea is strengthened by the fact that the rows often end at larger stones set at right angles to the axis of the rows. Archaeologists call them *blocking stones*, and perhaps that is just what they were—blocking the passage of spirits beyond the ends of the "roads." This echoes the concepts of Feng Shui, which calls for straight-line spirit travel to be blocked or diverted by various means.

Another archaeological enigma is the long earthen avenue line

"Blocking stones" at one end of a Bronze Age double stone row at Merrivale, Dartmoor, England. *(Paul Devereux)*

known as a *cursus*. These have so far been found only in the British Isles. The first one to be noticed was a half mile north of Stonehenge: the eighteenth-century antiquarian William Stukeley detected the easily overlooked vestiges of an earthwork nearly two miles long, running in a straight line and with its eastern end terminating at a Neolithic burial mound of the type known as a *long barrow*. He thought it was the remains of a racecourse (*cursus* in Latin) dating to the times of Roman Britain. Archaeological investigations in the twentieth century, however, have shown the Stonehenge cursus to date to the second or third millennium B.C., and its purpose is unknown. Archaeologists have noted, however, that if the cursus's alignment is extended beyond the eastern terminus, it passes through a standing stone and a Neolithic henge enclosure called "Woodhenge," forming a three-mile alignment overall, almost two-thirds of it marked on the ground by the cursus. Aerial photography has now revealed about fifty of these types of site, most of them completely invisible at ground level. Some are perfectly straight, while others are straight in sections, but change directions at each junction. Virtually all the cursuses are associated with burial sites of one kind or another, and usually link groups of mounds, so, yet again, a spirit-line function could reasonably be supposed. One of the most dramatic cursuses is a dead-straight two-mile section running immediately to the west of London's Heathrow Airport, dwarfing even the longest runways there.[64]

A third mysterious line feature of prehistory is the "Sweet Track" in Somerset, in southwestern England. This is one of the oldest roads in the world, dating back some six thousand years; it was discovered hid-

One of William Stukeley's eighteenth-century sketches of the Stonehenge Cursus.

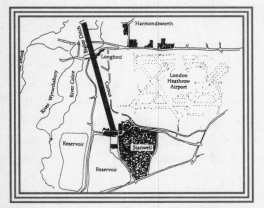

The long two-mile section of a cursus (shown as bold line) to the west of London's Heathrow Airport. Comparison of its size to the size of the runways designed for international jets gives some sense of scale. The full length of this feature is not known, as built-up areas have covered where its ends are assumed to have been.

den deep in the Somerset peat bogs, not far from the famed Glastonbury. A long section of it was uncovered, and found to consist of long poles of ash, hazel, elm, and alder, laid on the boggy surface, with pegs driven in at angles on either side of the poles every yard or so, forming V-notches. Planks were placed end to end on these supports, a foot or two above the poles, and were notched so they could lock onto the pegs. "The track was found to run in a remarkably straight line," investigating archaeologists Bryony and John Coles reported.[65] Various intriguing finds were found secreted along it, including a polished, jadeite ax blade—clearly a ceremonial object, thus indicating that the road may have had some ceremonial function. Pins made of yew were also found, similar to ones found in Neolithic burial sites, and are thought to have been from bags (which would have rotted away) that held cremated remains. This suggests that the Sweet Track may have been used for ceremonial processions carrying the remains of the dead. The road is believed to have led to the Mendip Hills, where it is known that funerary and ceremonial activities were conducted in the Neolithic period.

A medieval *doodweg* or death road near Hilversum, Holland. *(Paul Devereux)*

There are a few other odd prehistoric linear features no one today understands. But there is also considerable spirit-line evidence from the early and late medieval periods, and from the immediately post-medieval centuries. The straight "tracks" dating from these times also seem related to death roads or corpse ways in one form or another, and all are probably (and some are undoubtedly) spirit lines.

An interesting example is the Viking cult or death road that was unearthed by archaeologists at Rösaring, in Laassa, Uppland, Sweden. It is a dead-straight track of smoothed clay almost four feet wide that runs a third of a mile from what had been a timber chapel or "death house" to a group of Bronze and Iron Age and Viking burial cairns (stone mounds). The body of a dead Viking chieftain was drawn along the ritual road in a ceremonial wagon to its rest.[66]

In the Netherlands, there were the *doodwegen,* or death roads (also known as *spokenwegen,* or "ghost roads"), which converged on medieval cemeteries. Some of these survive in fragments to this day, such as the three well-kept sections now used as recreational pathways on Westerheide, Hilversum. They are notable for their straightness. Indeed, it was actually illegal to carry a corpse in anything other than a straight line to burial in medieval Holland.[67] These paths are likely barely Christianized reflections of the "the proto-typical path of spirits,"[68] the way to the underworld, of old northern European pagan lore. In fact, the old tradition recorded two paths, the God-way (*godvegr*) and the Hel-way (*helvegr*); the first was straight and led to the heaven worlds; the other was twisted, and led to the underworld, ruled by the dark goddess, Hel.[69] (It seems that the medieval Dutch dead were given the benefit of the doubt, as the *doodwegen* all seem to be straight Godways—no twisted Hel-ways have yet been found.)

In Britain, the idea of the death road seems to have been maintained in the church path or corpse way, along which walking funerals made their way to churchyard cemeteries from the outlying countryside. On the Penwith Peninsula of western Cornwall, at the very southwestern-most tip of England, an oral tradition of the "coffin line" survives, with emphasis on its linearity, as the term implies.[70] The course of some of these Cornish corpse ways can still be traced, running to a church or even connecting several churches, and they tend toward straightness, or are

St. Levan's path, with a short Celtic cross alongside it, leading to the ancient enclosure of St. Levan's Church, in the distance. Cornwall, England. *(Paul Devereux)*

straight in sections. They are marked out by, among other things, very old Celtic crosses, giving some idea of their antiquity. In certain cases they miss the church they serve by hundreds of yards, hinting that perhaps those paths were *older* than the medieval churches themselves.[71]

One particularly interesting Cornish "coffin line" aligns directly to the churchyard of the old church of St. Levan's, and is known as St. Levan's path. It is said to have been walked by the sixth-century saint, behind whom the grass grew greener where he walked. It leads to a giant split boulder in the middle of the ancient churchyard (sacred enclosure or *llan* in Welsh), clearly originally a pagan holy feature. A tall Celtic cross a thousand or more years old stands alongside to "Christianize" the stone. St. Levan's path is marked by short Celtic crosses, and where it crosses the boundary of the churchyard there is a stone the size and shape of a coffin or casket.[72]

Church paths in Britain sometimes ran across difficult terrain, awkward for the bearers of the coffin, but even where easier alternative routes existed, the old corpse paths continued to be used, right up until modern times, for it was considered unlucky to take the corpse to burial by any other way.[73] It was also traditional to carry the corpse feet-first in the direction of the graveyard, so the ghost of the deceased wouldn't be able to make its way back home—again the idea that one moves along a spirit line. Not all church paths or corpse ways in Britain are straight, by any means, and where this is the case it may be supposed that the corpse ways are more recent, being made after the ancient spirit-line concept had been forgotten or dismissed as superstitious, or was simply too old and weak a tradition to be upheld. The older corpse ways are, the straighter they seem to be. By Mont Ventoux, near Avignon in France, for example, an exceedingly old road leads down "deep and straight" from an isolated chapel, which houses one of the mysterious Black Madonna statues, to a large group of fifth-century Merovingian tombs.[74]

The apparent association between spirits, the dead, and straightness seems to have been universal. In Laos the Hmong peoples have a rule that a new house in a village should not be built directly in front or directly behind another house. This is because spirits travel in straight lines, and when corpses are moved from the house for burial they must go straight out of the house. Often the coffin will go through an opening specifically made in the wall and down to an open space at the other side of the village without passing around any other house.[75] One can hardly help but recall that the Indian tracks in the Costa Rican rain forest described earlier in this chapter were also used as corpse ways. It would appear that the association among spirits, death, and straightness was fundamental, spanning cultures and times.

In Old Europe the various forms of death roads appear to have carried the concept of the spirit way through the medieval period, and probably account for some of Alfred Watkins's leys. It is, however, clear that the idea was more generally applied too, over long periods of time, as is indicated by a road in Steeple Barton, Oxfordshire, which was known as Demnesweye (Demon's way) in Anglo-Saxon times.[76] Some roads, too, showed their spirit nature in that they actually became shrines—a pagan path in France called Yries, for example, was marked with votive offerings up until the seventeenth century.[77]

Other "paths" of Old Europe include the *Geisterwege*, ghost or spirit paths, of medieval (or earlier) Germany. German researcher Ulrich Magin found a reference to them in the 1933 edition of *Handwortbuch de deutschen Aberglaubens:* "These are always in the same place; on them one meets with ghosts quite often. The paths, with no exception, always run in a straight line over mountains and valley and through marshes. . . . In the towns they pass the houses closely or go right through them. The paths end or originate in a cemetery."[78]

Magin was subsequently able to confirm that references to *Geisterwege* go back to at least the nineteenth century, relating, of course, to older traditions. The places where these ghost path traditions were strongest—Saxony, the Voigtland, Silesia, and parts of the Oberpfalz—were outside the great early medieval German empire, and so were closer to pagan and Slav traditions, which might indicate great antiquity for the concept of *Geisterwege.* Though these "paths" are themselves invisible, they seem to relate in one way or another to the death roads, for as we noted, the Dutch *doodwegen* were also known as "ghost roads."

Another such example is the folk memory of an invisible or "lost" path said to exist between Brailes Hill in the central English county of Warwickshire and Bredon Hill in the neighboring county of Worcestershire.[79] This lost road was said to be a corpse way, but as the distance between the hills is twenty-three miles, this is almost certainly a reference to a ghost way rather than any kind of physical death road.

There are also spirit ways that are not related to death roads. In Ireland, there were the famous "fairy passes," invisible straight paths that ran from one *rath* (prehistoric earthwork) to another. In Irish folk tradition, it was considered unwise to build on the course of a fairy pass; to do so would be to invite bad luck. Irish writer Dermot McManus tells the story of one Paddy Baine of County Mayo, who built his croft without consulting anyone "wise or otherwise." Shortly after Baine and his family moved in, they suffered illnesses, domestic disputes, and, to cap it all, poltergeist activity. The crofter was obliged to call in the local wise woman, Mairead ni Heine. She told Baine that a corner of his house protruded onto a fairy pass, and was interfering with the progress of the "good people." The only answer was to lop off the offending corner of the building, a feature that can be seen to this day.[80] This solution is consistent with Chinese Feng Shui: straight features in the landscape—roads, ridges, river courses, lines of trees, and such like—all facilitate the passage of troublesome spir-

A Chinese illustration showing a Feng Shui geomancer going about his task in selecting and preparing a site for a tomb or dwelling.

its, so if a tomb or building is on the course of such an "arrow" in the land, then preventive measures must be taken, such as putting up physical barriers to mask the entrance to the building, placing fearsome "door guardians" on either side of the door, or placing a special mirror on the front door so that any horrible spirits will scare themselves off by their own reflections. This same basic idea is found all around the Pacific Rim. We have already mentioned the Hmong beliefs in Laos. In Indonesia temples have low walls inside their main entrances to deflect any straight-moving spirits from getting in. In the Gilbert Islands in the western half of the Pacific, Makin Meang, the northernmost island, is considered the halfway house between the living and the dead. On whatever island within the archipelago a person died, it was believed that the soul traveled northward in a straight line to a sand spit on Makin Meang known as the "Place of Dread." From there, the soul departed across the ocean and over the western horizon en route to Matang, the land of the ancestors, and the location of the Tree of Life. Long ago, a supernatural being, Nakaa the Judge, gave the islanders a ritual called Te Kaetikawai, "Straightening the Way of the Dead."[81] This ritual needed to be enacted around the body of the recently deceased, otherwise the departing spirit might not travel in a straight line, in which case Nakaa would ensnare it. As with the Hmong, houses in villages were situated to allow the straight passage of any departing soul.

In Europe, the folk link between the physical corpse way and invisible ghost path might have been maintained through the tradition of holding vigils at the church door (or lych—corpse—gate) on New Year's Eve or St. Mark's Eve (April 24), when the spirits of all the parishioners who are to die in the coming year are said to become visible, parading by in a line.

The Church seems to have ultimately taken over the concept of spirit lines, according to further research by Ulrich Magin. Between A.D. 900 and 1300 in Germany and Switzerland, at least, the Church created its own "sacred geography," aligning churches in a cross formation—one central cathedral with churches in each of the cardinal directions. Sometimes this formation would be enhanced by church roads running out along the alignments too. At Worms, for instance, Magin counted seven churches on a two-mile alignment, with a third of that distance being followed by a road.[82] Such arrangements have been noted at Speyer and Zurich among other cathedral cities. These features seem to have been a more purposeful and sophisticated version of church paths, and Magin has speculated that they were envisaged as conduits of the Christian Holy Spirit.[83]

EVERY WITCH WAY

The spirit ways that crossed the landscape of Old Europe in a variety of forms at various periods of time were, in fact, only one manifestation of the way Europeans, like traditional people elsewhere, populated their environment with spirits. Old paths and crossroads would be swept at certain times to rid them of spirits (reminiscent of the "road-cleaning" operations of the Native Americans cited earlier in this chapter). Spirit traps consisting of threads crisscrossed over a hoop—similar to Native American "dream catchers"—would be placed on stakes along old pathways, especially cemetery paths. These thread webs or labyrinthine arrangements of stones would be used to "bind" spirits caught moving along the straight paths. (Indeed, throughout Eurasia, including in Siber-

Part of an esoteric "church line" and pilgrimage route in Zurich, Switzerland, much of it still visible today. There is a church, the Fraumunster, in lower right foreground, a shrine on the bridge, a church at the other end (the Wasserkirche), a small circular geomantic marker known as a "blue stone" just beyond that, and then the Grossmunster (upper center). *(J. Murer, 1576)*

ian shamanic traditions, straight threads were considered "roads" that spirits could travel along.) These old straight ways, visible and invisible, almost certainly had shamanic origins, though it is hard to prove due to the opaque depth of Old World history. There are clues, however. Scholar Bruce Lincoln traces the Norse theme of the "two paths" leading to the afterworlds to the "Path of the Fathers" of the Vedas and Upanishads, as well as to the "Bridge of Separation" (the Cinvat Bridge) of Zoroastrian tradition.[84] This pushes the origins of the concept that appears as the physical *doodwegen* on the Dutch countryside, for instance, back into early Indo-European times. The Cinvat Bridge, which has to be negotiated by the deceased soul, is a shamanic concept applicable not only to the dead but also to ecstatics.[85] Hints may also reside in arcane witch lore—the lingering traces of archaic shamanism in Europe. In Germany's Harz Mountains, for example, which were notorious as the gathering place of night-flying witches, there are stone rings containing burial kists dating to the Iron Age, or even possibly to the Neolithic. Leading to one of these on the summit plateau of the Wurmberg (Dragon Mountain) is a straight section of rock-paved road known as the Steinweg. This road is oriented exactly east-west, and leads from the stone steps known as the Heidentreppe ("pagan stairs") or Hexensteppe ("witch stairs") at the edge of the summit plateau to the burial kist in the center of the stone ring. Another stone ring nearby is joined by another straight stretch of paved track. Despite the presumed prehistoric dates of the stone rings, however, pollen analysis shows that the Steinweg is, strangely, more recent, dating to between the eleventh and thirteenth centuries A.D.[86] Could it have been associated with folk-shamanic ("witch") ritual activities? We may never know, but the question inevitably arises as to whether or not the *myrkridas* of Europe had landscape "ways" like their shamanic counterparts in Native America. No sustained work has yet been done on this question, but a Spanish folk tale suggests that such research might be rewarded. The story concerns the Heathen Stone (Piedra de Gentil), a Neolithic dolmen at Vallgorguina in Catalonia. The witches of Montseny and Maresma used to assemble at this stone monument (a kind of box with uprights supporting a massive capstone) when they wanted to create storms. They jumped over the capstone of the dolmen, and when they touched it they became weightless and turned into clouds that floated away. Disastrous hail would pelt down from these "witch clouds." Close to Vallgorguina, on the road to Montnegre, is the Pla de Bruixes, Catalan for the "place of the witches." Another legend says that the dolmen is linked to a nearby church by an underground passage (a feature attributed to prehistoric monuments throughout Europe). Taken together, Ulrich Magin has suggested, these legends may well be "a folk memory of shamanic flight and the straightness connected with it."[87] Recent research suggests that vampire legends in eastern European lore may also be folk memories of shamans,[88] and there are hints in that material too of special "roads" for vampiric spirit flight.[89]

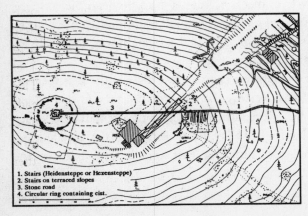

Map showing the Steinweg rising up the eastern slope of the Wurmberg and crossing the summit plateau to stone ring.

1. Stairs (Heidensteppe or Hexensteppe)
2. Stairs on terraced slopes
3. Stone road
4. Circular ring containing cist.

SITTING OUT

There is clearly much more we can try to learn, but the association between shamanism and the old straight ways of Europe is already evident beyond a reasonable doubt. Icelandic folklore contains considerable detail on northern magical traditions, far more than can now be recovered in documenting the folklore of Scandinavia and Europe. There was a magical practice in the northern tradition called "sitting out." In this activity, the magician, shaman, or seer would sit in an entranced state and summon spirits for divination, or "go on seers' journeys."[90] In Norway this tradition is recorded in accounts of men sitting out on burial mounds in order to receive occult wisdom. The record of the tradition in Iceland, which can be traced back to various medieval texts, is much more specific. On New Year's Eve or on the Eve of St. John's Day (June 24), the shaman (or seer, or magician) would go to a crossroads "where four roads run, each in an a straight unbroken line, to four churches."[91] He would take with him a gray cat, a gray sheepskin with its fleece on, the hide of a walrus or of an old bull, and an ax. At the crossroads he would lie down and spread the hide over him, then hold the ax before his eyes and stare fixedly at the sharp, shining edge of its blade. He would lie entranced in that position, still as a corpse, throughout the night, using incantation to summon spirits from the churchyards to which the roads led. In an alternative procedure, the shaman might summon elves for his divinatory requirements rather than the spirits of the dead: the elves or "hidden folk" file past crossroads on New Year's Eve, much as the soon-to-be-dead file past the church door. In the surviving records of such traditions we have all the essential, combined elements of spirit paths, straightness, the death association, and shamanic practice.

If we look hard enough, we can still just discern the disappearing traces of the web of trance ecstasy that covered both the Old and New Worlds in ancient times. Bequeathed, it is part of a remarkable legacy that holds special value for us today, for it deals with the very areas of human awareness that our culture is least knowledgeable about and least comfortable discussing.

Something Is Happening Here—But Do We Know What It Is?

(Memoranda)

Only in recent years have we begun to grasp the full, awesome extent of the Long Trip that has been taken by so much of humanity in cultures and societies that existed long before our own. It has left its mark—on the land, engraved in stone, in monuments, artifacts, and rituals—testament to the fact that the yearning to reach other, alternate states of consciousness is a powerful and irrepressible human instinct. It is as strong as hunger or the sexual drive, as Andrew Weil has pointed out,[1] and the evidence of that is deeper and more widespread than we had ever supposed. It is a legacy we are going to have to deal with, sooner or later, in our brave yet in many ways rather immature modern Western culture, because no "war on drugs" or slogan is ever going to defeat such a primal urge. The present-day prohibitionist approach to "drugs" (which is itself a reductionist and inadequate word) will only drive into criminal and pathological channels a subject that should be seriously studied.

Nobody in his or her right mind likes the current situation regarding "hard drugs" in society, with the street violence, human misery, and international organized crime. The indiscriminate prohibitionist approach of recent decades has actually managed to make this situation worse. It does not help to exaggerate the dangers of a "drug" such as cannabis, putting it in the same legal and conceptual category as crack cocaine. This only serves to weaken the valid case for prohibiting the truly dangerous narcotics, and undermines respect for the law. One element that helps explain Western society's attitude toward cannabis is the historical fact, which Andrew Sherratt pointed out, that the West is a "drinking complex" culture, whereas other societies are more attuned to a "smoking complex," a schism we can crudely label as the "Christian West" and the "Islamic East" respectively. There is no absolute good or evil, white or black, about this: it is simply a cultural reflex, and there are unnecessary problems when this factor cannot be perceived. Drinking scotch and beer are acceptable in the West. The staggering number of people killed in drunk-driving episodes is accepted. (In terms of fatalities, cannabis, in contrast, has an almost pristine record.) The prohibitionist approach to cannabis and other nonaddictive mind-altering drugs is a general Western phenomenon, but it is particularly unremitting in the United States. It may not be clearly perceived within the USA just how earnestly the government tries to persuade—some would say coerce—other nations into adopting its one-dimensional "no drugs" policy. The Dutch seem to have developed a perfectly workable alternative: controlled, monitored tolerance of cannabis use. As a result, cannabis now no longer poses a significant sociological difficulty in that society. In 1995, even some British police chiefs and politicians called for the noncriminalization of cannabis, to release police time and resources, to remove otherwise perfectly law-abiding people from a criminal context (and therefore danger of criminal influence and contamination), and thus to partially but significantly disenfranchise the drug syndicates.

The core of the issue is that developing intelligent policy requires that we "know drugs." The taking of hallucinogenic substances for medical and psychological research or with the serious intent of expanding direct personal psychological and spiritual experience ought not to be lumped together with "substance abuse"—the irresponsible ingestion of substances purely for "kicks," as psychosocially-driven escapism, or because of the demands of physical addiction. Hallucinogens *are* powerful substances, and do need to be subject to social control. This should not be beyond the ability of society to organize. Cultures throughout history have managed to channel and use the human interest in these substances and experiences. We saw early in this book that Czechoslovakia at the time Stanislav Grof left was managing controlled access to the tremendously important and informative psychedelic experience without unfortunate social effects.

In his island utopia of Pala, Aldous Huxley envisaged a mind-altering substance, the moksha-medicine, which would be taken by every individual in his or her rite of passage of puberty. Thus everyone would have the opportunity—the obligation, even—to at least once in his or her life directly experience the profound levels of mind exposed in the psychedelic experience.[2] It's not unreasonable to think that a society where every mind has a sense of deeply dimensioned other states of consciousness as a backdrop to everyday concerns, and, indeed, where it could go and refresh its acquaintance with those states when the glow fades, would not be plagued as we are by people who use filthy hypodermic needles filled with dangerous drugs bought illegally from the lackeys of organized drug cartels on street corners using criminally obtained funds. In such a society, it would be less likely that young men would be mindlessly violent and aggressive, having faced awesome forces in the hyperdimensions of other states of consciousness. In such a society, positive personal and social patterns would quite definitely assume greater prominence, as they do in tribal societies where regular access to the otherworld is made. At this point it seems a complete fantasy to imagine such a society, and yet it is helpful to do so, to imagine how these experiences could be put to society's good. Of course, this kind of change could not occur until the social and, even more importantly, the political will to seek it came first.

We have seen that other, older societies used the psychedelic experience to *strengthen, renew, and heal* the spiritual underpinning of their social structures. The ever-deepening social unease that Western civilization seems to be caught in is the real source of our "drug problem": natural hallucinogens are not the problems in themselves; it is the context in which they are used that matters. If there were orderly and healthy structures and mechanisms for their use and the cultural absorption of the powerful experiences—and knowledge—we could separate these experiences from the culture of crime that surrounds them now. The problems are not in the psychoactive substances themselves, but in society.

WHISPERING LEAVES: INTERSPECIES COMMUNICATION

Perhaps only a shock of some kind could break our society free from the patterns of thought and prejudices that lock it into the crisis. The desire for such a shock may be hidden within the widespread belief in extraterrestrial intervention. In fact we do not have to look to science fiction for a real otherworld contact: it already exists in the form of plant hallucinogens. If we see them in the context of a "problem," it is only because they hold up a mirror in which we see our spiritual, social, and mental condition reflected. And they hold that mirror up to us as one species to another just as surely as if they were from another planet. Indeed, Terence McKenna has argued that the ancestral spores of today's hallucinogenic mushrooms may have originated on some other planet![3] The psilocybin family of hallucinogens, says McKenna, produces a "Logos-like phenomenon of an interior voice that seems to be almost a superhuman agency . . . an entity so far beyond the normal structure of the ego that if it is not an extraterrestrial it might as well be."[4]

It is a remarkable fact that plant hallucinogens are hallucinogenic precisely because they contain the same, or effectively the same, chemicals as are found in the human brain, and so act on us as if we were indeed engaged in an interspecies communication. "The chemical structure of the hallucinogenic principles of the mushrooms was determined . . . and it was found that these compounds were closely related chemically to substances occurring naturally in the brain which play a major role in the regulation of psychic functions," Schultes and Hofmann have observed, for instance.[5] This challenges the view held by many people that taking a plant hallucinogen is somehow "unnatural." Certainly, it takes the brain-mind to states that are not "normal" by the standards of our culture, but the "normal" state of Western consciousness cannot claim to be the one and only "true" state of consciousness. (Indeed, judging by the mess we manage to make of our societies and of the natural world around us, it may even be an aberrant or pathological state of mind that we are locked into.)

"If one were to reduce to its essentials the complex chemical process that occurs when an external psychoactive drug such as psilocybin reaches the brain, it would then be said that the drug, being structurally closely related to the naturally occurring indoles in the brain, appears to interact with the latter in such a way as to lock a nonordinary or inward-directed state of consciousness temporarily into place. . . . There are obviously wide implications, biological-evolutionary as well as philosophical, in the discovery that precisely in the chemistry of consciousness we are kin to the plant kingdom," writes Peter Furst.[6]

These are probably the same kind of chemical changes that occur during the course of long and intensive spiritual exercises, but it takes a rare person in our culture to achieve sufficient expertise in such techniques to have experiences that match those accessible through hallucinogen usage, which are certainly very "real" in a subjective sense. It is a culturally engineered cliché to dismiss such states as being somehow delusional. They are subjectively no more delusional than the experience of daily life. The human body takes in material from the environment and expels matter into it all the time, and we really shouldn't think of taking in natural chemicals for visionary and mind-expanding functioning as any less natural than taking in gases from the air for their chemical benefits to the body, or chemicals and compounds in animal and vegetable matter to provide food, or fermented fruits and vegetables to provide delicious and inebriating beverages, or vitamins to augment healthy functioning, or medicines when we are ill or caffeinated teas and coffees when we want to be energized. "Ethnobotanists now realize that psychotropic plant species extend further than had been suspected, as though nature truly wanted the human species to get in touch with its floral neighbors," Richard Gehr muses. "As plant species die off at a furious rate, the issue is no longer what they are trying to tell us, but whether we will get the message in time."[7]

That message may have to do with the need for us to change our minds, or, at least, to broaden our cognitive horizons. The plant kingdom could be urging us to allow the ability to "switch channels" in consciousness terms, to let them become a recognized and acceptable part of our emerging global culture. Hallucinogen-using ancient and traditional societies had and have exceptional sophistication when it comes to understanding and navigating alternate states of consciousness, whereas we are still quite primitive and inexperienced in this regard. The manual for using expanded consciousness is an ancient textbook we have not yet read—or, more accurately, recalled. Not that widening our collective experience of consciousness will act like a magic wand and remove all problems and obstacles, but it would help us to make wiser, more whole-some decisions in coping with them. If Western civilization is truly to advance, we surely must learn to operate using the multidimensional capacities of our minds, rather than using the police to conduct an indiscriminate war on the means of doing so. A workable balance has to be struck between protecting the well-being and the orderly functioning of society as a whole, and allowing the human brain-mind to explore its full potential. We are smart enough, and complex enough and able enough, to make it possible to do both.

THE PSYCHEDELIC POTENTIAL

As a culture, we have barely scratched the surface of the potential enhancements that greater, more socially-integrated access to psychedelic states could provide—and we may already owe the psychedelic experience more than we would care to know. Gordon Wasson questioned whether it could have been soma that triggered the qualities "that alone make man unique ... memory, language, and self-consciousness."[8] Richard Rudgley remarks that it is at the beginnings of our species that we need to seek the basis of civilization, not arbitrary points such as ancient Greece.[9] Did early human beings, in discovering the doorway to the alternate mental realities of the psychedelic universe guarded by the plant kingdom, have to develop greater intellectual powers and a greater vocabulary, a more sophisticated use of language, to cope with the profound experiences of the expanded states of mind that flooded in on them? Did the psychedelic encounter *provoke* the traits that we now see as characteristically human?

There seems to have been a relatively sudden development in the size of the human brain during our evolution that is puzzling to evolutionary biologists. Could it be that contact with the psychedelic experience over several thousand generations contributed to this growth? Certain hallucinogens, especially the mushrooms, do seem to promote language. Henry Munn, who lives with the Mazatec Indians of Oaxaca, has made a special study of this. "The Mazatecs say that the mushrooms speak," he writes. "If you ask a shaman where his imagery comes from, he is likely to reply: I didn't say it, the mushroom did. No mushroom speaks, that is a primitive anthropomorphization of the natural, only man speaks, but he who eats the mushrooms, if he is a man of language, becomes endowed with an inspired capacity to speak."[10] It is, says Munn, "as if the mushrooms revealed a primordial activity of signification." With regard to psilocybin, the active element in most hallucinogenic mushrooms, and DMT, Terence McKenna refers to "a kind of *Ursprache*; a language scripted into the bone and meat of the organism, rather than a very superfluous software language of the sort that we teach our children."[11] These substances "work directly on the language centers," he observes. With the languages of vast vocabularies now developed, and the many means of mass communication now available to us, to what mental levels could we be provoked were we to engage with the plant kingdom again on a full, cultural level? What language of the future could be seeded? What cognitive tools fashioned? What evolutionary leaps of mind achieved? What new, high civilizations created . . . civilizations worthy of a species becoming global in its worldview and actions?

And then there is creativity. We saw in the "Psychedelic Sixties" how the hallucinogenic experience charged our society with creativity—in art, in music, in fashion, in literature, in film, in intellectual daring—in all sorts of ways. Indeed, the effects of those years are so pervasive as to have become irreversible. The creative potential of the psychedelic state has been remarked on often, but prevailing political attitudes have prevented serious research on the subject. Right in the midst of the 1960s psychedelic revival, psychologist Stanley Krippner could identify a number of instances in which psychedelically provoked creativity was suggested.[12] In 1966, Navy captain John Busby reported the use of LSD in his solving of a difficult problem in pattern recognition while developing equipment for a navy research project. "With LSD, the normal limiting mechanisms of the brain are released and entirely new patterns of perception emerge," Busby stated. A mental hospital was designed by psychiatrist Humphry Osmond and architect Kyo Izumi with the aid of psychedelic drugs. A series of pilot studies conducted at that time into the effects of psychedelic creativity showed positive subjective aesthetic shifts (though often more in the areas of appreciation than performance). One program studied problem solving with a group of professionals who had labored over intractable problems for some months. The use of mescaline helped them come to satisfactory solutions. In another study, fifty-four percent of a group of ninety-one artists reported an improvement in their work through the use of psychedelic substances. Krippner concluded that the subject was worthy of further study. And so it remains.

We have noted in earlier chapters how the songs, music, and decorative art of many traditional societies are said to originate with hallucinogenic experience. With assistance from a musicologist, Marlene Dobkin de Rios studied the music from *ayahuasca* sessions held by rain forest Indians, and found that it played a crucial role in bridging ordinary and nonordinary realms of consciousness.[13] That will not come as a great surprise to many people in our own societies, but what a rich field of inquiry beckons here! With new, extensive studies, we might find that the psychedelic experience could unleash a new renaissance of creativity.

The essence of the psychedelic experience is spiritual, which can mean religious (though not necessarily). It takes the psyche, the soul, into realms far beyond material reality, where the workings of the mind and the very universe are revealed. These experiences are by no means always blissful and serene. They can be painful and terrifying. But they can also be transcendental. For many people, just one such experience may be enough—especially if it is undergone in a supportive environment where the maximum benefit can be obtained and retained. No hallucinogen can endow a soul with "permanent spiritual enlightenment." No drug is a substitute for spiritual discipline and attainment.

But when the mind or soul has once been in these transcendental realms, it "wakes up," as it were, and the far-reaching potential of human spiritual experience becomes direct knowledge. Subsequent spiritual effort, by whatever means or disciplines, is thus *informed*. Spiritual reality isn't merely belief or guesswork anymore, it is certainty, it becomes actual memory. This, of course, is the nature of initiation. This seems to have been the principle behind the Eleusinian Mysteries (chapter 2), the only really instituted psychedelic experience the West has ever had. It is cause for profound regret that our culture does not encompass such an experience within its mainstream structure now. Nevertheless, with four decades of widespread psychedelic experience within our modern society, there have to be more people alive on Earth at this time with direct knowledge of transcendental realms than at any other single period in the history of the planet. This weight of experience clearly has and will inevitably continue to find its ways to influence the mainstream culture. But mainstream recognition and accommodation would transform such a cautious growth into a phenomenal flowering.

Because the psychedelic experience is a spiritual one, it has been suggested, most notably by the Wassons, that perhaps plant hallucinogens were the spur, the trigger, for the birth of religious sensibility in the human species. Perhaps the hallucinogenic plants gave the human soul its wake-up call—the generous gesture of one species to another. If this distinctly possible scenario is *at all* true, then, on the one hand, mainstream culture seriously needs to correct its jaded view of "hallucinogens," and, on the other hand, users of illicit hallucinogens should ponder their responsibility in contributing to the decline of such substances from sacraments to mere recreational mind-toys, a decline psychologists such as Andrew Weil and Ralph Metzner have drawn attention to.[14]

Finally, the potential of hallucinogens to help with the healing of certain dysfunctions needs to be explored. For example, LSD interacts with dopamine, a neurotransmitter in the brain. This may have implications regarding diseases such as schizophrenia and Parkinson's disease.[15] Who knows what healing capacities might be found in them if such substances were released from the politico-cultural condemnation that, until recently at least, has crippled even bona fide research efforts?

WHAT IS REALLY REAL?

What is the nature of the experiences encountered in the psychedelic state? What is their ontological status? The mainstream view is that all such experiences are hallucinatory (whatever that term actually means), implying that they are delusional. But such confident statements are usually made by those who have never directly experienced these alternate mental realities, or who have done so only in limited, unfortunate conditions. Our cognitive scientists, despite their reductionist selves, are showing that our perception of the "real world" is but a mental construction, a model, made from the information supplied by raw data impinging upon our senses, and the brain-mind processes that put this together are the same as those that present "hallucinations" to our consciousness.[16] We could easily speculate that our culture is itself a hallucination, and that our reality is only real so long as we are culturally and physically "locked" into it. In sleep and the trance or psychedelic state it may be that this binding is loosened and we can more freely engage with other realities, even if they come to us through the restrictive doorways of our personal and cultural psychology, sensory memory, and the processing idiosyncrasies of our organ of consciousness, the brain. Who knows but that in death we are released from these attachments and can enter into the experience of the direct nature of realities that appear to us only in their symbolic forms, dressed in imagery familiar to us in our "waking" lives?

What are we to make of experiences such as those reported by the anthropologist Kenneth Kensinger, for example, where six members of a tribal *ayahuasca* session told him that his faraway father-in-law had died, a fact later confirmed by field radio? The *ayahuasca* experience of flying in spirit, perhaps in the form of a bird, to other parts of the world is readily explained by our psychologists as a remodeling of sensory data—essentially hallucinatory material. So it might well be, but does that stop it being a vehicle for obtaining "real" information? The body of anthropological and anecdotal material is too overwhelming to dismiss these phenomena. Science should take up the challenge: it must come up with better explanations.

Our science also tells us that the imagery seen in hallucinations is largely determined by set and setting, so that the elements of, for instance, a rain forest tribe's *ayahuasca* hallucinations would be different from the imagery seen by hallucinogen takers in a desert group in Africa. By and large, this cultural influence on hallucinatory material is pretty well confirmed. But the basic functions of different hallucinations—communication with an ancestral spirit, say—may be essentially the same. In other words, the role of a hallucination as a vehicle of information is not necessarily changed by its outward appearance. But even at this superficial level of imagery, there are exceptions to the rule. An intriguing, even disturbing, example of this was provided by research conducted by psychiatrist Claudio Naranjo in the 1960s, mentioned earlier. Naranjo administered harmaline, one of the alkaloids of the South American rain forest hallucinogenic brew *yagé*, to a group of thirty-five urban Chilean volunteers who knew nothing of the experiences of rain forest Indians with *yagé*. "Strangely enough," reported Naranjo, "tigers, leopards, or jaguars were seen by seven of the subjects even though big cats are not seen in Chile."[17] Some subjects reported other equally alien serpents and reptiles. Serpent forms and large cats, notably the jaguar, feature prominently in Indian *yagé* visions. How did they appear to these humans from another culture? "This result was unexpected and remains unexplained," commented Michael Harner on the study.[18] Naranjo noted that these results "invite us to regard some shamanistic conceptions more as the expression of universal experiences than in terms of acculturation to local traditions."[19]

There are hints in other research on hallucinogenic visions, too, that transpersonal elements can occur that transcend available explanations. We have already noted that psychotherapist Stanislav Grof is one of the most experienced researchers in the use of LSD and other hallucinogens, and he has observed session content that represents "a serious challenge for Western science and the philosophical assumptions upon which it is based":

Persons who report transpersonal experiences [under the influence of hallucinogens] often obtain access to detailed and relatively esoteric knowledge about . . . the material universe which vastly exceeds their general level of education. . . . Experiences of collective and racial unconscious in the sense of Jung, and memories of previous incarnations often contain quite astounding details concerning specific historical events and costumes, architecture, weaponry, art or religious practices of the societies concerned. Persons who relive phylogenetic memories or consciously identify themselves with a living species of animal not only report on the unusual authenticity and convincingness of these events, but also obtain in this manner unusual insights into animal psychology, ethnology, species-specific habits, complex reproductive cycles, and the mating customs of the most diverse species.

Persons who consciously experience identification with plants or botanical processes occasionally report remarkable knowledge about the germination of seeds, the process of photosynthesis, the role of auxins in the growth of plants, pollination, or the exchange of minerals and water in the root system.[20]

Such experiences suggest to Grof that we all have "in some unexplained manner . . . information concerning the entire universe and every type of existence at our disposal." Once the existence of transpersonal phenomena is admitted, Grof argues, then "the fine line between psychology and parapsychology disappears." The sort of experiences described above, Grof reports, have led many subjects, including well-educated ones, to independently suggest that consciousness is not a product of the central nervous system but rather an attribute of existence as a whole, "which can neither be reduced to nor derived from anything else."[21]

The psychedelic experience precipitates us into a mental reality that may be another realm of existence, or another way of allowing our brain-minds to model the input of "Mind-at-Large." A subject observing-participating in an indescribable visual pattern while under the influence of DMT reported:

I was seeing the "true universe" or the universe as it really exists. . . .
That is to say, I was seeing directly the vibrations of every particle
in the universe without ordering it into an arbitrary reality tunnel,
i.e., a perceived "solid, objective reality." The visual pattern seemed
to be a sort of n-dimensional Lissajous curve, formed by the inter-
section of "I" with the shock wave of space-time causality.[22]

D. M. Turner calls the realm that the psychedelic experience takes
us to "CydelikSpace." Another psychedelic writer and researcher, Jim
DeKorne, calls it "the Imaginal Realm,"[23] using a phrase developed by
Henri Corbin. Turner insists that it is not a fictional dimension:

It is accessible now, and even appears to be the underlying reality
behind all existence. It is of this state that one becomes aware, to a
greater or lesser degree, during deep psychedelic experiences, and
any other mystical or spiritual experience.

. . . CydelikSpace supports the notion that the manifest universe is a construct of consciousness, and not the other way
round. . . .

Not only is CydelikSpace a complete depository of my own
life's perceptions, it similarly contains all thoughts and experiences
of every human, animal, plant, and molecular life form that has existed in the universe since time began, including the life experience
of individual cells and galactic star systems. . . .

But this entire storehouse of universal experience is but a frac-
tion of CydelikSpace's magnitude.[24]

Wolfgang Coral considers this psychedelic dimension to be "the space
between the spirit and matter," but comments ruefully that because in
Western industrialized societies "spiritual experiences are no longer an
immediate aspect of our culture, it is hard for us to understand the
unity of this continuum of experience."[25] He points out that it is a
common error to think that such states of experience are the products
of the drugs themselves. In fact, they are the products of our nervous
systems, since both drugs and nondrug techniques are capable of ush-

ering us into various parts of this hyperdimensional domain. Any specific hallucinogenic experience may lead us for a time along the lines laid out by that substance's particular "molecular script," Coral admits, but the core of the experience belongs to us, not an outside agent.

Even from this brief summary, it can be seen that experienced psychedelic researchers are independently arriving at a very similar model, in which the appearance of the world, of the universe, is constructed in our brain-minds as but one cognitive model out of many that could be drawn from the "n-dimensional" matrix of which we are a part, and that we are culturally locked onto one model as being "reality." This consensus hints that perhaps the psychedelic experience can offer a whole new paradigm of consciousness, of the very nature of what we perceive as "reality." If the disciplined analytical skills of our science could be fully combined with the experiential knowledge that currently has only been fully explored in shamanic societies, we might well arrive at vital new models of consciousness, drastically different from those to which we currently adhere.

I sometimes wonder if our culture, acting in the manner of a single organism—in the way a crowd of people or a classroom of students sometimes can—somehow senses a deep threat to its own philosophical foundations residing in the psychedelic experience. This might help account for the otherwise irrational hatred and repression of the use of hallucinogens, and the smirking dismissal of the psychedelic experience as a trivial one by so many of our intellectuals. Consequently, our cognitive scientists do not explore alternate states of consciousness with the neutrality good science demands, and the important writing and research produced by many psychedelic experts remains on the fringe of our intellectual life.

THE ROAD AHEAD

Although there has been a sharp break in the Long Trip, significant elements within our Westernized societies are still treading the trail, especially since the 1960s psychedelic revival. There are two destinations marked on the signpost we are passing: scientific research into hallucinogens, and the social application of the psychedelic experience.

Because of the powerfully reinforced political attitudes against mind-altering substances generated in the 1970s and 1980s, even bona fide scientific research into hallucinogens has been drastically hindered. But the 1990s has seen something of a psychedelic renaissance, both scientifically and socially. In 1995, Rick Doblin, founder and president of the Multidisciplinary Association for Psychedelic Study (MAPS) of Charlotte, North Carolina, a group dedicated since 1986 to advancing the study of psychedelics by assisting scientists to design, obtain governmental approval for, fund, and conduct research, was able to announce a number of new or pending official psychedelic research projects.[26] Since 1994, for instance, Dr. Charles Grob had been conducting the first study of MDMA since it was made illegal in 1985. The effects of the substance on volunteers was monitored with high-tech brain-scanning techniques and other physiological and psychological monitoring methods, and higher doses were being administered and studied in March 1995. No obvious signs of any MDMA-related brain damage was recorded, and plans were afoot to use MDMA in conjunction with guided imagery to reduce physical and psychological pain in cancer patients, and to hopefully boost their immune systems—a continuation of successful initial work in this field that was curtailed when the substance was criminalized. Research by doctors Juan Sanchez-Ramos and Deborah Mash started with ibogaine. In 1995, Drs. Richard Yensen and Donna Dryer were planning to initiate a study into the use of LSD in substance abusers and in cancer patients. MAPS also brought over to America Dr. Evgeny Krupitsky, a Russian scientist studying the effects of ketamine in the treatment of alcoholics and neurotics, to meet with U.S. researchers into mind-altering drugs. (Ketamine is a legal anesthetic drug in the USA, so its study is not so curtailed as with other substances; several research teams at Yale University and the University of Washington are apparently currently studying the drug with regard to attempting to understand the biochemical basis of schizophrenia.)

The research program that effectively broke the drought of psychedelic research in the USA was a study of the effects of DMT conducted at the University of New Mexico by Dr. Rick Strassman, commenced in 1990. It began with collecting dose-response information about DMT's physiological and psychological effects—the latter using the Hallucinogen Rating Scale (HRS) designed by Strassman. Then tests to determine whether subjects could develop tolerance to repeated doses of DMT were conducted, and within the terms of the tests carried out, it was found that they did not. This had a bearing on the possible role of natural, body-produced DMT (endogenous DMT) in mental illness. The Strassman program went on to study what brain receptor sites were used by DMT for its effects. This program came to an end in 1996. Strassman was planning to go on to study LSD and psilocybin, but family matters forced a move to Canada after preliminary dose range-finding work was performed with psilocybin. Even if he had stayed in New Mexico, Strassman was becoming increasingly concerned about the unsuitability of a hospital-based setting for the longer-acting drugs, such as LSD and psilocybin. The smells, sounds, and sights of the hospital, and the lack of natural surroundings to relax in at various times during the eight-hour sessions, combined to make many of his first psilocybin volunteer anxious and uncomfortable. When he resumes this work, Strassman will use his hospital-based psilocybin information to argue against a hospital setting for work with this and other long-lasting psychedelics—though he actually preferred the hospital setting for DMT. The intense cardiovascular effects (blood pressure and pulse) could seriously stress someone with unknown heart disease, and the availability of immediate response teams for medical emergencies, while never used, added a safety net to a drug that inherently makes many people feel as if they are dead or dying.

Strassman feels that it is unwise to proceed in less than ideal circumstances, and had in any case been considering winding down the type of work he has been doing. (He has been studying effects in healthy, experienced hallucinogen-using volunteers, doing descriptive psychopharmacology work, and studying effects and mechanisms of action—which often involved blockading drug effects by another, often unpleasant, pretreatment drug.) He is now beginning to consider how the therapeutic utility of these drugs might be best explored. "As a clinical researcher, the therapeutic potential of these drugs were what drew me to their study, and I was not impressed with how 'therapeutic' the drugs were in and of themselves," Strassman informed me. "Odd, novel, compellingly weird were their effects, but in our group, already rather sated with psychedelic and/or other unusual experiences, the 'therapeutic' end results, on the longer term, were pretty thin." I asked Strassman how he would like to see the field develop as a whole, in the light of his experienced and well-informed role on the crest of the new wave of psychedelic research. "There are several areas in which I can see the field moving, but this differs from how I'd *like* to see it develop!" was his initial response, but he went on to comment on several aspects of the question.

First, there is the well-worn adage of "enhancing mind-brain studies." However, I am less enthusiastic about this than I was when I started out. First of all, it puts an enormous stress on the need to perform "brain" studies, which translates into thousands of animals being injected with psychedelics, then radioactivity, then decapitated, having their brains removed and sliced into thin sections, and pictures taken of the results. This is clearly an indirect, and some might argue, cruel, method to study drugs whose primary effects are on human mentality. On the other hand, there are imaging techniques of brain function which show something going on when people are altered (hallucinating on their own in, say, a schizophrenic state; or visualizing something they've just seen). However, this is so high tech, and so far removed from what common sense is telling us is going on in the first place, it seems that there really is ultimately little to be gained by all this machinery. Are people any nicer to each other knowing how the brain works? I think better yet is if they enhanced "mind" studies, and therefore helped us return to valuing introspective, subjective data, which certainly can be measured if one applies oneself to measuring these things. (For example, our rating scale, the HRS, was much more capable of discerning subtle dose effects, or drug-drug combination effects, than were the multiple biological variables we exhaustively measured in our volunteers.)

Secondly, while I do not see these drugs as inherently therapeutic, they have properties which when other factors are brought to bear on them (therapeutic intent, therapeutic circumstances) can magnify certain processes that occur within a therapeutic context: for example, increasing symbolic productions in a clear sensorium, freeing associations, derepressing imagery and memories, enhancing certain aspects of the interpersonal dynamic, and the like. And, when people have bona fide problems (abuse, drug problems, depression, marital problems) perhaps in the right hands, set, and setting, something good can come out of working with these drugs in a therapeutic situation. Maybe with using lower doses than we're used to thinking of as being "psychedelic," at least in the beginning, to build people up to, and familiarize themselves with, some of the more peculiar states.

Third, a lot of people, even the so-called "a-religious," "atheist" types, will describe psychedelic drug effects in terms that people, for lack of anything else, call "religious" or "spiritual." This is probably their property that causes the most alarm in the most people. Be that as it may, it's true, and to deny it is to deny what people are saying, which of course is bad clinical practice, and even worse clinical research. This has recently gotten me to thinking about who should sit for sessions, and what should the feedback be to people who are tripping? Are psychiatrists alone up for it? I don't think so, since they have no religious training, and are trained actually to look at religious sensibilities as more primitive than everyday sensibilities. So, it might be easier to conceive of physician/clergy "teams" working with patients. But they would have to include clergy who can hold both a mystical and materialistic world view at the same time.

This leads to the fourth issue, which is the use of psychedelics in religious training/discipline. Not every denomination will send their minions out to help with psychedelic research cheek-to-jowl with a medical psychiatrist. It would take unusually open schools, which are hard to find, as I have discovered from personal experience. I would hope not all religions would react negatively, but most will. There are "religious" sects in Latin America where these plant/drugs are used in a responsible, socially acceptable and useful manner, and help moral, religious, behavioral sensibilities. But, in the West, and I guess in the East, there's no model for occasional use of psychedelics to enhance the religious discipline's results. I think this possibility ought to be discussed openly, widely, and broadly, and examined without preconceptions.

And finally, there are issues related to non-material realms . . . but I'll let that one lie for a while.[27]

Clearly, there are problems not only with what have been the political and legal circumstances besetting psychedelic research, but also with its recognition as a valuable tool in spiritual areas, and in the challenges it poses regarding scientific methodology. In other words, the powerful and potentially paradigm-shifting perspectives the psychedelic experience creates are presenting as many difficulties across the whole spectrum of our culture's outlook as did the invention of the telescope for societies in medieval Europe.

Hopefully, the new glimmerings of official tolerance toward research with psychedelic substances will continue to develop, and the scope of permitted research will extend beyond the potential therapeutic aspects into the area of consciousness study *in its own right*. This would be very much in the spirit of the times, for the 1990s has seen a tremendous explosion of serious interest in many areas of consciousness studies within the international scientific community—indeed, the most important area of study there can be has begun to properly engage Western science. It is to be hoped that the newly charged inquiry into the nature of consciousness will go the full distance, and fully include the psychedelic experience. To not do so would be like a college of old-line astronomers managing to ignore the existence of the telescope.

But however the legal authorities and the scientific establishment finally decide to conduct themselves, the Long Trip will not be halted. The Long Trip is an essential part of the journey of the human mind in its quest for its full expression, and will continue even if it meets opposition. We can see this happening now, in the last decade of the twentieth century, as a new generation of psychedelically aware young Westerners and Westernized, psychedelicized Pacific Rim youth is again emerging, a new wave building up after the trough that followed the Psychedelic Sixties. Old-style psychedelia helped spawn the high technology of the nineties, and has produced hybrid "cyberpunks," "techno-ravers" and "zippies." In the 1980s "rave" scene in Britain, networked information would result in hundreds or even thousands of young people descending on open fields or vast, impromptu venues such as warehouses, to hold all-night parties with dancing, "acid house" music, MDMA ("Ecstasy"), LSD, cannabis, and computerized laser light shows. Despite the relatively small number of problems with violence or "bad trips" at such vast events, and despite the general absence of "hard" drugs, the authorities did their best to clamp down on the raves, whose sheer size, use of mind-altering drugs, and impressively effective decentralized "systems" organization clearly rattled them. But some elements of the scene moved on and clubs were opened and groups specializing in trancing effects using music, sound, and electronic technology became, and remain, popular and increasingly effective. Luminaries of psychedelic thought and New Science, such as Terence McKenna and Rupert Sheldrake, are invited to speak about their research to the new psychedelic generation at such venues.

This is the growing, now international context of popular psychedelia, which will doubtless continue to develop, chameleonlike, as it needs to. Interestingly, the late Timothy Leary, original prophet of the sixties psychedelic revolution, became something of a guru for the new techno-psychedelic generation too, with slogans like "the PC is the LSD of the nineties." His book *Chaos and Cyber-Culture* (Ronin Publishing, 1994) has apparently been an element in the new hybridization of psychedelia and computerized high technology.

Another element in the continuing story of the Long Trip is the fact that some individuals went on from their own experiences during the Psychedelic Sixties and became highly expert and, indeed, scholarly researchers on the nature of psychedelic substances and their effects. One of these "hands-on" experts is Jonathan Ott. He has started to present his research into *ayahuasca* pharmacology, which has resulted in his identifying very simple ways of creating the same hallucinogenic effects by using combinations of different plants containing the appropriate alkaloids that are found in those comprising *ayahuasca* brews. "With careful experimentation, we will discover ways of making *ayahuasca* analogues with plants from all continents and from every climate zone," he writes. "Inasmuch as this technology is not much more difficult than, and employs equipment already available for, home extraction of coffee beans, I expect it will revolutionize the world entheogen [hallucinogen] market. This technique will allow users to prepare their own entheogenic potions in the safety of their own homes, using legally and commercially available plants."[28] Such resourceful research could put the use of plant hallucinogens beyond the reach of both government legislation and criminal cartels simultaneously.

The best course for all concerned would be to seek ways to order and harness the quest for alternate mind states through the use of physically harmless or relatively harmless hallucinogens, to remove them from the criminal sphere of influence and profit, to encourage the positive effects of the psychedelic experience to be harvested for the good of all, and to minimize the potential psychological dangers by arranging a nonalienating, nonthreatening monitored context for their use. If this were done, criminal organizations would have the carpet pulled from beneath them, and the marketing of genuinely dangerous substances would be exposed and isolated as never before, while the social, intellectual, scientific, and philosophical benefits of relatively organized psychedelic experience could at long last be allowed to flow to the culture at large. By the same token, those who use, or who demand the right to use, hallucinogens have the responsibility to become more active in restoring deep psychedelic experience to a more sacramental status, such as it enjoys in tribal, non-Western societies. To fulfill its potential the psychedelic experience needs to be seen and used in a higher context than merely as another choice for recreational hedonism.

Whatever the decisions that are made in these matters, however, one thing is certain: the Long Trip will continue in one form or another into the haze of the future just as surely as it has emerged out of the mists of the past.

Reference Notes

INTRODUCTION

1. Huxley, Penguin 1959.
2. First published in *The Realist*, September 1965; reprinted in Leary, *The Politics of Ecstasy* 1965/1970.
3. *The Best of High Times* 1995, 19.
4. Stafford 1978/1992, 48.
5. John Beresford, in the introduction to the first edition of ibid.
6. Hofman 1983, 15.
7. Ibid., 18.
8. Ibid., 19.
9. Grof 1980/1994.
10. Grof, cited in Stafford 1992.
11. Grof 1980/1994, 11.
12. Stafford 1992, 42.
13. Ibid., 44.
14. Lee and Shlain 1985/1992, 58.
15. *Acid Dreams* by Lee and Shlain is recommended to anyone who would like a detailed account of the extraordinary role of the intelligence services in the LSD story.
16. Grof 1975, ix.
17. Furst 1976/1992, 60n.
18. Wasson 1963/1965.
19. Hofmann 1983, 124.
20. Ibid., 125.

21. Devereux 1992a, 62–66.
22. Hofmann in interview, *The Best of High Times* 1995, 61.

CHAPTER ONE

1. Patton 1993, 24.
2. Sherratt 1991.
3. Emboden 1972, 219.
4. Latimer and Goldberg 1981, 18, 21.
5. Ibid., 22.
6. La Barre 1975, 30.
7. Sherratt 1991, 52.
8. Burl 1993, 20.
9. Sherratt 1991.
10. Rudgley 1993/1995, 31–35.
11. Sherratt 1995, 11–46.
12. Rudgley 1995.
13. Rudgley 1993/1995, 26.
14. Ibid., 27.
15. Sherratt 1991, 54.
16. Patton 1993, 123.
17. Ibid., 75.
18. Emboden 1972, 219.
19. Rudenko 1953/1970; see also Abel 1980, 24.
20. Rudgley 1993/1995, 38.
21. Mark Patton, personal communication 1995.
22. Godwin 1967.
23. Robert Jones, personal communication 1995, citing the investigations of Forrest and Rault (unpublished research at the time of this writing).
24. Furst 1976, 34.
25. Rudgley 1993/1995, 31.
26. Weil and Rosen 1983/1993, 85.
27. De Quincey 1856/1960, 241.
28. Cited in Hogshire 1994, 19.
29. Latimer and Goldberg 1981, 7.
30. Cited in von Bibra 1855/1995, 119.
31. Gautier 1845, cited by W. Reininger, in Andrews and Vinkenoog, (eds.), 1967, 35–37.

32. Siegel 1990, cited in Bennett et al. 1995, 249.
33. Cited in Bennett et al. 1995, 250.
34. Bibra 1855/1995, 153.
35. Cited in ibid., 156.
36. Nahas 1975, 9.
37. Burroughs, cited in Stafford 1978/1992, 201.
38. Patton 1993, 96.
39. Ibid., 168.
40. Ibid., 123.
41. Sherratt 1995, 28.
42. Jaynes 1976.
43. Ibid., 139–44.
44. Patton 1993, 94.
45. Jaynes, personal communication 1993.

CHAPTER TWO

1. Schultes and Hofmann 1979/1992, 64.
2. Hui-Lin Li 1975, in Rubin 1975, 52.
3. Abel 1980, 4.
4. Emboden 1972, in Furst 1972, 217.
5. Ibid., 225.
6. Furst 1986/1992, 57.
7. Vladimir Jochelson, quoted in ibid., 65.
8. Taylor 1980/1994, 2.
9. Wasson 1986, in Wasson et al. 1986, 68.
10. Rudgley 1993/1995, 42.
11. Furst 1986/1992, 46.
12. Kaplan 1975, 72–79.
13. Rätsch 1992, 83.
14. Wasson 1986, in Wasson et al. 1986, 72–73.
15. La Barre 1975, in Siegel and West, (eds.), 1975, 25.
16. Taylor 1980/1994, 1–4.
17. Ott 1993, 347.
18. Rudgley 1993/1995, 54.
19. Daniel H. H. Ingalls 1971, quoted in Furst 1976/1992, 101.
20. Ott 1993, 258–59.
21. Ibid., 259.

22. Rudgley 1993/1995, 62.

23. McKenna 1992, 110.

24. Ott 1993, 346–47.

25. McKenna 1992, 113.

26. Ott 1993, 346.

27. Rudgley 1993/1995, 52.

28. Sherratt 1995, in Goodman, Lovejoy, and Sherratt, (eds.), 1995, 29–30.

29. Ibid., 30.

30. Ibid., 28.

31. Scully 1962.

32. Devereux 1992b, 12–23.

33. Kerényi 1960/1967, 20–21.

34. Ibid., 185.

35. Rätsch 1992, 154.

36. Kerényi 1960/1967, 179.

37. Ruck 1986, in Wasson et al. 1986, 162n.

38. Wasson, cited in Ott 1993, 142.

39. McKenna 1992, 136.

40. Fontenrose 1978.

41. Cited in Ruck 1986, in Wasson et al. 1986, 231n.

42. Jaynes 1976, 323.

43. Rätsch 1987.

44. Rätsch 1992, 99–101.

45. Schenk 1955, 44–48.

46. Bibra 1855/1995, 78.

47. Schenk 1955, 39–40.

48. Rätsch 1992, 185.

49. Ibid.

50. Musès 1989, in Rätsch, (ed.), 1989, 143–59.

51. Wagner 1991, 61–63.

52. Devereux 1992c, in Rätsch, (ed.), 1992, 189–91, for example.

53. Furst 1976, 41n.

54. Dobkin de Rios 1984/1990, 164.

55. Ndong Asseko, quoted in Stafford 1978/1992, 363–64.

56. Stafford 1978/1992, 363.

57. Dobkin de Rios 1984/1990, 164.

58. Silva, in *Psychedelic Illuminations* 1, no. 7: 24–26.

59. Quoted in ibid., 26.
60. Katz 1982, 284–93.
61. Schultes and Hofmann 1979/1992, 72–73.
62. Toit 1975, in Rubin, (ed.), 1975, 81–118.
63. Jonathan Ott, technical note, in Bibra 1995, 240.
64. Dobkin de Rios 1984/1990, 23.
65. Alfred Gell, quoted in Rudgley 1993/1995, 153–54.
66. Rudgley 1993/1995, 96.
67. Ashton 1990, 14.
68. Cited by Rätsch 1992, 84.
69. See Duerr 1978/1985 for a classic discussion of the night travelers, the precursors of the Church's "witches," and the profound psychosociological meaning of "wilderness" and the boundary between that and civilization.
70. Ibid., 156.
71. Jackson 1992a, 17.
72. Duerr 1978/1985, 155.
73. Ibid., 4.
74. Rätsch 1992, 95.
75. La Barre 1975, in Siegel and West, (eds.), 1975, 25.
76. Harner 1973b, in Harner, (eds.), 1973, 128.
77. Kreig 1964, 93.
78. Peuckert, quoted in Rätsch 1992, 190.
79. Harner 1973b, in Harner, (ed.), 1973, 131.
80. Hesse, quoted in ibid., 142.
81. Naranjo 1973, in Harner, (ed.), 1973, 185.

CHAPTER THREE
1. Schultes and Hofmann 1979/1992, 26–27.
2. Ibid., 27.
3. La Barre 1975, in Siegel and West, (eds.), 1975, 39.
4. La Barre 1970/1972, 143.
5. Fagan 1991, 70.
6. Ibid., 77.
7. Schultes and Hofmann 1979/1992, 57.
8. Furst 1976, 8, for example.

Reference Notes

9. Furst 1994, 23.

10. La Barre 1970/1972, 123–26.

11. Ibid., 126.

12. La Barre 1938/1989, 263.

13. La Barre 1970, 160.

14. Ibid., 149.

15. Ibid., xv.

16. Wasson 1961/1965, in Weil, Metzner, and Leary, (eds.), 1965, 27.

17. Ibid., 38.

18. Richardson 1988/1990, in Reidlinger, (ed.), 1990, 197.

19. Furst 1986/1992, 93.

20. Hofmann 1980/1983, 111.

21. Ibid., 112–13.

22. Ibid., 116.

23. Richardson 1988/1990, in Riedlinger, (ed.), 1990, 199.

24. María Sabina, cited in Allen, *Psychedelic Illuminations*, no. 6: 30.

25. Furst 1976, 81.

26. Cited in Schultes and Hofmann 1979/1992, 85.

27. Furst 1976, 108.

28. Rudgley 1993/1995, 78.

29. Cited in ibid.

30. Wasson et al. 1986, 39–40.

31. La Barre 1975, in Siegel and West, (eds.), 1975, 35.

32. Schultes and Hofmann 1979/1992, 111.

33. Schultes 1972, in Furst, (ed.), 1972, 47.

34. Schultes and Hofmann 1979/1992, 36.

35. Schultes and Raffauf 1992, 50.

36. Metzner 1992, in Rätsch, (ed.), 1992, 193–98.

37. Hadingham 1987, 40.

38. Frank Joseph, "The Candelabra of the Andes," 1995, in *The Ancient American* 2:10, no. 10, cited in *Science Frontiers*, no. 102 (Nov./Dec. 1995).

39. Schultes 1972, in Furst, (ed.), 1972, 33.

40. Duerr 1978/1985, 202n.

41. Kensinger 1973, in Harner, (ed.), 1973, 11.

42. Schultes and Raffauf 1992, 24.

43. Rätsch 1992, 49–50.

44. Manuel Villavicencio, cited by Harner 1973a, in Harner, (ed.), 1973, 155–56.
45. Gorman, in *The Best of High Times* 1995, 83.
46. Kensinger 1973, in Harner, (ed.), 1973, 10n.
47. La Barre 1938/1989, 20.
48. Schultes 1972, in Furst, (ed.), 1972, 13.
49. Stewart 1989, in Seaman and Day, (eds.), 1994, 186.
50. La Barre 1938/1989, 257.
51. Myerhoff 1978, in Berrin, (ed.), 1978, 56.
52. Furst 1976, 113–33.
53. Myerhoff 1978, in Berrin, (ed.), 1978, 57.
54. Prem Das 1978, in ibid., 135.
55. Myerhoff 1978, in ibid., 60–61.
56. Stone-Miller 1995, 32.
57. Isabelle Druc, personal communication.
58. Stone-Miller 1995, 28–29.
59. Ibid., 40.
60. Dobkin de Rios 1984/1990, 93.
61. Ott 1993, 165.
62. Furst 1976, 155.
63. Schultes and Hofmann 1979/1992, 116–17.
64. Ott 1993, 168.
65. Ibid., 171.
66. Furst 1976, 153.
67. Ibid., 154.
68. Wilbert 1994, in Seaman and Day, (eds.), 1994, 50.
69. Ibid., 64.
70. Ibid.
71. Rätsch 1992, 186.
72. Dobkin de Rios 1984/1990, 120–24.
73. Schultes 1972, in Furst, (ed.), 1972, 32.

CHAPTER FOUR

1. Klüver 1928.
2. Ibid., 30–31.

3. Ibid., 94.

4. Ibid., 40.

5. Horowitz 1975, in Siegel and West, (eds.), 1975, 178.

6. Siegel and Jarvik 1975, in Siegel and West, (eds.), 1975, 81–162.

7. Cited in ibid., 110.

8. Ibid., 115.

9. Ibid., 125.

10. Ibid., 128.

11. Knoll and Kugler 1959, 1823–1824.

12. Oster, cited in Lyttle and Smith 1990, 51. See also Knoll and Kugler 1959.

13. Lyttle and Smith 1990, 53–58.

14. Ibid., 54.

15. Cited in Siegel and Jarvik, in Siegel and West, (eds.), 1975, 105.

16. Lewis-Williams and Dowson 1988, 204.

17. Ibid., 203.

18. Lewis-Williams and Dowson 1989, 12.

19. Ibid., 14.

20. Dowson 1992, 1.

21. Lewis-Williams and Dowson 1989, 7.

22. Breuil, cited in Brodrick 1963, 254–57.

23. Lewis-Williams and Dowson 1989, 8.

24. Ibid., 23.

25. Katz 1982, 42.

26. Lewis-Williams and Dowson 1992, 41.

27. Lewis-Williams and Dowson 1989, 36.

28. Ibid., 75.

29. Dowson 1992, 74.

30. Ibid.

31. Campbell 1988, xi–xiii.

32. Lewis-Williams and Dowson 1989, 90.

33. Katz 1982, 180.

34. Ibid., 281–96.

35. Schultes and Hofmann 1979/1992, 72–73.

36. La Barre 1975, in Siegel and West, (eds.), 1975, 24–37.

37. Whitley 1994a, 359.

38. Whitley, in Lewis-Williams and Dowson 1988, 238.

39. Ibid.
40. Whitley 1994a, 361.
41. Whitley, in Lewis-Williams and Dowson 1988, 238.
42. M. Zigmond 1977, cited in Whitley 1994a, 363. Also note Whitley 1994b on this and other factors associated with Coso rock art.
43. Grant 1965, 77.
44. Ibid., 124.
45. Krupp 1983, 130.
46. Patterson 1992, 84, for example.
47. Wellmann 1978, 1526.
48. Eger and Collings, in Berrin, (ed.), 1978, 39.
49. Siegel and Jarvik 1975, in Siegel and West, (eds.), 1975, 138.
50. Polia and Bianchi 1991, 65.
51. Reichel-Dolmatoff, in Greenhalgh and Megaw, (eds.), 1978, 291.
52. Ibid., 291–93.
53. Ibid., 297.
54. Ibid., 302.
55. Schultes and Raffauf 1992, 233.
56. Patton 1990, 554–58.
57. Patton 1993, 88.
58. Bradley 1989, 68–75.
59. Brennan 1983.
60. Devereux 1992d, 117–126.
61. Lewis-Williams and Dowson 1993, 60.
62. Dronfield 1995a, 261–75. See also Dronfield 1995b, 539–49.
63. Syal, in *Sunday Times* (London) 1996.
64. Jahn et al. 1995.
65. Jahn et al. 1996.
66. Jahn 1995.
67. Lewis-Williams and Dowson 1988, 205.
68. Cited in Lewin 1991, 33.
69. See Marshack 1972, for instance, 198–99.
70. Lewis-Williams and Dowson 1988, 208.
71. Marshack 1972.
72. Lewis-Williams and Dowson 1988, 216.
73. Eliade 1951/1964, 481.
74. Wasson, in Wasson, Kramrisch, Ott, and Ruck 1986, 39.

75. Sherratt, in Goodman, Lovejoy, and Sherratt, (eds.), 1995, 30.
76. Fischer 1969, cited in Lyttle and Smith 1990, 46.

CHAPTER FIVE
1. Alfred Watkins's main book on the topic was *The Old Straight Track* (1925), which has had many subsequent editions.
2. Devereux 1993.
3. Lepper 1995, 52–56.
4. L. Sample, "Trade and Trails in Aboriginal California," in *Reports of the University of California Archeological Survey* 8 (1950), cited in Robertson 1983, in Kincaid, (ed.), 1983, 1.
5. S. A. Barrett and E. W. Gifford, "Miwok Material Culture," *Bulletin of the Public Museum of the City of Milwaukee* 4 (1933), cited in ibid.
6. Kincaid 1983.
7. Lekson et al. 1988, in *Scientific American* (July 1988), 100–109.
8. Sever and Wagner 1991, in Trombold, (ed.), 1991, 51.
9. Sever 1990.
10. Sever and Wagner 1991, in Trombold, (ed.), 1991, 42.
11. Frazier 1986, 127.
12. Ibid., 210–12.
13. Gabriel 1991, 154–83.
14. Windes 1991, in Trombold, (ed.), 1991, 124.
15. Ibid., 118.
16. Trombold 1991a, in Trombold, (ed.), 1991, 6.
17. Earle 1991, in Trombold, (ed.), 1991, 13.
18. Hyslop 1991, in Trombold, (ed.), 1991, 29.
19. Lyon 1828, quoted in Trombold 1991b, in Trombold, (ed.), 1991, 155.
20. Ibid., 151–54.
21. Gann, cited in Robertson 1983, in Kincaid, (ed.), 1983, 2–5.
22. Folan 1991, in Trombold, (ed.), 1991, 225.
23. Ibid., 226.
24. Sheets and Sever 1991, in Trombold, (ed.), 1991, 53–65.
25. Ibid., 62.
26. Ereira 1990.
27. Beck 1991, in Trombold, (ed.), 1991, 66–79.
28. See Reiche 1968 or Morrison 1987.

29. Hawkins 1973.
30. Aveni, (ed.), 1990.
31. Aveni 1990, in Aveni, (ed.), 1990, 111.
32. Clarkson 1990, in Aveni, (ed.), 1990, 151.
33. Ibid., 170.
34. Silverman 1990, in Aveni, (ed.), 1991, 240.
35. Urton 1990, in Aveni, (ed.), 1991, 173–206.
36. Morrison 1978.
37. Denevan 1991, in Trombold, (ed.), 1991, 230.
38. Ibid., 234–35.
39. Ibid., 235.
40. Ibid., 232.
41. Ibid., 232, 238–39.
42. David Browne, personal communication.
43. Trombold 1991a, in Trombold, (ed.), 1991, 5.
44. Silverman 1990, in Aveni, (ed.), 1990, 169.
45. Dobkin de Rios 1977, in Toit, (ed.), 240.
46. Hoskinson 1992, in Williamson and Farrer, (eds.), 133.
47. Thomas 1993, in Bender, (ed.), 20.
48. Ibid., 21–22.
49. Susan Ford 1991, cited in ibid., 24–25.
50. Thomas 1993, in Bender, (ed.), 1993, 25.
51. Tilley 1994, in Tilley, (ed.), 1994, 9–11.
52. Humphrey 1995, in Hirsch and O'Hanlon, (eds.), 1995, 151.
53. Ibid., 154.
54. Ibid., 150–51.
55. Ibid., 153.
56. Silverman 1990, in Aveni, (ed.), 1990, 240.
57. Dobkin de Rios 1977, in Toit, (ed.), 237.
58. Ibid., 246.
59. Zuidema, cited in Silverman 1990, in Aveni, (ed.), 1990, 239.
60. Hoskinson 1992, in Williamson and Farrer, (eds.), 1992, 142.
61. BBC TV 1990.
62. Ereira 1990.
63. Ereira, personal communication.
64. For a full account of cursuses, see my "Prehistoric Lines in Britain," in Pennick and Devereux 1989, 47–91.

65. B. Coles and J. Coles 1986, 43.
66. Saward 1986.
67. Palmer 1989, 1990, 1991.
68. Jackson 1992b, 8.
69. Lincoln 1991, 119–27.
70. Hawkes and Henderson-Smith 1992, 12–15.
71. Weatherhill 1993, 28–29.
72. Weatherhill and Devereux 1994, 154–55.
73. Hole 1961/1974, 83–84.
74. Barker 1992.
75. Ashton, citing anthropologist Nick Tapp, 1993, 11–12.
76. Blair 1994, 18.
77. Pennick and Devereux 1989, 231.
78. Magin 1992a, 14.
79. Atkins 1981.
80. MacManus 1959/1973, 102–103.
81. Grimble 1952.
82. Magin 1992c, 11.
83. Magin 1992b, 1–4.
84. Lincoln 1991, 119–27.
85. Eliade 1951/1964, 397–98.
86. H. A. Lauer 1979, and other sources cited in Magin 1992d, 16.
87. Juan Atienza, cited in Magin 1993, 32.
88. Jackson 1994, 67–71.
89. Ibid, 68.
90. Jon Arnason (1862–64), cited in Simpson 1972, 177.
91. Ibid.

EPILOGUE
1. Andrew Weil 1972, cited in Furst 1976, 7.
2. Huxley 1962/1964.
3. McKenna 1991, 39–40.
4. Ibid., 158.
5. Schultes and Hofmann 1979/1992, 22.
6. Furst 1976, 15.
7. Gehr 1995.

8. Wasson 1986, 80.

9. Rudgley 1993/1995, 11–12.

10. Munn, in Harner, (ed.), 1973, 88.

11. McKenna, *Psychedelic Illuminations* 1994.

12. Krippner 1969, in Tart, (ed.), 1969, 271–90.

13. Dobkin de Rios 1975, in Rubin, (ed.), 1975, 408.

14. For example, Metzner 1989, in Rätsch, (ed.), 1989, 73–88.

15. Furst 1976, 57–58.

16. Devereux 1996.

17. Naranjo 1973, in Harner, (ed.), 1973, 183.

18. Harner, in Harner, (ed.), 1973, 153.

19. Naranjo 1973, in Harner, (ed.), 1973, 190.

20. Grof 1989, in Rätsch, (ed.), 1989, 65–66.

21. Ibid., 67.

22. Gracie and Zarkov, cited in "The Mind's Eye," *Psychedelic Illuminations*, no. 6 (1994), 56.

23. DeKorne 1994.

24. Turner 1994, 97–98.

25. Coral 1989, in Rätsch, (ed.), 1989, 133, 141.

26. Doblin 1995, *Psychedelic Illuminations* 1995.

27. Laura Mansnerus, *New York Times* News Service 1995.

28. Ott 1994, *Psychedelic Illuminations* 1994, 55. See also Jonathan Ott, *Ayahuasca Analogues*, (Kennewick, Wash.: Jonathan Ott Books 1994).

Bibliography

Abel, Ernest L. *Marihuana—The First Twelve Thousand Years*. New York: Plenum Press, 1980.

Allen, John. "Chasing the Ghost of Maria Sabina." *Psychedelic Illuminations*, no. 6 (1995).

Andrews, George, and Simon Vinkenoog. *The Book of Grass*. New York: Grove Press, 1967.

Ashton, Chris. "Meditation, Temples, and Asian Death Roads." *The Ley Hunter*, no. 118 (1993).

———. "Quicksilver Messenger Column." *The Ley Hunter*, no. 113 (1990).

Atkins, Meg Elizabeth. *Haunted Warwickshire*. London: Hale, 1981.

Aveni, Anthony, ed. *The Lines of Nazca*. Philadelphia: American Philosophical Society, 1990.

———. "Order in the Nazca Lines." In *The Lines of Nazca*. Philadelphia: American Philosophical Society, 1990.

Barker, Paul. "Lavender Daze." *Weekend Guardian*, 29–30 August 1992.

BBC TV. *From the Heart of the World*. 4 December 1990.

Beck, Colleen M. "Cross-cutting Relationships: The Relative Dating of Ancient Roads on the North Coast of Peru." In *Ancient Road Networks and Settlement Hierarchies in the New World*, edited by Charles D. Trombold. Cambridge: Cambridge University Press, 1991.

Bender, Barbara, ed. *Landscape: Politics and Perspectives*. Providence and Oxford: Berg, 1993.

Bennett, Chris, Lynn Osburn, and Judy Osburn. *Green Gold the Tree of Life: Marijuana in Magic & Religion*. Frazier Park, Calif.: Access Unlimited, 1995.

Berrin, Kathleen, ed. *Art of the Huichol Indians*. New York: Harry N. Abrams in association with Fine Arts Museums of San Francisco, 1978.

Bibra, Ernst von. *Plant Intoxicants*. 1855. Rochester, Vt.: Healing Arts Press, 1995.

Blair, John. *Anglo-Saxon Oxfordshire*. Stroud, England: Alan Sutton, 1994.

Bradley, Richard. "Deaths and Entrances: A Contextual Analysis of Megalithic Art." *Current Anthropology* 30, no. 1 (1989).

Brennan, Martin. *The Stars and the Stones*. London: Thames & Hudson, 1983.

Brodrick, Alan Houghton. *The Father of Prehistory: The Abbé Henri Breuil: His Life and Times*. New York: William Morrow, 1963.

Burl, Aubrey. *From Carnac to Callanish*. New Haven, Conn.: Yale University Press, 1993.

Campbell, Joseph. *Historical Atlas of the World*. Part 2, *Mythologies of the Great Hunt*. New York: Harper & Row, Perennial Library, 1988.

Clarkson, Persis B. "The Archaeology of the Nazca Pampa, Peru: Environmental and Cultural Parameters." In *The Lines of Nazca*, edited by Anthony Aveni. Philadelphia: American Philosophical Society, 1990.

Coles, Bryony and John Coles. *Sweet Track to Glastonbury*. London: Thames & Hudson, 1986.

Coral, Wolfgang. "Psychedelic Drugs and Spiritual States of Consciousness in the Light of Modern Neurochemical Research." In *Gateway to Inner Space*, edited by Christian Rätsch. Bridport, England: Prism Press, 1989.

Das, Prem. "Initiation by a Huichol Shaman." In *Art of the Huichol Indians*, edited by Kathleen Berrin. New York: Harry N. Abrams, 1978.

DeKorne, Jim. *Psychedelic Shamanism*. Port Townsend, Wash.: Loompanics Unlimited, 1994.

Denevan, William M. "Prehistoric Roads and Causeways of Lowland Tropical America." In *Ancient Road Networks and Settlement Hierarchies in the New World*, edited by Charles D. Trombold. Cambridge: Cambridge University Press, 1991.

De Quincey, Thomas. *Confessions of an English Opium-Eater*. 1821, 1856. London: Dent, 1960.

Devereux, Paul. "An Apparently Nutmeg-Induced Experience of Magical Flight." 1992c. In *Yearbook for Ethnomedicine and the Study of Consciousness*, edited by Christian Rätsch. Berlin: VWB, 1992.

———. *Earth Memory*. Slough, U.K.: Quantum/Foulsham, 1992d.

————. *Re-Visioning the Earth: Guide to Opening the Healing Channels Mind & Body*. New York: Simon & Schuster, 1996.

————. *Secrets of Ancient and Sacred Places*. London: Blandford, 1992a.

————. *Shamanism and the Mystery Lines*. Slough, U.K.: Quantum/Foulsham, 1993.

————. *Symbolic Landscapes*. Glastonbury, U.K.: Gothic Image, 1992b.

Dobkin de Rios, Marlene. *Hallucinogens: Cross-Cultural Perspectives*. 1984. Bridport, U.K.: Prism Press, 1990.

————. "Man, Culture and Hallucinogens: An Overview." In *Cannabis and Culture*, edited by Vera Rubin. The Hague: Mouton, 1975.

————. "Plant Hallucinogens, Out-of-Body Experiences and New World Monumental Earthworks." In *Drugs, Rituals and Altered States of Consciousness*, edited by Brian M. Du Toit. Rotterdam: A. A. Balkema, 1977.

Doblin, Rick. "Psychedelic Research in 1995." *Psychedelic Illuminations* 1, no. 7 (1995).

Dowson, Thomas A. *Rock Engravings of Southern Africa*. Johannesburg: Witwatersrand University Press, 1992.

Dronfield, Jeremy. "Migraine, Light and Hallucinogens: The Neurocognitive Basis of Irish Megalithic Art." 1995a. *Oxford Journal of Archaeology* 14, no. 3 (1995).

————. "Subjective Vision and the Source of Irish Megalithic Art." 1995b. *Antiquity* 69 (1995).

Duerr, Hans Peter. *Dreamtime: Concerning the Boundary between Wilderness and Civilization*. 1978. Oxford: Blackwell, 1985.

Earle, Timothy. "Paths and Roads in Evolutionary Perspective." In *Ancient Road Networks and Settlement Hierarchies in the New World*, edited by Charles D. Trombold. Cambridge: Cambridge University Press, 1991.

Eger, Susan, with Peter R. Collings. "Huichol Women's Art." In *Art of the Huichol Indians*, edited by Kathleen Berrin. New York: Harry N. Abrams, 1978.

Elgar, Frank. *The Rock Paintings of Tassili*. 1962. Cleveland: World Publishing, 1963.

Eliade, Mircea. *Shamanism: Archaic Techniques of Ecstasy*. 1951. Princeton, N.J.: Princeton University Press, Bollingen, 1964.

Emboden, William A. "Ritual Use of Cannabis Sativa L.: A Historical-Ethnographic Survey." In *Flesh of the Gods*, edited by Peter T. Furst. New York: Praeger, 1972.

Ereira, Alan. *The Heart of the World*. London: Jonathan Cape, 1990.

Fagan, Brian M. *Ancient North America*. London: Thames & Hudson, 1991.

Folan, William J. "Sacbes of the Northern Maya." 1991. In *Ancient Road Networks and Settlement Hierarchies in the New World*, edited by Charles D. Trombold. Cambridge: Cambridge University Press, 1991.

Fontenrose, Joseph. *The Delphic Oracle*. Berkeley: University of California Press, 1978.

Frazier, Kendrick. *People of Chaco*. New York: W. W. Norton, 1986.

Furst, Peter T., ed. *Flesh of the Gods*. New York: Praeger, 1972.

————. *Hallucinogens and Culture*. Novato, Calif.: Chandler & Sharp, 1976.

————. "Introduction: An Overview of Shamanism." 1994. In *Ancient Traditions: Shamanism in Central Asia and the Americas*, edited by Gary Seaman and Jane S. Day. Niwot, Colo.: University Press of Colorado, 1994.

————. "The Mara'kame Does and Undoes: Persistence and Change in Huichol Shamanism." 1994. In *Ancient Traditions: Shamanism in Central Asia and the Americas*, edited by Gary Seaman and Jane S. Day. Niwot, Colo.: University Press of Colorado, 1994.

————. *Mushrooms: Psychedelic Fungi*. 1986. New York: Chelsea House, 1992.

————. "The Roots and Continuities of Shamanism." *ArtsCanada*, (Dec. 1973/Jan. 1974): 33–60.

Gabriel, Kathryn. *Roads to Center Place*. Boulder, Colo.: Johnson Books, 1991.

Garwood, P., D. Jennings, R. Skeates, and J. Toms, eds. *Sacred and Profane*. Oxford: Oxford University Committee for Archaeology, 1991.

Gehr, Richard. "Notes from a Psychedelic Revival Meeting." *Village Voice*, 5 July 1995.

Godwin, H. "Pollen-Analytic Evidence for the Cultivation of Cannabis in England." *Rev. Palaeobotan. Palynol.* 4 (1967): 71–80.

Goodman, Jordan, Paul Lovejoy, and Andrew Sherratt, eds. *Consuming Habits*. London: Routledge, 1995.

Gorman, Peter. "Ayahuasca." In *The Best of High Times*. 1995.

Grant, Campbell. *The Rock Paintings of the Chumash*. Berkeley: University of California Press, 1965.

Greenhalgh, Michael, and Vincent Megaw, eds. *Art in Society*. London: Duckworth, 1978.

Grimble, Arthur. *A Pattern of Islands*. London: John Murray, 1952.

Grof, Stanislav. "Beyond the Brain: New Dimensions in Psychology and Psychotherapy." In *Gateway to Inner Space*, edited by Christian Rätsch. Bridport, U.K.: Prism Press, 1989.

————. *LSD Psychotherapy*. 1980. Alameda, Calif.: Hunter House, 1994.

————. *Realms of the Human Unconscious*. 1975. London: Condor/Souvenir, 1979.

Hadingham, Evan. *Lines to the Mountain Gods*. New York: Random House, 1987.

Harner, Michael J. "Common Themes in South American Indian Yagé Experiences." In *Hallucinogens and Shamanism*. New York: Oxford University Press, 1973a.

————, ed. *Hallucinogens and Shamanism*. New York: Oxford University Press, 1973.

————. "The Role of Hallucinogenic Plants in European Witchcraft." In *Hallucinogens and Shamanism*. New York: Oxford University Press, 1973b.

————. *The Way of the Shaman*. 1980. San Francisco: HarperSanFrancisco, 1990.

Hawkes, Gabrielle, and Tom Henderson-Smith. "Coffin Lines: And a Cornish Spirit Path?" *The Ley Hunter*, no. 117 (1992).

Hawkins, Gerald. *Beyond Stonehenge*. London: Hutchinson, 1973.

Herodotus. *The Histories*. Harmondsworth, U.K.: Penguin Books, 1954.

Hirsch, Eric, and Michael O'Hanlon, eds. *The Anthropology of Landscape*. Oxford: Clarendon Press, 1995.

Hofmann, Albert. *LSD: My Problem Child*. 1980. Los Angeles: Tarcher, 1983.

Hogshire, Jim. *Opium for the Masses*. Port Townsend, Wash.: Loompanics Unlimited, 1994.

Hole, Christina, ed. *Encyclopaedia of Superstitions*. London: BCA, 1974.

Hoskinson, Tom. "Saguaro Wine, Ground Figures, and Power Mountains: Investigations at Sears Point, Arizona." In *Earth and Sky*, edited by Ray A. Williamson and Claire R. Farrer. Albuquerque: University of New Mexico Press, 1992.

Humphrey, Caroline. "Chiefly and Shamanist Landscapes in Mongolia." In *The Anthropology of Landscape*, edited by Eric Hirsch and Michael O'Hanlon. Oxford: Clarendon Press, 1995.

Huxley, Aldous. "The Doors of Perception" (1954) and "Heaven and Hell" (1956). One-volume collection. Harmondsworth, U.K.: Penguin, 1959.

————. *Island*. 1962. Harmondsworth, U.K.: Penguin, 1964.

Hyslop, John. "Observations about Research on Prehistoric Roads in South America." In *Ancient Road Networks and Settlement Hierarchies in the New World*, edited by Charles D. Trombold. Cambridge: Cambridge University Press, 1991.

Jackson, Nigel. *Call of the Horned Piper*. Chieveley, U.K.: Capall Bann, 1994.

————. "Trance Ecstasy and the Furious Host." *The Ley Hunter*, no. 117 (1992b).

————. "Witch Ways." *The Ley Hunter*, no. 117 (1992a).

Jahn, Robert G. "The Old Stones Speak" *The Ley Hunter*, no. 123 (1995).

Jahn, Robert G., Paul Devereux, and Michael Ibison. "Acoustical Resonances of Assorted Ancient Structures." Technical Report PEAR 95002, March 1995, Princeton University, Princeton.

————. "Acoustical Resonances of Assorted Ancient Structures." *Journal of the Acoustical Society of America* 99, no. 2 (February 1996).

Jaynes, Julian. *The Origins of Consciousness in the Breakdown of the Bicameral Mind*. Boston: Houghton Mifflin, 1976.

Kaplan, Reid W. "The Sacred Mushrooms in Scandinavia." *Man*, no. 10 (1975).

Katz, Richard. *Boiling Energy: Community Healing among the Kalahari Kung*. Cambridge, Mass.: Harvard University Press, 1982.

Kensinger, Kenneth M. "Banisteriopsis Usage among the Peruvian Cashinahua." In *Hallucinogens and Shamanism*, edited by Michael J. Harner. New York: Oxford University Press, 1973.

Kerényi, Carl. *Eleusis: Archetypal Image of Mother and Daughter*. 1962. Princeton, N.J.: Princeton University Press, Bollingen, 1967.

Kincaid, Chris, ed. *Chaco Roads Project Phase I*. Albuquerque: U.S. Dept. of the Interior, Bureau of Land Management, 1983.

Klüver, Heinrich. *Mescal: The 'Divine' Plant and Its Psychological Effects*. London: Kegan Paul, Trench, Trubner, 1928.

Knoll, M., and J. Kugler. "Subjective Light Pattern Spectroscopy in the Encephalographic Frequency Range." *Nature*, no. 184 (December 1959).

Kreig, Margaret B. *Green Medicine*. Chicago: Rand McNally & Co., 1964.

Krippner, Stanley. "Psychedelic States, Hypnotic Trance, Creative Act." In *Altered States of Consciousness*, edited by Charles Tart. New York: John Wiley, 1969.

Krupp, E. C. *Echoes of the Ancient Skies*. New York: Harper & Row, 1983.

La Barre, Weston. "Anthropological Perspectives on Hallucination and Hallucinogens." In *Hallucinations*, edited by R. K. Siegel and L. J. West. New York: John Wiley, 1975.

————. *The Ghost Dance*. New York: Dell, 1970/1972.

————. "Hallucinogens and the Shamanic Origins of Religion." 1972. In *Flesh of the Gods*, edited by Peter T. Furst. New York: Praeger, 1972.

————. *The Peyote Cult*. 1938. 5th ed. Norman: University of Oklahoma Press, 1989.

Latimer, Dean, and Jeff Goldberg. *Flowers in the Blood.* New York: Franklin Watts, 1981.

Leary, Timothy. *The Politics of Ecstasy.* 1965. London: Paladin, 1970.

Lee, Martin A., and Bruce Shlain. *Acid Dreams.* 1985. New York: Grove Weidenfeld, 1992.

Lekson, Stephen H., Thomas C. Windes, John R. Stein, and W. James Judge. "The Chaco Canyon Community." *Scientific American* 259, no. 1 (July 1988).

Lepper, Bradley T. "Tracking Ohio's Great Hopewell Road." *Archaeology* (Nov/Dec. 1995).

Lewin, Roger. "Stone Age Psychedelia." *New Scientist,* no. 1772 (June 1991).

Lewis-Williams, J. D., and T. A. Dowson. *Images of Power.* Johannesburg: Southern Book Publishers, 1989.

———. "On Vision and Power in the Neolithic: Evidence from the Decorated Monuments." *Current Anthropology* 34, no. 1 (February 1993).

———. *Rock Paintings of the Natal Drakensberg.* Pietermaritzburg, South Africa: University of Natal Press, 1992.

———. "The Signs of All Times." *Current Anthropology* 29, no. 2 (April 1988).

Li, Hui-Lin. "The Origin and Use of Cannabis in Eastern Asia: Their Linguistic-Cultural Implications." 1975. In *Cannabis and Culture,* edited by Vera Rubin. The Hague: Mouton, 1975.

Lincoln, Bruce. *Death, War and Sacrifice.* Chicago: University of Chicago Press, 1991.

Lyttle, Thomas, and Elvin D. Smith. "Neostructuralism and Hallucination." In *Psychedelic Monographs and Essays,* no. 5. Boynton Beach, Fla.: PM&E Publishing Group, 1990.

MacManus, Dermot. *The Middle Kingdom.* 1959. Gerrards Cross, U.K.: Colin Smyth, 1973.

Magin, Ulrich. "Church Lines." *The Ley Hunter,* no. 117 (1992c).

———. "Geisterwege: Are Medieval Ghost Paths the Reality behind Alfred Watkins' Leys?" *The Ley Hunter,* no. 116 (1992a).

———. "The Medieval Christianisation of Pagan Landscapes." *The Ley Hunter,* no. 116 (1992b).

———. "The Old Straight Track on Dragon Mountain." *The Ley Hunter,* no. 117 (1992d).

———. "Spanish Witch Flight?" *The Ley Hunter,* no. 118 (1993).

Mandell, Arnold J. "The Neurochemistry of Religious Insight and Ecstasy." In

Art of the Huichol Indians, edited by Kathleen Berrin. New York: Harry N. Abrams, 1978.

Marshack, Alexander. *The Roots of Civilization.* New York: McGraw-Hill, 1972.

McKenna, Terence. *The Archaic Revival.* San Francisco: HarperSanFrancisco, 1991.

———. *Food of the Gods.* London: Rider, 1992.

———. "Glossolalia, Novelty, and the Great Timestream Bifurcation." *Psychedelic Illuminations,* no. 6 (1994).

Metzner, Ralph. "Divinatory Dreams Induced by Tree Datura." In *Yearbook for Ethnomedicine and the Study of Consciousness,* edited by Christian Rätsch. Berlin: VWB, 1992.

———. "Molecular Mysticism: The Role of Psychoactive Substances in the Transformation of Consciousness." In *Gateway to Inner Space,* edited by Christian Rätsch. Bridport, U.K.: Prism Press, 1989.

Morrison, Tony. *The Mystery of the Nasca Lines.* Woodbridge, U.K.: Nonesuch Expeditions, 1987.

———. *Pathways to the Gods.* Shaftesbury, U.K.: Michael Russell, 1978.

Munn, Henry. "The Mushrooms of Language." In *Hallucinogens and Shamanism,* edited by Michael J. Harner. New York: Oxford University Press, 1973.

Musès, Charles. "The Sacred Plant of Ancient Egypt." 1989. In *Gateway to Inner Space,* edited by Christian Rätsch. Bridport, U.K.: Prism Press, 1989.

Myerhoff, Barbara G. "The Religious Experience." 1978. In *Art of the Huichol Indians,* edited by Kathleen Berrin. New York: Harry N. Abrams, 1978.

Nahas, Gabriel G. *Marihuana: Deceptive Weed.* New York: Raven Press, 1975.

Naranjo, Claudio. "Psychological Aspects of the Yagé Experience in an Experimental Setting." In *Hallucinogens and Shamanism,* edited by Michael J. Harner. New York: Oxford University Press, 1973.

Ott, Jonathan. "Ayahuasca and Ayahuasca Analogues." *Psychedelic Illumination,* no. 6 (1994).

———. *Pharmacotheon.* Kennewick, Wash.: Natural Products Co., 1993.

Palmer, John. "Deathroads." *The Ley Hunter,* no. 113 (1990).

———. "Deathroads III." *The Ley Hunter,* no. 114 (1991).

———. "The Deathroads of Holland." *The Ley Hunter,* no. 109 (1989).

Patterson, Alex. *Rock Art Symbols of the Greater Southwest.* Boulder, Colo.: Johnson Books, 1992.

Patton, Mark. "On Entoptic Images in Context: Art, Monuments, and Society in Neolithic Brittany." *Current Anthropology* 31, no. 5 (December 1990).

————. *Statements in Stone*. London: Routledge, 1993.

Pennick, Nigel, and Paul Devereux. *Lines on the Landscape*. London: Hale, 1989.

Polia, M., and A. Bianchi. "Ethnological Evidences and Cultural Patterns of the Use of Trichocereus pachanoi B.R. among Peruvian Curanderos." *Integration*, no. 1 (1991).

Rätsch, Christian. *The Dictionary of Sacred and Magical Plants*. Bridport, U.K.: Prism Press, 1992.

————, ed. *Gateway to Inner Space*. Bridport, U.K.: Prism Press, 1989.

————. "Der Rauch von Delphi. Eine ethnopharmakologische Annaherung." *Curare* 10, no. 4 (1987).

————, ed. *Yearbook for Ethnomedicine and the Study of Consciousness*. Berlin: VWB, 1992.

Reiche, Maria. *Mystery on the Desert*. Stuttgart: Private, 1968.

Reichel-Dolmatoff, G. "The Cultural Context of an Aboriginal Hallucinogen: Banisteriopsis Caapi." In *Flesh of the Gods*, edited by Peter T. Furst. New York: Praeger, 1972.

————. "Drug-Induced Optical Sensations and Their Relationship to Applied Art among Some Colombian Indians." In *Art in Society*, edited by Michael Greenhalgh and Vincent McGraw. London: Duckworth, 1978.

Reininger, W. "Two Celebrated Hashish Eaters." In *The Book of Grass*, edited by George Andrews and Simon Vinkenoog. New York: Grove Press, 1967.

Richardson, Allan. "Recollections of R. Gordon Wasson's 'Friend and Photographer.'" In *The Sacred Mushroom Seeker*, edited by Thomas J. Riedlinger. Portland, Oreg.: Dioscorides Press, 1990.

Riedlinger, Thomas J., ed. *The Sacred Mushroom Seeker*. Portland, Oreg.: Dioscorides Press, 1990.

Robertson, Benjamin P. "Other New World Roads and Trails." In *Chaco Roads Project Phase I*, edited by Chris Kincaid. Albuquerque: U.S. Dept. of the Interior, Bureau of Land Management, 1983.

Rubin, Vera, ed. *Cannabis and Culture*. The Hague: Mouton, 1975.

Ruck, Carl A. P. "Mushrooms and Philosophers." 1986. In *Persephone's Quest*, edited by R. Gordon Wasson et al. New Haven, Conn.: Yale University Press, 1986.

Rudenko, Sergei I. *Frozen Tombs of Siberia: The Pazyryk Burials of Iron-Age Horsemen*. 1953. Berkeley: University of California Press, 1970.

Rudgley, Richard. "The Archaic Use of Hallucinogens in Europe: An Archaeology of Altered States." *Addiction* 90 (1995): 163–4.

————. *Essential Substances: A Cultural History of Intoxicants in Society.* (1993, as *The Alchemy of Culture: Intoxicants in Society*.) New York: Kodansha International, 1995.

Saward, Deb. "The Rösaring Road." *Caerdroia* 18 (1986).

Schaafsma, Polly. *Indian Rock Art of the Southwest.* Albuquerque: University of New Mexico Press, 1980.

Schenk, Gustav. *The Book of Poisons.* New York: Rinehart, 1955.

Schultes, Richard Evans. "An Overview of Hallucinogens in the Western Hemisphere." In *Flesh of the Gods*, edited by Peter T. Furst. New York: Praeger, 1972.

Schultes, Richard Evans, and Albert Hofmann. *Plants of the Gods*. 1979. Rochester, Vt.: Healing Arts Press, 1992.

Schultes, Richard Evans, and Robert F. Raffauf. *Vine of the Soul.* Oracle, Ariz.: Synergetic Press, 1992.

Scully, Vincent. *The Earth, the Temple, and the Gods.* New Haven, Conn.: Yale University Press, 1962.

Seaman, Gary, and Jane S. Day, eds. *Ancient Traditions: Shamanism in Central Asia and the Americas.* Niwot, Colo.: University Press of Colorado, 1994.

Sever, Thomas L. "Remote Sensing Applications in Archaeological Research; Tracing Prehistoric Human Impact upon the Environment." Ph.D. diss., University of Colorado, 1990.

Sever, Thomas L., and David W. Wagner. "Analysis of Prehistoric Roadways in Chaco Canyon Using Remotely Sensed Digital Data." In *Ancient Road Networks and Settlement Hierarchies in the New World*, edited by Charles D. Trombold. Cambridge: Cambridge University Press, 1991.

Sheets, Payson, and Thomas L. Sever. "Prehistoric Footpaths in Costa Rica: Transportation and Communication in a Tropical Rainforest." In *Ancient Road Networks and Settlement Hierarchies in the New World*, edited by Charles D. Trombold. Cambridge: Cambridge University Press, 1991.

Sherratt, Andrew, "Introduction" and "Alcohol and Its Alternatives." 1995. In *Consuming Habits*, edited by Goodman et al. London: Routledge, 1995.

————. "Sacred and Profane Substances: The Ritual Use of Narcotics in Later Neolithic Europe." In *Sacred and Profane*, edited by P. Garwood et al. Oxford: Oxford University Committee for Archaeology, 1991.

Siegel, R. K., and L. J. West, eds. *Hallucinations.* New York: John Wiley, 1975.

Silva, Arjuna da. "Stalking the Spirit of Ibogaine." *Psychedelic Illuminations* 1, no. 7.

Silverman, Helaine. "The Early Nazca Pilgrimage Center of Cahuachi and the

Nazca Lines: Anthropological and Archaeological Perspectives." In *The Lines of Nazca*, edited by Anthony Aveni. Philadelphia: American Philosophical Society, 1990.

Simpson, Jacqueline. *Icelandic Folktales and Legends*. Berkeley: University of California Press, 1972.

Stafford, Peter. *Psychedelics Encyclopedia*. 1978. 3d ed., Berkeley: Ronin Publishing, 1992.

Stewart, Omer C. "Peyote Religion." In *Ancient Traditions: Shamanism in Central Asia and the Americas*, edited by Gary Seaman and Jane S. Day. Niwot, Colo.: University Press of Colorado, 1994.

Stone-Miller, Rebecca. *Art of the Andes: From Chavín to Inca*. London: Thames & Hudson, 1995.

Syal, Rajeev. "Raves in the Caves: Stone Age Britons Took Drugs." *Sunday Times* (London), 28 January 1996.

Tart, Charles T., ed. *Altered States of Consciousness*. New York: John Wiley, 1969.

Taylor, Rogan. "Who Is Santa Claus?" *The Ley Hunter*, no. 122 (1994).

Thomas, Julian. "The Politics of Vision and the Archaeologies of Landscape." In *Landscape: Politics and Perspectives*, edited by Barbara Bender. Providence and Oxford: Berg, 1993.

Tilley, Christopher, ed. *Interpretative Archaeology*. Providence and Oxford: Berg, 1993.

———. "Introduction: Interpretation and a Poetics of the Past." In *Interpretative Archaeology*.

Toit, Brian M. du. "Dagga: The History and Ethnographic Setting of Cannabis sativa in Southern Africa." 1975. In *Cannabis and Culture*, edited by Vera Rubin. The Hague: Mouton, 1975.

———. *Drugs, Rituals and Altered States of Consciousness*. Rotterdam: A. A. Balkema, 1977.

Trombold, Charles D., ed. *Ancient Road Networks and Settlement Hierarchies in the New World*. Cambridge: Cambridge University Press, 1991.

———. "Causeways in the Context of Strategic Planning in the La Quemada Region, Zacatecas, Mexico." 1991b. In *Ancient Road Networks and Settlement Hierarchies in the New World*, edited by Charles D. Trombold. Cambridge: Cambridge University Press, 1991.

———. "An Introduction to the Study of Ancient New World Road Networks." 1991a. In *Ancient Road Networks and Settlement Hierarchies in the New World*, edited by Charles D. Trombold. Cambridge: Cambridge University Press, 1991.

Turner, D. M. *The Essential Psychedelic Guide*. San Francisco: Panther Press, 1994.

Urton, Gary. "Andean Social Organization and the Maintenance of the Nazca Lines." In *The Lines of Nazca*, edited by Anthony Aveni. Philadelphia: American Philosophical Society, 1990.

Wagner, Johanna. "Das 'dawa' der mamiwata." *Integration*, no. 1 (1991).

Wasson, R. Gordon. "The Hallucinogenic Fungi of Mexico." In *The Psychedelic Reader*, edited by Gunther M. Weil et al. New Hyde Park, N.Y.: University Books, 1965.

————. "Notes on the Present Status of Ololiuhqui and the Other Hallucinogens of Mexico." In *The Psychedelic Reader*, edited by Gunther M. Weil et al. New Hyde Park, N.Y.: University Books, 1965.

————. "Persephone's Quest." In *Persephone's Quest: Entheogens and the Origins of Religion*, edited by R. Gordon Wasson et al. New Haven, Conn.: Yale University Press, 1986.

Wasson, R. Gordon, Stella Kramrisch, Jonathan Ott, and Carl A. P. Ruck. *Persephone's Quest: Entheogens and the Origins of Religion*. New Haven, Conn.: Yale University Press, 1986.

Watkins, Alfred. *The Old Straight Track*. London: Methuen, 1925.

Weatherhill, Craig. "The Zennor Churchway." *The Ley Hunter*, no. 118 (1993).

Weatherhill, Craig, and Paul Devereux. *Myths and Legends of Cornwall*. Wilmslow, U.K.: Sigma, 1994.

Weil, Andrew, and Winifred Rosen. *From Chocolate to Morphine*. 1983. Boston: Houghton Mifflin, 1993.

Weil, Gunther M., Ralph Metzner, and Timothy Leary, eds. *The Psychedelic Reader*. New Hyde Park, N.Y.: University Books, 1965.

Wellmann, Klaus F. "North American Indian Rock Art and Hallucinogenic Drugs." *Journal of the American Medical Association* 239, no. 15 (April 1978).

Whitley, David S. "By the Hunter, for the Gatherer: Art, Social Relations and Subsistence Change in the Prehistoric Great Basin." 1994a. *World Archaeology* 25, no. 3 (February 1994).

————. "Shamanism, Natural Modeling and the Rock Art of Far Western North American Hunter-Gatherers." 1994b. In *Shamanism and Rock Art in North America*. San Antonio, Tex.: Rock Art Foundation, Special Publication 1, 1994.

Whitley, David S., in Lewis-Williams and Dowson, "The Signs of All Times." *Current Anthropology* 1988, op. cit.

Wilbert, Johannes. "The Cultural Significance of Tobacco Use in South America." In *Ancient Traditions: Shamanism in Central Asia and the Americas*, edited by Gary Seaman and Jane S. Day. Niwot, Colo.: University Press of Colorado, 1994.

Williamson, Ray A., and Claire R. Farrer. *Earth and Sky*. Albuquerque: University of New Mexico Press, 1992.

Windes, Thomas C. "The Prehistoric Road Network at Pueblo Alto, Chaco Canyon, New Mexico." In *Ancient Road Networks and Settlement Hierarchies in the New World*, edited by Charles D. Trombold. Cambridge: Cambridge University Press, 1991.

Young, M. Jane. *Signs from the Ancestors*. 1988. Albuquerque: University of New Mexico Press, 1990.

Index